"Jairo de Oliveira's work provides a sensitive and moving portrait of the plight of Fur people from Sudan living as asylum seekers and refugees in Jordan. De Oliveira's motivation is not simply to inform. His desire to communicate the life-changing news of Jesus the Savior is evident in the approach to evangelism and discipleship he proposes. I hope it will be widely read with the result that others will take up the author's challenge to communicate the gospel appropriately to the Fur people and others."

—**Alistair I. Wilson**, professor in mission and New Testament,
Edinburgh Theological Seminary

"*Hope for the Afflicted* is a groundbreaking effort to look at mission strategy and outreach to one of the most neglected and needy Muslim refugee groups worldwide. This book allows us to hear the voices of the Fur people, what they have suffered, and the tenuous circumstance of being refugees in a second land that discriminates against them. I highly recommend this book as an example of how ethnography and contextualization to unreached peoples should be done."

—**David G. Cashin**, professor of intercultural studies,
Columbia International University

"In his meticulous study, Jairo de Oliveira points out that suffering, migration, Islamic peoples, and UPGs all converge over and again. Unfortunately, the body of Christ is usually unprepared to respond in a way that mixes compassion with disciple making and church planting. This well-written book offers one such way and is therefore well worthy of our prayerful consideration."

—**Dick Brogden**, co-founder, Live Dead Movement

"What every reader encounters while in the mind of brother Jairo de Oliveira is the enriching experience of both a researcher and a practitioner. What every reader takes away from his book is an integrity to every principle, counsel, and conviction as each has been personally practiced by his own hand and heart. That is the kind of scholarship we need more of in the church. That is the scholarship you find in these pages."

—**Jami L. Staples**, founder and CEO, The Truth Collective

"We live in the age of the refugee, surrounded by massive numbers of peoples on the move—peoples with a diverse array of needs, hurts, concerns, fears, and hopes. No one ministry method is effective at reaching everyone. Jairo de Oliveira has provided the church a glimpse into one of the neediest refugee populations. *Hope for the Afflicted* offers cutting-edge study and specific ministry guidance for those serving among asylum seekers and refugees."

—**J. D. Payne**, professor of Christian ministry, Samford University

"Through profound research, Jairo de Oliveira inspires us to explore the context of a specific ethnic group to embrace these realities with empathy, love, compassion, and tenderness. The methodology and the content applied in this research stands as a practical guide for mission agencies and local churches to contextualize the word of God in the majority world. I strongly recommend it."

—**Jeferson Chagas**, founder and president, Hikmah International Ministries

"This accessible and engaging study opens a window into the Fur people of the Darfur region of Sudan, whose experience of persecution and suffering has few parallels in the modern day. Through a multidisciplinary approach combining text-based research and direct interviews, Jairo de Oliveira gives a voice to the voiceless community of Fur refugees who have found temporary safety in Amman, Jordan."

—**Peter Riddell**, senior research fellow, Australian College of Theology

"Based on an insightful ethnography of Fur asylum seekers and refugees from Sudan currently located in Jordan, *Hope for the Afflicted* exemplifies a fascinating intersection of clear definitions, careful methodology, and perceptive recommendations for a contextualized approach to ministry that significantly contributes to the field of missiology. I will be recommending this book to my students and colleagues in missiology!"

—**Robin Harris**, president, Evangelical Missiological Society

Hope for the Afflicted

Hope *for the* Afflicted

A Framework for Sharing the Good News
with Asylum Seekers and Refugees

Jairo de Oliveira

FOREWORDS BY
Edward L. Smither
AND Warren Larson

WIPF & STOCK · Eugene, Oregon

HOPE FOR THE AFFLICTED
A Framework for Sharing the Good News with Asylum Seekers and Refugees

Wipf & Stock
An Imprint of Wipf and Stock Publishers
199 W. 8th Ave., Suite 3
Eugene, OR 97401

www.wipfandstock.com

PAPERBACK ISBN: 978-1-6667-7362-0
HARDCOVER ISBN: 978-1-6667-7363-7
EBOOK ISBN: 978-1-6667-7364-4

06/26/23

This book is dedicated with love and gratitude to
my wife, Vania, and my two sons, Mateus and David,
my faithful ministry partners.

But God will never forget the needy;
the hope of the afflicted will never perish.

Ps 9:18

Contents

Foreword

THE BIBLE IS A story about peoples on the move—those who are displaced and who migrate in search of a better life. While God allows peoples to be scattered, we always see in Scripture the hope of redemption. The children of Israel depart Egypt toward a land of promise. A vulnerable gentile widow like Ruth migrates to Israel where she becomes a believer in and worshiper of Israel's God. At the day of Pentecost, diaspora Jews from around the world believe the gospel amid tongues of fire descending on the apostles. God scatters and God gathers.

Human history further testifies to peoples on the move—those leaving their homelands and migrating because of war, famine, poverty, political tyranny, religious persecution, and hopes of a better life. In the last few decades, global migration has greatly accelerated. Today, it is impossible for governments to ignore the needs of asylum seekers and refugees. It is also impossible for the church, especially those churches with a vision for the Great Commission (Matt 28:18–20), to think about and approach God's mission without considering how to reach international students, international business people, refugees, and asylum seekers. We live in a diaspora world with peoples on the move.

Although the global refugee crisis only grows, many displaced peoples remain hidden and forgotten. This is true of the Fur people of Sudan, the subject of this study. In Jairo de Oliveira's work, he has told their story, beginning with their oppression and displacement within the borders of Sudan. Jairo de Oliveira has further recounted the plight of those who have crossed borders as refugees and settled in the largely Arab Muslim nation of Jordan. Though the Fur people are Muslims, they have not always been welcomed warmly in Jordan. While they live in a safer place now, this does not mean that their lives are easy or that they have begun to flourish.

While faithfully recounting their story, the author, a Brazilian Christian and cross-cultural worker, shares a vision for what compassionate Christian ministry to the Fur people looks like. While his research about the plight of the Fur is thorough, his perspective as an on-the-ground teacher and advocate for refugees is wise.

Hope for the Afflicted is not an easy read (in fact, it's heartbreaking in many places), but it is a necessary read for God's people on mission today. This book will greatly benefit those considering cross-cultural ministry among refugees, especially among displaced peoples from Sudan. This book would also benefit global pastors and mission organizations who have a vision for global mission in a twenty-first century diaspora world.

—**Dr. Edward L. Smither**, Dean, College of Intercultural Studies,
Columbia International University

Foreword

THE CONTENT OF THIS book reminded me of an image on the cover of *Christianity Today*, September 1984. It depicted Ralph Winter as a scholarly scientist peering through his magnifying glass trying to find hidden people groups in some remote place on earth. Jairo de Oliveira has found one such group: Fur asylum seekers in Jordan. They are an ethnic group from Western Sudan, connected to the Darfur region. The author gives a comprehensive historical account and analysis of their painful history, beginning with a civil war in 2003 that killed 300,000 and uprooted millions. Sadly, the Fur have faced incredible suffering by the Khartoum regime, but also neglect, discrimination, and racism as they languish in deplorable conditions before resettlement. Reasons for such harsh treatment in Jordan include the facts that they are outsiders and have a dark complexion. Hence, many are not happy with Islam and wonder how fellow Muslims could treat them so badly. Yet this creates opportunities for kingdom work. The author develops five themes (discrimination, war, displacement, exile, and suffering) and explains how the gospel alone can meet their felt needs. He describes various aspects of Fur culture and the kind of Islam practiced (Sufism). He even provides an apologetic for answers to common objections such as to the Son of God, the divinity of Jesus, and the Trinity. As of this writing, there are no known believers among the Fur, and this underscores the great need for workers. The author anticipates that in the coming years there will be a group of believers who know and worship the Lord Jesus. This book will serve as a manual and practical guide for all those who feel called to disciple the Fur for Christ.

—**Warren Larson**, Senior Research Fellow and Professor,
                    Zwemer Center for Muslim-Christian Relations,
                    Columbia International University

Acknowledgments

First and foremost, I want to express my sincere gratitude to God for giving me the strength to overcome each challenge along the journey and complete this project.

Many thanks to my advisors Dr. Edward Smither and Dr. Warren Larson from Columbia International University (CIU). I am thankful to Dr. Smither not only for encouraging me to explore the world of doctoral studies, inspiring me with his love for the kingdom of God, but also for his esteemed encouragement, guidance, and advice during the whole research process. I am thankful to Dr. Larson, too, for helping me to fine-tune ideas throughout the entire research experience, even though he was not able to remain as my advisor beyond my first semester of studies. I am also thankful to Dr. David Cashin from Columbia International University for introducing me to the world of ethnographic research. I am grateful to Columbia International University's faculty, staff members, donors, and students for the pleasant interactions, investment, and all the lessons I have learned from them.

I am indebted to my wife, best friend, and co-worker, Vania, for her patience, prayers, and encouragement along the way. I would not have been able to conclude this study without her priceless support and sacrifice. Likewise, I am grateful for my sons Mateus and David, great partners in the ministry with refugees.

I am grateful for my wonderful friends Ruth Buchanan, Carla Foote, D. William Keller, and Audrey Frank for the editorial assistance they provided.

I must thank my local churches, Segunda Igreja Batista na Taquara in Rio de Janeiro, Brazil, and Arsenal Hill Presbyterian Church in Columbia, South Carolina, for their example, fellowship, support, and encouragement over the years. I am thankful to our partner organizations World Witness and PMI (Muslim Peoples International), which allowed me to synthesize my work on the field and my studies.

I am also thankful for my dearest team members in Jordan, who instructed, prayed for, and encouraged me in my journey. I greatly appreciate my Fur asylum seekers and refugee friends in Jordan who welcomed me in their homes, invested their precious time in this study, and have become like family to me in a foreign land. I have learned much from them and deeply admire their example of resilience in the face of the tremendous suffering they have experienced in life.

Finally, I would like to express my appreciation for my supporters, who have been investing in my life, ministry, and studies. May the Lord extend his generosity to all of you and "bless you abundantly, so that in all things at all times, having all that you need, you will abound in every good work" (2 Cor 9:8).

Abbreviations

ASC	Asylum seeker certificate
BBC	British Broadcasting Corporation
COVID-19	Coronavirus disease 2019
ESL	English as a Second Language
FGM	Female genital mutilation
ICC	International Criminal Court
IDPs	Internally displaced persons
JEM	Justice and Equality Movement
POC	Persons of concern
RC	Refugee certificate
RSD	Refugee status determination
SLA	Sudan Liberation Army
THI	Trauma Healing Institute
UN	United Nations
UNHCR	United Nations High Commissioner for Refugees
UNICEF	United Nations Children's Fund
UNMIS	United Nations Mission to Sudan
UNRWA	United Nations Relief and Works Agency for Palestine Refugees in the Near East
UPG	Unreached people group
US	United States

Introduction

OVER FIVE THOUSAND FUR men, women, and children are living in Jordan as asylum seekers and refugees. This people group has been displaced because of the armed conflict that took place in Darfur, their homeland, in Sudan. Who exactly are these people? What can we learn about their history, culture, and worldview? What can we do regarding their displacement? How can we carry out the Great Commission among them?

In this book, I present a contextualization model for evangelism and discipleship designed for Fur asylum seekers and refugees living in Jordan. The work is based on academic research that I conducted for my PhD dissertation in intercultural studies at Columbia International University. I am confident that the propositions of this contextualization model can be applied to other contexts and displaced people groups across the world. Therefore, I want to challenge the reader to explore the pages of this book with one question in mind: "How can I apply this content to my own living and working context?"

The first chapter talks about the hope the afflicted can find in God and the church's role as God's partner in bringing hope to the world. The second chapter discusses the challenge of developing a contextualization model to make the gospel available to the Fur people in a language they can understand. The third chapter analyzes Sudan's history, focusing on the Islamic influences during the modern period and narrating how the never-ending conflict in Darfur has dramatically impacted the lives of the Fur people. Chapter 4 examines the real-life environment of Fur asylum seekers and refugees residing in Jordan. The fifth chapter introduces the five main themes (discrimination, war, displacement, exile, and suffering) that emerged from the interviews. Chapter 6 presents a contextualization model for evangelism and discipleship, addressing each one of the five main themes. The final chapter shares insights, personal reflections, research implications, and lessons that Christians from both inside and outside the Arab world can learn from the contextualization model suggested in this study.

The core of this book is field research based on face-to-face communication. I am convinced that determining the most effective approaches for evangelism and discipleship of any people group requires both foundational understanding and personal connection. Consequently, in the following pages, the reader will learn much from the relationships I have established with beloved Fur asylum seekers and refugees. All my interactions and further observations are based on residing in their host city, observing their ways of life, and conducting interviews with members of their community.

The interviews were designed to capture the voices of Fur asylum seekers and refugees so that the research could accurately reflect their embodied realities. The questions were formulated to give the participants the opportunity to reflect on their own personal experiences and express their overall understanding of their life journey.

Ethnography was the method I chose to effectively learn about the Fur and explore a much-needed field of study; as de Waal points out: "The ethnography and history of the Fur remain desperately under-studied."[1] In summary, ethnography is a study tool based on the practice of living in proximity to people and allowing them to express their culture through their own perspective, using the descriptions and language of the participants themselves.

Why is it important to study the people group we want to reach with the gospel? Among other critical factors, understanding the life, culture, and context of the people group is foundational for evangelizing and discipling new believers as part of the process of church planting among them. When Jesus, sitting by a well, talked with the Samaritan woman in John 4:1–45, he engaged in a conversation about water. The Lord spoke of a spring of living water to the woman who held an empty water jar in her hands, to provide context for the gospel. Jesus's example shows us how understanding the themes and context of our audience can help us connect, faithfully share the good news, and make disciples among them.

---

1. de Waal, "Who Are the Darfurians?," 184.

I hope that this book will serve as a manual and practical guide for those who feel called to engage the current migration crisis by proclaiming the hope of the gospel and discipling asylum seekers and refugees worldwide.

1

There Is Hope

*Our world today so desperately hungers for hope, yet
uncounted people have almost given up. There is despair
and hopelessness on every hand. Let us be faithful in
proclaiming the hope that is in Jesus.*

—BILLY GRAHAM

THE GOSPEL OF JESUS Christ provides hope to the hopeless of the world . . .
and to the afflicted.

Is this still true in the face of abuse, violence, persecution, loss, and
grief? Can Amira, a name that means "princess," and Amina, a name that
means "safe one, protected," find such hope after dealing with life circumstances that brought them so much pain and suffering?

Amira was born in the village of Oringa in southern Nyala, the capital
of South Darfur State (see Appendix C, "Map of States of Sudan"). In 2003,
when she was only thirteen years old, her village was attacked by an armed
group. The Janjaweed fighters, an Arab militia that operates in western Sudan in association with the Khartoum government, arrived on horseback
before sunrise to surprise the residents of the village, who were mostly
members of the Fur tribe. Amira, her father, and her four brothers were
asleep in the backyard of the house on one of the hottest nights of the year
when they were met with a merciless form of terror.

Amira and her family members woke up to the sound of the militiamen moving around their property. Even though Amira's father and

brothers had no means with which to resist an attack, the Janjaweed killed each of them. As all this evil took place around her, Amira was unable to express any reaction. She was so frightened that only silent tears ran down her face. At first, she didn't understand why the fighters had spared her life. Soon, their intentions became clear. Immediately after the men stopped firing their weapons, they approached Amira, tore her clothing, and started abusing her sexually, one after the other.

A few hours later, Amira's neighbors found the teenager and brought her to Kalma, the nearest camp for internally displaced persons (IDPs) in Darfur. There, Amira joined thousands of people from her people group, most of them women and children.

As a result of the sexual abuse she endured, Amira discovered four months later that she was pregnant. However, in the sixth month of her pregnancy, she miscarried due to malnutrition. Her hope faded as she fought for the strength to keep going. We can envision that after all she had been through, she might have cried out as Jesus did: "My God, my God, why have you forsaken me?"

* * *

Amina was born in a small village in the Greater Upper Nile region of what is now South Sudan (see Appendix A, "Map of Sudan"). Like Amira, she also came to be familiar with hardship and suffering. When she was fourteen years old, she was given as a wife to a man more than twice her age. Despite this difference, Amina loved her husband. He treated her with kindness, and, in a context in which women can do little for themselves, he provided for all her needs.

During their honeymoon, Amina and her husband dreamed of having ten children: five boys and five girls. They were determined to grow their family, and within their first three years of marriage, they had two children. However, Amina's life changed dramatically nearly one year after the birth of her second child when her husband died of lung cancer and left her in a vulnerable position with her children. Even in the face of this difficulty, things were about to get worse for Amina. A few days after her husband's burial, Amina's mother-in-law reminded her that, in their cultural system, a widow must marry one of her husband's brothers.

To follow this tradition, Amina agreed to marry her brother-in-law and became his third wife. Unfortunately, her second husband did not relate to her in the same way as the first. In fact, he was so abusive and violent that she feared for her life and had to flee. In the eyes of her husband's family, this was viewed as a rejection and as bringing shame on the family, so they were determined to find and kill her. She ran from city to city, fleeing the people her family had sent after her. Amina had no choice but to cross her country's border in search of refuge and a new life. However, not long after becoming a refugee in a neighboring country, she learned that her in-laws were on her trail. So, to save her own life, she was once again forced to flee. Amina moved to a third foreign country after leaving her home and the children she loves. Amina must think that there is no safe place for her anywhere in the world as she walks through the valley of the shadow of death regularly. We can picture her praying a biblical prayer, "Look on me and answer, LORD my God. Give light to my eyes, or I will sleep in death" (Ps 13:3).

* * *

Heartbreakingly, Amira and Amina are not anomalies. They are among the over one hundred million displaced people who currently make up the largest migration crisis of all time. Their stories mirror the trauma and suffering that several refugees face all over the world. These two women exemplify the experience of individuals in Sudan, Syria, Iraq, Yemen, Somalia, Congo, Afghanistan, Palestine, Myanmar, Ukraine, and other nations where conflict forces people out of their homes and into a journey on the edge of life and death itself.

The God of Hope

When we hear stories of people like Amira and Amina, it's easy to lose hope in humanity. However, there is a God of hope who assures us that the suffering people experience in this world is not the end of their story. The God of all grace is calling people to his eternal glory in Christ, and no matter how much they have suffered, the Lord is powerful to restore their lives and make them "strong, firm and steadfast" (1 Pet 5:10). Therefore, God is not indifferent to human suffering, nor does he ignore its consequences. On the contrary, God loves the afflicted. The Almighty "has not despised or scorned the suffering of the afflicted one; he has not hidden his face from him but has listened to his cry for help" (Ps 22:24).

The Lord Jesus understands what it is like to be rejected, persecuted, and even forcibly displaced from his homeland (Matt 2:13–15). Jesus suffered in different ways throughout his life, and in a special way at his death. Christ has much to teach us about suffering (Matt 27:28–29) because he did not deviate from the cross and did not make his victory an act of triumphalism, but instead acted in obedience to God for the redemption of humanity (Phil 2:8). The Lord took our suffering on himself (Isa 53:4–5) to bring light to those who are in the darkness and give them hope through his works (Matt 4:16).

God's presence is a safe place for those who are afflicted: "God is our refuge and strength, an ever-present help in trouble" (Ps 46:1). Furthermore, the Bible is full of words of hope and encouragement: "For everything that was written in the past was written to teach us, so that through the endurance taught in the Scriptures and the encouragement they provide we might have hope" (Rom 15:4).

Although our world is filled with stories of millions of people who are victims of fear, discrimination, violence, and pain, everywhere we look, we can also spy surprising signs of the kingdom of God everywhere. In the face of Russia's war against Ukraine, I recently gave an assignment to the refugees at the community development center where I teach ESL in Jordan. I asked them to write a message of hope for Ukrainians who have also been forced to leave their country and become refugees. The messages they wrote were posted on social media, aiming to reach Ukrainian hearts. They wrote such words of encouragement that show how God is keeping, healing, and blessing them with hope. I share here three messages written by my students:

> I am very sorry for the war in Ukraine and the destruction it has produced in your country, to the point of making you become a refugee. I am a refugee from Sudan, and I know how you are feeling at this moment. Be aware that you are not alone. Millions of refugees around the world sympathize with your suffering. Stay strong, and do not give up! You have the power to offer the world a lesson on overcoming difficulties and rewriting one's own life story.
>
> Ukrainian refugees, I know your pain as I am one of the victims of the war in Sudan. I ask you to be patient and stay focused on your future. Dear ones, the war will end, and you will return to your country. You will be successful.
>
> I am Somali, and I was forced to leave Somalia in 2009 because of the war. The war has not ended, and I am still a refugee. My heart goes out to people who suffer, and face difficulties caused by war. My prayers are with you, Ukrainian refugees.

Even in the most remote, unlikely, and hostile locations, God is working in the lives of those who are suffering, providing them with a glimmer of hope, a precious ointment, and a healing balm. In the Scriptures, God promises hope and a future to a group of captives who were experiencing great suffering and living in exile: "For I know the plans I have for you, declares the LORD, plans for welfare and not for evil, to give you a future and a hope" (Jer 29:11). The same promise is being fulfilled today. Through the gospel, the Lord is promoting divine encounters, healing wounded hearts, and providing rest for those who are weary and burdened. I remember an experience I had with my students a few months ago that illustrates God's work in the hearts of refugees. I was almost ready to start teaching and had already listed all the new vocabulary on the whiteboard. The lesson was based on material that introduces basic family terminology to ESL students. Given that I still had five minutes before starting the class, I opted to leave the classroom for a few moments. On the way to the room next door, I was stopped by Aziza, one of my refugee students, who made an unexpected request: "Teacher, I just noticed the vocabulary for the lesson. Please don't teach about family members. For me, approaching this subject is quite challenging. Talking about family causes me suffering." Despite not having much time to alter the content of the class, I decided to respond positively to the student's request. I chose another topic and began improvising each activity, avoiding the subject that could cause Aziza distress. Once I finished teaching, she approached me privately, expressed gratitude, and justified her request. "Teacher, I have no family. All my family members were killed in Somalia's war. I live alone because I don't have anyone else in this life." Aziza discussed how the loss of family members occurred and how it has impacted her life profoundly. After narrating her story of suffering, she concluded, "I'm relieved now that I've shared my heart with you. In fact, I have the sense that I am a new person. I believe I am ready to deal with this matter. So, feel free to teach about family in the next class. Dealing with this subject is no longer an issue for me."

A few months later, Aziza was sitting right in front of me when I started teaching about family members, as Aziza had encouraged me to do so. I then asked my refugee students: "Do you all believe in God?" Since they were all Muslims, they unanimously responded positively. Then I asked another faith question: "Do you believe in miracles?" Again, I received a positive response. So, I came up with a suggestion: "How about we dream and consider some miracles together? If I close my eyes, I can see Aziza crossing the ocean, being resettled in Canada, and building a new life." I looked at her and saw a smile shining on her face. I continued. "I can also see Aziza finding a husband and getting married." This time, the smile had multiplied on the faces of all the students. "Who would like to go to Aziza's wedding in Canada?" They all raised a hand. Then together, we chose a name for Aziza's future husband. Ahmed was the name picked by the class with Aziza's approval. Then, I started teaching family vocabulary: "If Aziza marries Ahmed, she will be a wife, and he will be a husband.

Aziza will be a mother if they have children, and Ahmed will be a father. If their children have children, Aziza and Ahmed will be grandparents." In this way, I introduced the family vocabulary to my Sudanese, Somali, and Yemeni students without bringing up their past.

Fortunately, Aziza has been showing signs of restoration from the trauma of having lost all her family members in the war. She attended the entire class without expressing any discomfort. At the end of the class, Aziza said that she was happy to dream of a new family and that looking at the future had created hope in her heart.

By God's grace, there is healing, there is hope, and there is reason to celebrate even though we also have reason to lament, especially the lack of incarnate care and living solidarity that should characterize humanity in general—and particularly people of faith.

As the sovereign God works in the lives of people across the world, he calls his children to move beyond borders and become global ambassadors of eternal hope. Therefore, the church has a divine call to bless the nations with the good news that in Christ God has worked to "reconcile to himself all things" (Col 1:20). But who are we to bring hope to the afflicted? We are the people commanded by God to join him as he fulfills his promise to make a pathway through the wilderness and create rivers in the dry wasteland (Isa 43:19).

Even amid the current migration crisis, we are called to make disciples of all nations. Our God does not favor one nation or exclude one people group. Rather, the Lord extends his salvation to the entire world and embraces those who are willing to accept his love. In the Old Testament, God's people were told that the temple would be known as a "house of prayer" for all nations. God's words, "these I will bring to my holy mountain and give them joy in my house of prayer" (Isa 56:7), reverberate throughout history and in our ears today.

Bringing Hope to the World

As we join God in his work, we must recognize that we have no mission apart from his mission. We are called to be "co-workers in God's service" (1 Cor 3:9), who find the foundation and purpose of our own mission in God's mission. Therefore, we are mission partners rather than protagonists. As sophisticated as we are in terms of preparation, strategies, and work models, they are ineffective in transforming a sin-damaged world. On our own, we could never accomplish the work of the kingdom. We must always recognize that God's grace is made perfect in our weakness (2 Cor 12:9) and that his treasure is hidden in our jars of clay (2 Cor 4:7).

Our Lord Jesus demands that we move like him, in a spirit of humility and sacrificial service, that we speak up with prophetic courage for the oppressed and proclaim God's kingdom, justice, and hope for the afflicted. In Scripture, we are commanded to embody the gospel of Christ and to live our faith and all its implications. We are warned to constantly confess our own sins and reject any expression of arrogance, pride, and indifference. Likewise, we must resist the temptation of fulfilling our mission without caring about the people we are sent to serve. As we minister to people who are suffering, we are invited to learn from their stories, respect their experiences, and not stray from the cross—all of which is inherent to our calling. As we love those we serve, we will have the grace and privilege of building deep and genuine relationships as we break bread together, sharing our hopes and dreams. We are called to cry with those who cry, as we recognize that the pain of individuals like Amira and Amina is too great for a single person's tears. As we relate to those who are broken, we must faithfully witness the transformative power of the gospel, the power of grace that works in all areas of life. Only by God's grace can we make the whole gospel accessible to everyone and everywhere.

As we commit ourselves to planting seeds of hope in the lives of those who are afflicted, God promotes mutual consolation so that divine comfort can be shared, and we can become part of healing each other. After all, it is Jesus "who comforts us in all our troubles, so that we can comfort those in any trouble with the comfort we ourselves receive from God" (2 Cor 1:4). Thus, in our work as ambassadors of the gospel, we experience the reciprocity of the kingdom of God. In this way, we both promote transformation and are mutually transformed by welcoming, sharing, and walking with people for whom God has compassion and who are "harassed and helpless, like sheep without a shepherd" (Matt 9:36).

There Is Hope, No Matter What

As we turn our eyes to the millions of displaced people worldwide, we must recognize that even in the direst situations, there is hope. Also, we need to acknowledge that most of them have never had the opportunity to hear the good news. We are called to touch their lives. Through meaningful words and acts of love, they can come to know that they are made in God's image and likeness (Gen 1:26), formed with an everlasting love (Jer 31:3), and created for God's glory (Isa 43:7). Thus, they are precious to the Almighty. They need to realize that even though sin has separated them spiritually from God, in Jesus there is healing, forgiveness, justice, and hope. It matters not—the location of their homeland, their ethnicity, skin color, mother tongue, or any other identifying characteristic. Hope is intended for the afflicted; and in Jesus, the kingdom of God has come to them. For in Christ Jesus, all who believe become a new creation and are dead to the power of sin and alive to God (Rom 6:11). Therefore, all our hopes rest on the name of Jesus.

As disciples and ambassadors of the gospel in contexts of pain and suffering, vulnerability and discrimination, exclusion and persecution, we seek to assist people in their experience of faith and to strengthen their new identity of belonging to a new community. In this way, sitting at a table with Amira and Amina in Jordan, where they both now live, we may witness divine encounters, life transformation, and the birth of new communities that glorify the name of our Lord Jesus Christ and point to his kingdom.

May the Lord use us as salt and light in the lives of those we meet along the way. May we open our hearts to be inspired by the lives of these people, learn their stories of suffering and resilience, and share experiences and hope with them.

As we pray for the afflicted, may our prayer be influenced by the words given by God to the apostle Paul in Rom 15:13: "May the God of hope fill you with all joy and peace as you trust in him, so that you may overflow with hope by the power of the Holy Spirit."

Summary

This chapter has presented a tragic reality that affects over one hundred million people worldwide. Forcible displacement, often caused by violence and war, impacts individuals of all ages who are pushed from their homes and must run to save their lives. As they deal with constant death threats within their territory, some IDPs have no choice but to flee their homeland, cross their country borders, and become refugees. The stories of Amira and Amina illustrate the afflictions they face at various stages of their life journey. Additionally, the chapter emphasizes the hope available for the victims of the current migration crisis because God loves them, understands their pain, and has dealt with much suffering to provide the hope they need.

As people called by God, the church is commanded to join the Almighty as he works to reconcile with himself everything that has fallen because of sin. The church finds its mission within the mission of God and must reflect the example of Jesus Christ in serving a world marked by suffering. The body of Christ needs to resist the temptation of cooperating with

God in its own strength and joining those who suffer without having the same mindset as Christ Jesus.

The good news of Jesus Christ provides hope to all people, including the afflicted, no matter how complex the circumstances they have endured or how much suffering they have experienced. If they put their trust in Jesus, hope will come to them, embrace them, and lead them to experience a powerful new beginning.

Throughout this book, I will continue to examine *the hope that will never perish* (Ps 9:18) and introduce strategic approaches for bringing hope to asylum seekers and refugees from Sudan, people like Amira and Amina. Therefore, I welcome you to join me in exploring the upcoming chapters.

2

There Is Hope for
the Fur People

Hope is being able to see that there is light despite all of the darkness.

—DESMOND TUTU

THE POPULATION OF DISPLACED people worldwide continues to increase, and it doubled from 2012 to 2022. According to the global trends report on forced displacement, published in June 2022, the refugee population under UNHCR's mandate is 21.3 million,[1] up from 10.5 million in 2012.[2]

Sudan is one of the countries most affected by the world migration crisis. As reported by the UNHCR, more than 3 million Sudanese are internally displaced persons (IDPs), while 825,300 have been displaced across their borders.[3] Consequently, Sudanese represent the seventh-largest refugee community in the world.[4]

High Sudanese displacement is a direct consequence of an armed conflict that began on February 26, 2003. It started in Darfur, west of the country, in an area bordered by four nations: Libya, Chad, the Central African Republic, and South Sudan (see Appendix A, "Map of Sudan"). The conflict originated when the central government of Sudan reacted with

---

1. UNHCR, *UNHCR Global Trends 2022*, 2.

2. UNHCR, *UNHCR Global Trends 2012*, 2.

3. UNHCR, *UNHCR Global Trends 2021*, 24.

4. UNHCR, *UNHCR Global Trends 2012*, 17.

violence against a group of demonstrators: "The conflict began in 2003 when rebels launched an insurrection to protest what they contended was the Sudanese government's disregard for the western region and its non-Arab population. In response, the government equipped and supported Arab militias—which came to be known as *Janjaweed* (also *Jingaweit* or *Janjawid*)—to fight against the rebels in Darfur."[5]

Since the beginning of the conflict, 300,000 people have been killed, and over 2.7 million have been forced from their homes, including IDPs, asylum seekers, and refugees.[6] In 2005, the United Nations ranked the war in Darfur as the world's worst humanitarian crisis. Driven by these events, Luis Moreno-Ocampo, the chief prosecutor of the International Criminal Court (ICC), opened an international criminal investigation. On March 4, 2009, and July 12, 2010, the tribunal issued two arrest warrants against former President Omar al-Bashir for crimes against humanity, war crimes, and genocide committed in Darfur.[7]

As a result of the civil war in western Sudan, most Darfuris have become refugees in Chad: "Chad hosts around 370,000 Sudanese refugees from Darfur."[8] Other Darfuris have sought refuge in North Africa in countries such as Egypt and Libya. Some others have fled to countries in the Middle East, such as Jordan, Lebanon, and Israel.

As of December 2021, in Jordan, where this research occurs, 5,891 Sudanese live as refugees under UNHCR (United Nations High Commissioner for Refugees) protection.[9] Sudanese make up the country's fourth-largest group of refugees, and among them, the Fur tribe is the predominant people group.

Nearly all the Fur asylum seekers and refugees living in Jordan profess Islam as their religion. They barely have access to the gospel and are classified by evangelical Christian organizations such as the Joshua Project as an unreached people group (UPG).[10]

This study intends to examine how evangelism and discipleship can take form in this context. The results will enable Fur individuals to hear and understand the good news in a compelling way and come to faith in Christ. It will also equip those seeking to facilitate a church planting movement among the Fur.

---

5. Britannica, "Conflict in Darfur."

6. UN, "Sudan," para. 3.

7. ICC, "Al Bashir Case," para. 1.

8. ACAPS, "Chad Darfur Refugees," para. 1.

9. UNHCR, "Jordan," 1.

10. See https://joshuaproject.net/people_groups/11779.

A Significant Challenge

Before the current civil war began, when nearly no gospel witness was available to the people groups in the region, Darfur was closed to the Christian faith. The tribes living in the area acknowledged Islam as their sole professed faith, although they also observed various animistic practices. Since the war broke out in Darfur, several people groups have expressed an increasing disillusionment with Islam and a corresponding openness to the gospel.

Their dissatisfaction with Islam, as a religious system, stems from the fact that the people leading the massacre in Darfur share the same beliefs. Darfuris often stress that a Muslim should never kill another Muslim. Therefore, they perceive something wrong with the religion the Sudanese leaders are practicing.

Darfuris say they have shown themselves to be true Muslims by following their Islamic leaders and answering all the requests of the religious leaders of the Khartoum administration. Pointing to recent history, they claim to have contributed significantly to the government's plan to establish Sharia law in Sudan's whole territory and make the country an Islamic nation. Darfuris argue that some of them fought for Bashir during the decades of war (1983–2005) against Christians in the South. As a result, they don't understand why they are still seen as enemies by the Sudanese government. Consequently, they feel used, misled, and betrayed. "To become true Muslims, the government in Khartoum ordered us to kill the Christians in the South because they were infidels. Today, despite our Muslim faith, government forces and militias treat us in the same way they did their enemies at the time. The religious justification they often use is just an excuse," says one study participant.

Many Darfuris have become disillusioned with Islam and are willing to explore other faith expressions and even embrace the Christian faith. "There is an openness to the gospel among African Sudanese Muslims in Darfur who have suffered greatly in the war that has raged in Sudan since 2003."[11]

The number of conversions made public in Sudan is growing. Religious pressures and persecution against new converts are not stopping people from believing in Jesus. The high price of religious persecution these converts often pay is a strong indication that their conversions to the Christian faith represent genuine experiences.

Even though an increasing number of Sudanese from Darfur have been choosing to follow Christ since 2003, most of the Sudanese asylum seekers and refugees in Jordan have not yet had an opportunity to hear the

---

11. Barnabas Aid, "Christian Converts from Islam," para. 8.

gospel preached. If a follower of Jesus were to share the gospel with them, what elements should be highlighted in the presentation? What components would need to be considered in their discipleship process if they responded positively?

Facing the Challenge

Christians must communicate the gospel effectively to fulfill Jesus's command to make disciples of all nations and to follow his example. When preaching the gospel, Jesus used suitable language and scenarios to ensure that his audience understood his message. While at sea, he talked about fishing to fishers (Luke 5:1–11). In a pastoral setting, Jesus presented himself as the good shepherd who gives life for his sheep (John 10:1–18). When preaching the gospel and discipling individuals of a specific people group, such as Fur asylum seekers and refugees, understanding the key issues they face in their context of life makes the gospel relevant. This study will address these needs and enable more Christians to understand the Fur people group. Three groups of people will benefit from this study:

1. The *Sudanese believers* coming to Christ will benefit from this study by learning how evangelism and discipleship can be practiced among individuals from their people group. They will be encouraged to pursue growth in their new faith and consider reaching out to other Sudanese living in their community.

2. The *Jordanian believers* who are passionate about reaching out to the Sudanese community living among them will have access to resources that will equip them to present the gospel in a way that makes sense to their Sudanese neighbors. They will feel better prepared to disciple new Sudanese converts and integrate them into the local body of followers of Jesus.

3. The *international believers* serving in Jordan will be challenged to examine evangelism and discipleship from this context. Outsiders often bring foreign church planting ideas with them, which usually do not address some of the realities of their new setting. This study will enable them to learn approaches used in Jordan and stimulate them to develop their mission strategies based on what is already happening in the community they are trying to reach.

Developing a Contextualization Model

This book will develop a contextualization model for ministry among the Fur, a Sudanese people group living as asylum seekers and refugees in Jordan. The focus is based on a key question: *What are the best approaches for evangelism and discipleship to be employed in the process of planting a church among Fur asylum seekers and refugees in Jordan?*

The supporting questions are:

1. What is the spiritual worldview of the Fur people?

2. How do the Fur people in Jordan currently regard Islam?

3. What challenges that the Fur people face as asylum seekers and refugees in Jordan should be addressed during the pre-evangelism process?

4. In a gospel presentation, what themes will make the most sense to Fur asylum seekers and refugees in Jordan?

5. Which themes need to be discussed first in the discipleship process with Fur individuals?

6. What fruitful practices ought to be adopted for ongoing ministry among Fur asylum seekers and refugees in Jordan?

The individuals interviewed for this study live as urban refugees in Amman, Jordan, under UNHCR protection. While this study is rooted in the Fur community of Jordan, lessons will naturally emerge to benefit church planting initiatives in the country, across the Middle East, and throughout the Arab world.

Islam is the most widely professed religion among the Fur people of Sudan, and all the participants interviewed profess to be Muslims. None of them has ever been exposed to a gospel presentation.

The focus is on contextualizing the gospel message and developing a contextual theologizing process for the Fur asylum seekers and refugees residing in Jordan.

The content of this book will be shaped by three important concepts:

- *Ethnography:* A research method used by anthropologists to broadly study individual cultures. Ethnography requires the researcher to live in proximity to people and allow them to express their culture in their words and through their own perspective.

- *Contextualization:* The process of faithfully communicating the Christian message to a certain cultural context. The purpose of contextualization is to ensure that the gospel is clearly communicated to the listener. The missionary who contextualizes the gospel communicates the Christian message in ways that are appropriate for his audience.

- *Missiology:* The study of the Christian mission, also known as the Great Commission (Matt 28:16–20). Missiology is a branch of theology that teaches Christians how to communicate the gospel effectively to the world to make disciples of Jesus Christ in every nation.

Three key terms will be used throughout the book to describe the process of people on their faith journey:

- *Evangelism:* As Archbishop William Temple said, it is the task to "present Jesus Christ in the power of the Holy Spirit that men and women shall come to put their faith in God through Him, to accept Him as their Savior and to serve Him as their King in the fellowship of His church."[12]

- *Discipleship:* This is the life journey of a disciple during which he grows in his faith, learning to become more like Jesus by the power of the Holy Spirit, or, as Dallas Willard states, this is "the relationship I stand into Jesus Christ in order that I might take on his character."[13]

- *Gospel:* The term *gospel* literally translates as "good news" or "the good story." It is specifically used to refer to the first four books of the New Testament (Matthew, Mark, Luke, and John) that record the teachings of Jesus Christ, covering all the events of his incarnation, including his birth, baptism, death, burial, resurrection, and ascension into heaven. A more general definition of *gospel* prevalent in this study would be the message, or the "good news," of God's plan to reconcile humanity to himself through the work of Jesus.

In addition, the following ideas will help the reader understand the situation of the Fur people in Jordan and what they face in terms of their current life trajectory:

- *Refugee:* A person who, "owing to a well-founded fear of being persecuted for reasons of race, religion, nationality, membership of a particular social group, or political opinion, is outside the country of his nationality, and is unable to or, owing to such fear, is unwilling to avail himself of the protection of that country."[14]

---

12. Gangel, *Toward a Harmony*, 80.

13. Hull, *Complete Book of Discipleship*, 16.

14. According to the UN Convention Related to the Status of Refugees; see www.iom.int/key-migration-terms.

- *Asylum seeker:* "Someone whose request for sanctuary has yet to be processed."[15] Asylum seekers are individuals who have expressed a desire to be under the UNHCR mandate to receive refugee status. If the UNHCR approves their refugee status, they may obtain the right to permanent residence and access to public services, depending on the host country's legislation.

- *Displacement:* The condition of people who, for different reasons, but usually because of war, conflict, poverty, political upheaval, natural disaster, or persecution, are forced to leave their home. As a result, they move to another area inside or outside their country.

- *Internally Displaced Persons (IDPs):* People who have been forced to flee their homes but not their country. The United Nations High Commissioner for Refugees classifies IDPs as "people or groups of people who have been forced to leave their homes or places of habitual residence, in particular as a result of or in order to avoid the effects of armed conflict, situations of generalized violence, violations of human rights, or natural or man-made disasters, and who have not crossed an international border."[16]

- *Janjaweed:* An Arab militia that operates in Sudan, predominantly in Darfur. They have been fighting for the Khartoum administration against the African tribes in the war taking place in the region. *Janjaweed* means "devil on horseback" in Arabic. The group received this name because of the atrocities they have committed in Darfur, especially related to killing and raping.

Motivation for Understanding the Fur People

The motivation to conduct this study began twenty years ago. My wife and I first learned about the Fur people in 2002, a year before the Darfur civil war broke out. We were attending a Bible school in Brazil and seeking to become cross-cultural workers among an unreached people group (UPG). The facts that the Fur people had no gospel witness, that not a single portion of the Bible was available in their language, and that their mother tongue had no written script challenged our hearts. We continued our pre-field preparation in areas of study such as theology, missiology, anthropology, and linguistics, with a growing conviction that we had a divine calling to serve the Fur people. We

15. UNHCR, "Asylum-Seekers," para. 1.

16. UNHCR, *UNHCR Global Trends 2016,* 56.

went to Sudan for the first time in 2006 on an exploratory trip. We returned to the country for a second visit in 2008 as part of a permanent transition process. In 2010, we made Sudan our home and started working with internally displaced individuals from the Fur tribe and other people groups from Darfur. In addition, we worked with Fur individuals in Kenya and Morocco before coming to the Middle East to serve among them.

Over the years we have known the Fur, we have learned to admire many characteristics of their culture and worldview. We often highlight their gentleness, generosity, and hospitality, among many other qualities. We've also come to appreciate their resilience in response to the civil war they've experienced in Darfur. Since the first time we heard about the Fur, we've always wondered: how we can effectively communicate the gospel and make disciples among them? This study represents an attempt to deeply understand different aspects of their lives as asylum seekers and refugees in Jordan and answer this crucial question based on the context.

3

Examining the Background of the Fur People in Sudan

You will argue with yourself that there is no way forward.
But with God, nothing is impossible. He has more ropes and
ladders and tunnels out of pits than you can conceive. Wait.
Pray without ceasing. Hope.

—JOHN PIPER

Introduction

THE HISTORY, CULTURE, RELIGION, and geography of Sudan, and of the region of Darfur, home to the Fur tribe, is not well known outside of those who study the region and its people. While Darfur was in the popular media nearly fifteen years ago, the attention has faded over the years, even though the situation has not necessarily improved.

Understanding the Fur people of Sudan and the major components that shape their worldview, including background, language, religion, geography, and history, is an important first step in building relationships and connection.

Even though the attention of the world has turned elsewhere, the never-ending conflict in Darfur has impacted the lives of the Fur tribe to the present day, resulting in much violence and death and forcing many of their people to flee their country and become asylum seekers and refugees in Jordan and throughout the world.

Sudan: The Country of the Fur

The Fur tribe is one of the Republic of the Sudan's native people groups. Often referred to as Sudan, the country shares its border with seven countries: Egypt, South Sudan, Central African Republic, Chad, Eritrea, Ethiopia, and Libya (see Appendix A, "Map of Sudan").[1] As a geopolitical entity, Sudan lies in the northeastern part of the African continent.

According to historians, the name Sudan was given to the country by medieval Muslim geographers who used to call the belt of African territory to the south of the Sahara Desert territory *Bilad al-Sudan*—literally, "the land of the Blacks."[2]

Sudan has an expansive territory, occupying an area of 728,215 square miles (1,886,068 square kilometers). Sudan was Africa's largest country until it split in 2011. This turning point in Sudan's history led to the formation of South Sudan. The homeland of the Sudanese is now Africa's third-largest country.[3]

Sudan's geography is diverse and divided into three distinct zones:

> In the north is rocky desert and semi-desert; south of this is a belt of undulating sand, passing from semi-desert to savanna; south of this again a clay belt, which widens as it stretches eastwards from the south of Darfur to the rainlands and semi-desert lying east of the Blue and main Niles.[4]

Khartoum serves as Sudan's administrative capital (see Appendix C, "Map of States of Sudan"). Other well-known cities in Sudan are Omdurman (Khartoum), Nyala (South Darfur), El-Obeid (North Kordofan), Kassala (Kassala), Wad Madani (Gezira), El-Gadarif (Al Qadarif), Al-Fashir (North Darfur), Kusti (White Nile), and Port Sudan (Red Sea).

The city of Port Sudan hosts the principal seaport of Sudan. Khartoum hosts the confluence of the White Nile and the Blue Nile, which together create the longest river in the world, covering 4,258 miles (6,693 kilometers).[5]

Sudan is a culturally diversified country with an extraordinary history and a rich archaeological heritage, including the Nubian Meroe pyramids, which are part of the larger group of Nubian pyramids. They were constructed in different eras during the kingdom of Kush and are part of humanity's cultural heritage:

1. Berlatsky and Chalk, *Darfur*, 29.
2. Holt and Daly, *History of the Sudan*, 1.
3. See https://www.worldatlas.com/maps/sudan.
4. Holt and Daly, *History of the Sudan*, 1–2.
5. Dodd, "10 Longest Rivers," para. 2.

Sudan is one of the richest African countries in terms of archaeological sites. Ruins of the ancient kingdom of Kush are found at Gebel Barkal and associated sites in the Nile valley; they were collectively designated a UNESCO World Heritage site in 2003. The archaeological sites at Meroe, an ancient Kushitic city, were collectively designated a World Heritage site in 2011.[6]

Sudan is mentioned in the Bible in all references to Cush (Kush), a term used in ancient times that appears in thirty-two verses in the Old Testament, such as in Zeph 3:10: "From beyond the rivers of Cush my worshipers, my scattered people, will bring me offerings."

Demographics

As of January of 2022, Sudan had a population of 45,438,772. The Sudanese population is growing at a rapid rate of 2.42 percent per year. More than one million people are added to the country's population every year at this rate. "According to current projections, Sudan is estimated to reach 100 million people by 2064."[7]

Sudan is home to nearly six hundred tribes. Although Sudan is an African country, "approximately 70 per cent of Sudan's people are characterized as Sudanese Arabs."[8] Fur, Nuba, Beja, Masalit, and Zaghawa are some ethnic groups that form the remaining 30 percent of the population. The Sudanese Arabs, the largest group, are descendants of migrants from the Arabian Peninsula who first began moving to Sudan in pre-Islamic times. The two major routes that the Arabs used in later times were across the Red Sea or via Egypt.[9] According to Voll, the Sudanese Arabs can be classified into four main groups: Juhayna, Baqqara, Jallaba, and Rashayda.[10]

Language

Sudan is a multilingual country with a diverse population. Even though Sudan's official languages are Arabic and English, the country's population speaks approximately four hundred dialects and languages, including the

6. Economic Intelligence Unit et al., "Sudan."

7. According to 2021 edition of https://worldpopulationreview.com/countries/sudan-population.

8. See https://minorityrights.org/country/sudan.

9. Holt and Daly, *History of the Sudan*, 7.

10. Voll, *Historical Dictionary*, 146–47.

Fur language, a Nilo-Saharan language. Most of the dialects and languages that are spoken throughout the country are essentially unwritten.

As a result of efforts toward the Islamization and Arabization of Sudan, over half of the Sudanese people now speak Arabic as their native language.[11] The Fur are one of the people who value the Arabic language and understand it is part of their religious identity:

> Almost all the northern Sudanese agreed on the acceptance of the Arab heritage, and of the Islamic faith and way of life that go with it. Nor is there any significant demand among those whose mother tongue is not Arabic, whether Beja, Nubians, or Fur, that their language be adopted in place of Arabic for administrative, educational, or general use.[12]

By 2005, the English language had become one of the two official languages in Sudan. Up to the present day, English is not yet widely spoken by the Fur people but rather by individuals from other people groups who have greater access to formal education and the country's urban centers.

Religion

The Fur people follow Islam, the dominant religion in Sudan. A total of 97 percent of the Sudanese population profess to be Muslims. The remaining 3 percent of the population practice traditional animist religions or claim to be Christians.[13]

The Arab conquest of Egypt in AD 641 paved the way for the gradual process of the Islamization of Sudan.[14] However, the expansion of Islam in Sudanese territory occurred through Islamic invasions from the eighth century. A variety of factors, according to Searcy, contributed to the spread of Islam in Sudan's territory, including Muslim missionary activity, mainly through traders involved in proselytizing efforts, the construction of mosques, and the conversion of individual rules to Islam, all of which had an impact on the people.[15] Later, starting in the sixteenth century, during the Funj and Fur Sultanates, the northern and western parts of Sudan were

11. Sidahmed and Sidahmed, *Sudan*, 136.

12. Voll, *Historical Dictionary*, 91.

13. According to 2021 edition of https://worldpopulationreview.com/countries/sudan-population.

14. Searcy, *Formation*, 7.

15. Searcy, *Formation*, 10.

Islamized and largely Arabized.[16] In 1596, when the Darfur Sultanate was established, Islam was declared the state religion.[17]

Islam became the dominant religion of these areas through a process involving a combination of factors, including "demographic movements, particularly the migration of Arab tribes and their settlement in various parts of Sudan, commercial contacts, and preaching and educational efforts of individual Muslim scholars."[18]

Islam and animism coexist in Sudan, as they do in many other parts of the world, resulting in what is known as *popular Islam* or *folk Islam* in the anthropological literature. According to Samuel Zwemer, one of the most prominent missionaries of the twentieth century: "Islam and Animism live, in very neighborly fashion, on the same street and in the same mind."[19]

Even though Muslim scholars characterize Islam as a monotheistic faith and reject the concept of Muslims having mediators or intercessors between them and God, there are several practices observed throughout the Islamic world that suggest the opposite.

Muslims who are actively involved in the spiritual world do not consider their practices problematic because they also adhere to all the Islamic norms prescribed by orthodoxy: "Those who practice folk Islam rarely see themselves as syncretists. They view themselves as genuine Muslims. From their perspective, no conflict exists between their popular religion and its more orthodox variety."[20]

Among the Fur people, several practices are filled with animistic elements. Like many other Muslim people groups in Sudan, the Fur believe "in spirits as sources of illness or other afflictions and in magical ways of dealing with them."[21] A central figure in this regard is the "holy man," who functions as a shaman and is responsible for assisting the people in dealing with the spiritual world through magical elements:

> The imam of a mosque is not an intercessor but a prayer leader and source of sermons. He may also be a teacher and in smaller communities combines both functions. In the latter guise he is called a *feki*. A *feki* may not be an imam, but in addition to teaching in the local Quranic school (*khalwa*), he is expected to write texts (from the Quran) or magical figures to be used

16. Sidahmed and Sidahmed, *Sudan*, 6.

17. Government of Sudan, "Understanding Darfur Conflict," para. 1.

18. Sidahmed and Sidahmed, *Sudan*, 6.

19. Zwemer, *Influence of Animism*, 207.

20. Love, *Muslims, Magic, and Kingdom*, 10.

21. Nelson, *Sudan*, 122.

as amulets and cures. His blessing may be asked at births, marriages, deaths, and on other important occasions, and he may participate in wholly non-Islamic harvest rites in some remote places. All of these functions and capacities make the *feki* the most important figure in popular Islam. But he is not a priest. His religious authority is based on his putative knowledge of the Quran, the law, and techniques for dealing with occult threats to the health and well-being of the ordinary Muslim. The notion that the words of the Quran will protect against the actions of evil spirits or the evil eye is deeply embedded in popular Islam, and the amulets prepared by the *feki* are intended to protect their wearers against these dangers.[22]

Although the Fur people freely practice Islam, filled with animistic elements, they do not have free contact with other religions' teachings. Regarding their access to the gospel, they are classified as an unreached people group (UPG). According to the Joshua Project, "an unreached or least-reached people is a people group among which there is no indigenous community of believing Christians with adequate numbers and resources to evangelize this people group without outside assistance."[23]

A Fur song from the mid-nineteenth century expresses their pride in Islam and enthusiasm to share their faith with other people groups:

> *The people who live in Fartit are slaves and yet go free.*
>
> *They know nothing at all, neither good nor evil.*
>
> *These heathens who eat men are barbarians and go around naked.*
>
> *They cover their behinds with leaves; of clothes they know nothing.*
> *Or else they run around like cattle.*
>
> *We Fur go and bring them among us and teach them our Islam,*
>
> *And they live happily among us.*[24]

Like most Muslims in Sudan, the Fur people adhere to the Sunni Islam of Maliki school of jurisprudence, although they also observe practices from other Islamic schools of law. The Fur people practice a form of Islam deeply influenced by Sufism, which is also a characteristic found among most Muslim people groups in Sudan.

---

22. Nelson, *Sudan*, 122.

23. See "Unreached/Least Reached," at https://joshuaproject.net/help/definitions.

24. O'Fahey, *Darfur Sultanate*, 167–68.

Sunni Islam

Sunni Islam and Shia Islam have historically been the two most important branches of Islam. Sunni Islam regards Saudi Arabia as its most powerful propagator, while Shia Islam has Iran as its spiritual heart. Sunnis consider themselves as genuine followers of the Sunnah, which refers to Muhammad's behavior. Therefore, they claim to be the Muslim group most identified with orthodoxy in Islam.

The exact percentage of Sunni Muslims worldwide is undetermined, but it is usually calculated between 85 to 90 percent of the world's Muslims. Esposito and Mogahed specifically put the figure at 85 percent,[25] whereas Braswell puts it closer to 90 percent.[26]

The division between Sunni and Shia Muslims began following Mohammed's death. The two groups split because of the disagreement over who should succeed Muhammad as leader of the Muslim community: "The fundamental reason for this major split within the Muslim community was the belief of these Muslims that the leader of the Muslim community ought to be someone from within the family of the Prophet."[27] This disagreement divides the Muslim community worldwide to this day.

Maliki School

In Sunni Islam, there are four schools of religious law or jurisprudence (*fiqh*). The Maliki school is one of them, and the others are Hanafi, Shafii, and Hanbali.[28] The Maliki school derives from the work of its founder Imam Malik bin Anas from Medina. It is distinct from the other three schools of religious law because it is founded on the practice of the people of Medina: "This is the oldest of the schools and is very conservative. It regards the Quran and the *sunna* as the main sources of authority but allows some place for consensus."[29]

The Maliki school of thought or jurisprudence is recognized as the second largest of the four schools, followed by approximately 25 percent Muslims.

25. Esposito and Mogahed, *Who Speaks for Islam?*, 2.

26. Braswell, *Islam*, 90.

27. Chapman, *Cross and Crescent*, 174.

28. Ryle et al., *Sudan Handbook*, 18.

29. Chapman, *Cross and Crescent*, 124.

In North Africa, the Maliki school is the most widely practiced.[30] Maliki *madrasas* can be found in nations all over Western and Northern Africa.[31]

Sufism

Sufism is a popular movement within Islam found among Sunni and Shia Muslims worldwide and is regarded as a robust Islamic expression among the Muslim community in Sudan: "Sufism in the Sudan, as in the rest of the Muslim world, was never considered a religion in and of itself."[32] Sufism has grown in popularity among the Muslim community worldwide. According to scholars such as Ernst, approximately half of the world's Muslim population today practice a form of Sufism.[33]

By practicing Sufism, Muslims seek to discover truth, love, and knowledge of God through direct experience and personal encounters: "Sufism is the mystical aspect of Islam. Some consider it a reaction to the 'cold' and formalistic tenets of more scripturalist Islam, which places great emphasis on the absolute gulf between humans and God."[34]

However experiential their religious practice may be, Sufi Muslims still find a foundation for their religious expression in the Qur'an (the Islamic holy book) and the Hadith (the sacred traditions of Islam). One of the qur'anic verses Sufis often referenced to validate their practices is Sura 2:115, which reaffirms the reality that the presence of Allah is everywhere. Therefore, the presence of Allah can be sought, found, and experienced: "To Allah belong the East and the West: whithersoever ye turn, there is the Presence of Allah. For Allah is All-Pervading, All-Knowing." One of the most popular hadith used by Sufi Muslims to defend their approach is the Hadith of the Hidden Treasure, in which God expresses a desire to be known: "I was a hidden treasure that wished to be known, so I created the universe so that I might be known."[35]

Sufism is a controversial faith expression within Islam. According to some Muslims, it represents a form of religion outside Islamic orthodoxy.[36] Nevertheless, Sufism is an integral part of Islam in the Sudan and determines the kind of Islam practiced by Muslims in the country: "Although both

30. Netton, *Encyclopedia of Islamic Civilization*, 25.

31. J. Qureshi, "Muslim Law," 1–2.

32. Searcy, *Formation*, 39.

33. Ernst, *Shambhala Guide to Sufism*, xvii.

34. Searcy, *Formation*, 39.

35. Campo, *Encyclopedia of Islam*, 279.

36. Ernst, *Shambhala Guide to Sufism*, xvii.

traditions of Sunni—or 'orthodox' Islam, and Sufism—or mystical Islam—were introduced in the Sudan, the latter became the predominant form of Islamic religion and was widely known as 'popular Islam.'"[37]

In Sudan, some people believe that Sufism cannot be separated from Islam, both because it has traditionally coexisted with the Muslim faith worldwide and because Islam's founder was the one who initiated it: "In lands like Sudan, where Sufism is the dominant expression of Islam the Prophet Mohamed is seen as the first Sufi."[38] Chapman argues, "If Muhammad had had his 'journey to heaven' (the Mi'raj), could the believer not enjoy something of the same kind of experience?"[39]

The Fur People

The Fur people are a tribe of approximately 1.25 million people. They mainly inhabit the mountainous area of Jebel Marra, the highest region of Sudan. This area is positioned in the far south of the Darfur region, near the Sudan-Chad border.

The name *Fur* is the most common designation given to the people, but other names are also used to refer to them, such as Fora, Fordunga, Furawi, Konjara, or Kungara. Considering their origins, "they are kin to the Kanuri people of Nigeria, with whom they maintained contact over the centuries."[40] Moreover, the Fur tribe is divided mainly into the Keira and Kunjara clans.[41]

The first historical mention of the name Fur dates to 1664. The Fur monarchs used the name to refer to the people during the Keira Sultanate, and they "apparently used the term Fur to refer to the region's dark-skinned inhabitants who accepted both their Islamic religion and their rule. As the Keira dynasty itself intermarried, its members also became known as Fur."[42]

Regarding ethnicity, even though a portion of the population in northern Sudan has Arab ethnic identification, the Fur people have African ties. However, due to religious bonds, they have adopted Arab names and dress codes.

37. Sidahmed and Sidahmed, *Sudan*, 150.
38. Howard, *Modern Muslims*, 48.
39. Chapman, *Cross and Crescent*, 135.
40. Chapman, *Cross and Crescent*, 135.
41. de Waal, "Who Are the Darfurians?," 186.
42. Britannica, "Darfur."

The Darfur Sultanate

The Fur people are one of Sudan's most prominent ethnic groups. They have been involved in significant historical events, playing an essential role in Sudanese history at various times. Due to their prevalence, the Fur people's history is entwined with Sudan's.

One of the most significant historical events involving the Fur people was the formation of the Darfur Sultanate in 1603, which existed until October 24, 1874, when it fell to the Sudanese warlord Rabih az-Zubayr. Nevertheless, in 1898 the sultanate was restored under the leadership of Sultan Ali Dinar, a world-renowned leader noted for his loyalty to his homeland and people:

> Listen, in every part of my country where I find a hyena who kills someone's animal, a lion that eats someone's animal, a man of the people who seizes his brother's property, or something like this happening in my land, then I shall arouse myself against this. Thus, with God's support, the wild beasts will not kill the livestock; the hobbled camel will go from Fashir to Kutum without anything happening to it; the thief will neither interfere with nor touch it. The well-dressed woman will be able to go wherever she wishes without anyone bothering her. There will be true security, not partial security.[43]

The Darfur Sultanate continued to exist until 1916, when it was defeated by the British and its territory was merged into Anglo-Egyptian Sudan. Around 1650, the Darfur Sultanate became a political entity and from around 1680 to 1780 the Darfur Sultanate was developed into an expansionist dynastic state "of great vitality willing to war among themselves while pursuing war against the west and later the east."[44]

> The sultanate ruled as a fixed political entity firmly located at the capital covering a far-flung empire that incorporated a variety of ethnic groups and very different livelihoods and cultural traditions. The foundation of the perception of a specific Darfurian identity has its origins in the sultanate's ability to integrate various people of different ethnic backgrounds into a larger political entity.[45]

43. O'Fahey, *Darfur Sultanate*, 285.

44. O'Fahey, *Darfur Sultanate*, 41.

45. Hastrup, *War in Darfur*, 26.

The volcanic highlands of the Marrah Mountains were historically the seat of authority of the Darfur Sultanate. As time progressed, the sultanate shifted its capital to El Fasher, which is today the regional capital of North Darfur and where the tomb of Ali Dinar, the last sultan of Darfur, is located.[46]

As Hastrup points out, the Darfur Sultanate was magnificent and rose to the status of an international reference in those days: "The sultanate was prosperous and demanded respect and awe; even medieval European travelers wrote of its glories. The sultans distributed land estates to subjects, the so-called *hakura* (pl. *hawakiir*), and there was a governing responsibility attached to these estates."[47]

The rules of the Darfur Sultanate traced their origins back to early Islamic history. As an Islamic movement, it was critical for them to maintain a connection to Islam's historical development:

> The rulers of the Darfur Sultanate, like the Funj elite, claimed to be descendants of Arab nobility. However, unlike the Funj, the Fūr rulers claimed descent from the ʿAbbāsids . The legitimacy of the ʿAbbāsid caliphate (750–1258) was based on the claim that they were direct descendants of the Prophet's uncle, ʿAbbās; consequently, the ʿAbbāsids maintained that their rule was divinely ordained because of their relationship to the Prophet's family.[48]

Sudanese Modern History

Sudan's history is extensive, dating to the Pharaonic period. Historians like Berlatsky tend to divide Sudan's history into three main periods: ancient, medieval, and modern. "The ancient period extends from antiquity to about the fourth and fifth centuries AD, the medieval from the sixth to eighteenth centuries AD, and the modern history of Sudan from the nineteenth century onwards."[49]

This study examines the history of the Fur people in the context of Sudan's Modern History: beginning with the Turkiya period, continuing through the Mahdiya period and the Anglo-Egyptian Condominium, and

---

46. Hastrup, *War in Darfur*, 26.
47. Hastrup, *War in Darfur*, 27.
48. Searcy, *Formation*, 16.
49. Berlatsky and Chalk, *Darfur*, 30.

concluding with the Independent Sudan period, which includes recent events, some of which are related to the Darfur civil conflict.

The Turkiya Period (1821–1885)

On June 12, 1821, Muhammad Ali, the Turkish viceroy of the Ottoman sultan in Istanbul, conquered Sudan. At the time, he was the ruler of Egypt and decided to take control of Sudan (the territory that is now Sudan and South Sudan).[50]

Muhammad Ali had a significant political motive in undertaking the invasion of the Sudan. As a ruler in Egypt, his most dangerous opponents had been the Mamluks, who had controlled Sudan up to that time.[51] The decision also had economic motives, primarily the search for slave recruits and gold exploration. Ismail Kalil Pasha, the viceroy's third son, led the army that invaded Sudan and encountered minimal opposition. Funj Sultan, Badi IV, and all the other Jaaliyyin *makks* (Sudanese chiefs) had no choice but to recognize Muhammad Ali's power, surrender to the Turkish viceroy's troops, and let him take control of the country.[52]

As intended, Muhammad Ali's conquest of Sudan led to an increase in regional slave exploitation. Although the slave trade activity was already a reality throughout the Funj Sultanate, it reached a new dimension during Muhammad Ali's dynasty. Khartoum was founded in the same year of the invasion with this exploratory purpose in mind. Soon, the city became a hub, allowing the slavery commercial expansion to spread. "By 1860 an estimated 12,000 to 15,000 slaves were sent north every year."[53] The slave trade was most highly active in Darfur and Kordofan, and many were taken from these regions to be sold in Khartoum's slave markets.

The Turkiya period changed Sudan's political and economic scenario and brought significant religious transformation to the Sudanese form of Islam. Since its early years in Sudan, Islam had been shaped by local beliefs. Muslim leaders in Egypt and other parts of the Muslim world were very concerned that Sufism, which they did not see as the correct form of Islam, had gained significant influence in the country.

> Islam in Sudan had traditionally been dominated by the rituals of popular mysticism, *sufism*, for which the legalistic structure

50. Collins, *History of Modern Sudan*, 10.

51. Holt and Daly, *History of the Sudan*, 35.

52. Collins, *History of Modern Sudan*, 10.

53. Collins, *History of Modern Sudan*, 139.

of orthodox Islam in Egypt had no appeal. After the Turco-Egyptian conquest, each of the Viceroys had sought to reform Sudanese Islam by appointing to the highest offices of Islamic law orthodox religious leaders from Egypt who firmly excluded the *sufi* mystics they contemptuously regarded as ignorant peddlers of superstition.[54]

Sudan's new rulers struggled to implement their desired Islamic reformation. They worked hard to promote among Sudanese what was regarded as a more orthodox type of Islam in Egypt and suppress Sufism's expressions in Sudan.[55] However, they failed because Sudanese perceived their teachings as exceedingly foreign. Consequently, the Islamic reformation found significant opposition and moved more slowly than expected, mainly because Sufism was rooted in the religiosity of the Sudanese people:

> The religious reformation of the Sudanese to accept formal Islam had been very gradual during the Turkiya, and it was not until the reign of Ismail that the first Sudanese was appointed president of the Islamic teachers in Sudan, and the Sudanese began to emerge from their religious isolation through the relentless acceptance of Arabic, no longer Turkish, as the lingua franca of administration.[56]

During the Turkiya period, the British and French increased their influence and presence in Egypt, factors that upset the Egyptians and led to a nationalist movement. The main consequence was the Urabi Revolution, an attempt to end British and French influence in Egypt. In 1882, however, the British won the Anglo-Egyptian War and began a process that led to the occupation of Egypt and, consequently, of Sudan.[57]

In 1877, Charles George Gordon, an English general, was appointed governor-general of Sudan.[58] Gordon was a talented leader and was "famous for leading the Ever-Victorious Army in China that suppressed the Taiping Rebellion in 1864."[59] Gordon achieved even greater international notoriety in 1883 for determining a skull-faced cliff as the hill of Golgotha, which is located adjacent to what is now known as the Garden Tomb in Jerusalem.

---

54. Collins, *History of Modern Sudan*, 17.

55. Collins, *History of Modern Sudan*, 20.

56. Collins, *History of Modern Sudan*, 18.

57. Sidahmed and Sidahmed, *Sudan*, 136.

58. Holt and Daly, *History of the Sudan*, 57.

59. Collins, *History of Modern Sudan*, 19.

General Gordon assumed his leadership position, and the British government immediately tasked him with ending slavery in Sudan. In 1880, three years after Gordon had come to power, the Anglo-Egyptian Slave Trade Convention was signed for the purpose of ending slavery in Sudan.[60]

Despite some progress made by the country of Sudan under General Gordon's command, the Turkiya period ended in 1885. The fall of Khartoum to Muhammad Ahmad bin Abdallah, the self-proclaimed Mahdi, marked the end of the period.

The Mahdiya Period (1885–1898)

Although General Gordon was fighting slavery in Sudan, the Sudanese people were seeing the foreign domination as a compromise, especially regarding their religiosity. Also, they were disturbed by the corruption that "had long been endemic in Egyptian administration."[61]

The form of Islam introduced during the Turkiya period did not ultimately suffocate the Sufism that had been part of the Islamic faith of Sudanese for centuries.[62] Amid this period of dissatisfaction, a Muslim Sudanese named Muhammad Ahmad bin Abdallah promoted a rebellion against the ruling Anglo-Egyptian government.

In an Islamic context full of mysticism, Muhammad Ahmad's mission to combat European imperialism with political Islam found validation in a significant religious belief. He claimed to be the *Mahdi*: "the divine leader chosen by God at the end of time to fill the earth with justice and equity, even as it had been filled with oppression and wrong."[63] This prerogative was incredibly significant to the Muslims in Sudan and the world of Islam because Muslims (Sunnis and Shias) believe that, according to Sura 24:55, God is about to send a messianic figure, a redeemer of Islam, who in a time of chaos will lead the believers and reunite Islam:

> Allah has promised, to those among you who believe and work righteous deeds, that He will, of a surety, grant them in the land, inheritance (of power), as He granted it to those before them; that He will establish in authority their religion—the one which He has chosen for them; and that He will change (their state), after the fear in which they (lived), to one of security and peace:

---

60. Collins, *History of Modern Sudan*, 19–20.
61. Holt and Daly, *History of the Sudan*, 63.
62. Collins, *History of Modern Sudan*, 17–18.
63. Holt and Daly, *History of the Sudan*, 64.

"They will worship Me (alone) and not associate aught with Me."
If any do reject Faith after this, they are rebellious and wicked.

Among Muhammad Ahmad's most powerful supporters were the Baqqara nomads of Kordofan and Darfur, who were mobilized by his message, purpose, and charismatic approach. The Mahdi gained his support by forming a group of disciples and persuading people of his messianic calling to conquer and lead Sudan on a religious path.

> In March 1881, on Aba Island, located in the White Nile 150 miles south of Khartoum, Muhammad Ahmad ibn 'Abdallah experienced several visions in which the Prophet appointed him the Expected Mahdi (*mahadi*, guided one). He first informed his confidant, 'Abdallahi ibn Muhammad Turshain, of this revelation and then his small circle of disciples before proceeding to El Obeid, the Turco-Egyptian capital of Kordofan. Here he publicly proclaimed his Mahdiship and emotionally appealed to the notables and the *nas* alike to abandon this world for the new age of righteousness and justice to follow.[64]

Muhammad Ahmad boasted a significant reputation of commitment to Islam among the Sudanese people. His upbringing as a devout Muslim gave him credentials as a leader who began to claim to be a man raised by God to fight the foreign forces ruling the country, free the people, and lead Sudan into a new era:

> Muhammad Ahmad ibn 'Abdallah was a 40-year-old Dunqulawi who from childhood had been deeply religious and well-educated in the Sam-maniyya *sufi* order in a Sudan that he thought had become too worldly. He left the brotherhood and retired to Aba Island, where he led the life of a religious ascetic. He was a reformer, a *mujadid*, who claimed three Islamic titles—the Imam as head of the true Muslim community, the Successor of the Apostle of God to restore that community as the Prophet had done, and the Expected Mahdi who foreshadowed the end of a corrupt and unjust world, which coincided with the coming end of the thirteenth Muslim century.[65]

The Mahdi used revelations, visions, and dreams to convince the Sudanese people of the legitimacy of his mission. Frequently, he shared these supernatural accounts in his public appearances and Friday sermons. In one of them, he told the people that Muhammad, the founder of Islam, had

---

64. Collins, *History of Modern Sudan*, 21.
65. Collins, *History of Modern Sudan*, 21.

appeared in a vision to one of his disciples, Faqih Isa, exhorting all people to recognize the authority of the Mahdi:

> The Prophet (may peace be upon him) came and sat next to me, and said, your shaykh [Muḥammad Aḥmad, the Mahdī] is the anticipated *mahdī*. ʿĪsā responded that he was a believer in the Mahdī's authority, to which the Prophet responded by saying, "whosoever does not believe in the Mahdī is an infidel in the eyes of God and his Prophet." The Prophet said this three times.[66]

By October 23, 1884, the Mahdi had made substantial progress in confronting the ruling authorities: he "established his headquarters on the west bank of the Nile opposite Khartoum in what became known as Omdurman."[67] On January 26, 1885, the Mahdi invaded the city and his army defeated the British, killed General Gordon, and expelled the British and Egyptians from the country.[68]

Following his great victory over the British and Egyptian forces, the Mahdi became the absolute ruler of Sudan. The Mahadyia, the Mahdi's new governing system, rose as "both an anti-colonial struggle and a proto-nationalist movement."[69] Surprisingly, the Mahdi did not rule for long, as he died months after becoming the new country's leader:

> Six months later, on 22 June, the Mahdi died after a short ill-ness, leaving behind a skeletal administration controlled by his disciples, three of whom he had given the title of Com-panion of the Prophet. ʿAbdallahi ibn Muhammad was the *Khalifat al-Siddiq*, the successor to the Caliph Abu Bakr; ʿAli ibn Muhammad Hilu became *Khalifat al-Faruq*, the successor to the Caliph ʿUmar; and Muhammad Sharif was designated *Khalifat al-Karrar*, the successor to the Caliph ʿAli, cousin of the Prophet. As the prototype of Abu Bakr, the closest of the Prophet's Companions, the Khalifa ʿAbdallahi, confidant of the Mahdi, was thus his likely successor.[70]

The Mahdi's government lasted years after his death under heavy Is-lamic radical influences, setting the stage for Islamic fundamentalism in Sudan, which continues to impact the country today. The Mahdiya ruled

---

66. Abū Salīm, *Manshūrāt al-Mahdī*, 14.

67. Collins, *History of Modern Sudan*, 24.

68. Churchill, *River War*, 27.

69. Hastrup, *War in Darfur*, 31.

70. Collins, *History of Modern Sudan*, 24.

Sudan from 1885 to 1898, implementing the Mahdi concept in Islam while facing opposition from different people groups, including the Fur.[71]

The Mahdya period ended when General Herbert Horatio Kitchener's army prevailed against the Mahdists. Aided by Winston Churchill, a young lieutenant with the Twenty-First Lancers, the Anglo-Egyptian forces reclaimed Sudan by defeating the Dervish army at the Battle of Omdurman on September 2, 1898.[72]

The Anglo-Egyptian Condominium (1899–1936)

When the Mahdiya came to an end, there was a power void in Sudan and much uncertainty about who would rule the country: "The overthrow of the Mahdist state posed the immediate question of the future status and administration of the Sudan."[73]

The British and Egyptians reached a consensus regarding Sudan's independence, prompting them to collaborate on formalizing their intentions and devising a means of allowing the Sudanese to rule themselves: "This was embodied in two Anglo-Egyptian conventions of 1899, which came to be known as the Condominium Agreement since they created a theoretically joint sovereignty."[74]

The Anglo-Egyptian Condominium period, from 1899 to 1955, was based on the Anglo-Egyptian Condominium Agreements of January 19 and July 10, 1899. The agreement proposed a joint government between Britain and Egypt to rule eastern Sudan in preparation for its independence.

In practice, the British ruled Sudan throughout the Anglo-Egyptian Condominium period: "Although Egypt theoretically had equal status with Britain, in actuality it was the British alone who administered Sudan until it became independent in 1956."[75]

The British and Egyptians had consented to choose a Sudanese ruler according to the agreements' premises: "The Condominium agreements established an office of governor-general, to be appointed, on British recommendation, by the khedive of Egypt and vested with supreme civil and military command."[76]

---

71. Collins, *History of Modern Sudan*, 25.

72. Churchill, *River War*, 302.

73. Holt and Daly, *History of the Sudan*, 85.

74. Holt and Daly, *History of the Sudan*, 85.

75. Petterson, *Inside Sudan*, 7.

76. Britannica, "Anglo-Egyptian Condominium."

A significant event in the history of the Fur people occurred during the condominium. The former independent Fur Sultanate was restored. It was formally recognized by the government in 1900.[77] The Anglo-Egyptian Condominium period came to an end in 1955, giving way to the independence of the Republic of the Sudan on January 1, 1956.

The Independent Sudan Period (1956–2022)

On July 5, 1956, Abdallah Khalil was appointed as the country's second prime minister. He succeeded Ismail al-Azhari, who declared Sudan independent and became its first president; however, he was later forced to resign.[78]

In 1958, a military coup in the north, led by General Ibrahim Abboud, resulted in the dissolution of parliament. This event happened because of fear of regional destabilization and Arab radicalism.[79]

Sudan and Egypt signed a Nile River water agreement in 1959. The bilateral deal enhanced Egypt's and Sudan's water allotments, reiterating the stipulations of an earlier agreement, the 1929 Anglo-Egyptian Treaty.[80]

After several demonstrations and strikes, prompted by students at the University of Khartoum, the revolution deposed the Abboud regime in 1964. Sirr al-Khatim al-Khalifa established a transitional administration, and civilian administration was reestablished.[81]

New elections for parliament were held in 1965. An agreement between the National Unionist Party (NUP) and the Umma Party led to a government headed by Mohamed Ahmed Mahgoub. Representatives of the Southern Front in cabinet agreed that elections should be held only in the north.[82]

In 1966, an internal rift within the Umma Party pulled down the Mahjub government, replacing it with a new cabinet under the leadership of Sadiq al-Mahdi,[83] the grandson of Sayyid Abd al-Rahman al-Mahdi, founder of the Umma Party. Also, al-Mahdi was the great-grandson of

77. Collins, *History of Modern Sudan*, 35.
78. Holt and Daly, *History of the Sudan*, 115.
79. Holt and Daly, *History of the Sudan*, 117.
80. Holt and Daly, *History of the Sudan*, 119.
81. Holt and Daly, *History of the Sudan*, 122–23.
82. Holt and Daly, *History of the Sudan*, 122–23.
83. Holt and Daly, *History of the Sudan*, 126.

Muhammad Ahmad, the Mahdi who fought the Anglo-Egyptian armies during the Mahdist War.[84]

Five years later, in 1971, Gaafar Mohamed el-Nimeiri, major general, commander of the armed forces, and first elected Sudanese president, was confirmed to preside over the country in a referendum. In 1983, under the influence of the Muslim Brotherhood, the Sudanese president Nimeiri replaced the civil criminal code in Sudan with Islamic law (Sharia), imposing penalties such as amputating the hands of thieves. In the same year, Sadiq al-Mahdi was arrested for his opposition to the Islamization process.

On January 18, 1985, under Nimeiri administration, Mahmud Muhammad Taha, the elderly Sudanese Muslim reformer and peaceful Muslim activist, was executed on the charge of apostasy. Despite repeated appeals for mercy from the Muslim world and the international community, the revered leader of the Republican Brothers, an Islamic reform movement, was hanged at Khartoum prison.[85]

Nimeiri became unpopular for his radicalism. Even though he eventually softened his ideas and weakened Islamic law to gain popular support, he was deposed in a coup in April 1985 by a group of army officers led by Abd al-Rahman Muhammad Siwar al-Dahab, the defense minister and commander-in-chief of the armed forces.[86] In 1986, the new military government held elections that resulted in the return of Sadiq al-Mahdi to the position of prime minister. However, the subsequent three years were characterized by considerable political turmoil. On June 30, 1989, Omar al-Bashir, the military chief of Sudan, in collaboration with Islamist hard-liners, led a coup against Prime Minister Sadiq al-Mahdi, resulting in the dissolution of the government and all political parties. Bashir established himself as the country's leader, appointed himself as chairman of the Revolutionary Command Council for National Salvation—which ruled the country—and became the defense minister. As a career army officer, Omar al-Bashir had played a significant part in the war against insurgents in the South during the 1980s.

In 1990, Osama Bin Laden relocated from Afghanistan to Sudan, only three years after establishing Al-Qaeda as a terrorist organization. He lived in Khartoum from 1990 to 1996 at the invitation of Hassan al-Turabi, who became one of his mentors. Turabi orchestrated the 1989 military coup against his brother-in-law, Sadiq al-Mahdi, bringing Omar al-Bashir to power. He also championed radical Islam in Sudan in the early 1990s. Turabi was a

---

84. Hastrup, *War in Darfur*, 156.

85. Holt and Daly, *History of the Sudan*, 141.

86. Economist Intelligence Unit et al., "Sudan."

multilingual politician who spoke Arabic, English, French, and German fluently. He held a bachelor's degree in jurisprudence from the University of Khartoum, a master's degree from the University of London, and a doctorate in constitutional law from the University of Sorbonne in France.

In 1991, Omar al-Bashir and his Islamist allies, including Hassan al-Turabi, imposed strict Islamic law on the country, further dividing Sudan between the predominantly Muslim and Arabized northern region and the largely animist and Christian southern region.[87]

After the Revolutionary Council was disbanded, Omar al-Bashir was appointed president of Sudan in October of 1993.[88] Nearly five years later, Sudanese legislators wrote a new constitution in June 1998, which relaxed the country's ban on political parties for the first time.

In 2002, an agreement for a cessation of hostilities was signed by the North and South Sudan governments, marking a defining moment in recent Sudanese history. The deal gave the people of the South the choice to seek independence after a six-year period, which they did, resulting in the division of the country's territory.[89]

Demonstrations against the government erupted in Darfur in 2003. People were complaining of the neglect of the Khartoum administration. As a result, rebel groups in Darfur launched an uprising against the government forces. The government responded with significant violence, sending armed Arab militias to battle both the local population and the rebel organizations in the region.[90]

In 2004, the hostilities in Darfur escalated. Tens of thousands of civilians were killed, and hundreds of thousands became refugees. With another war front to contend with, in the following year, Omar al-Bashir signed an official peace agreement with the southern Sudanese rebel group, the Sudan People's Liberation Army.[91]

In 2009, the International Criminal Court (ICC) issued an arrest warrant for President Omar al-Bashir for crimes against humanity, war crimes, and genocide in Darfur. It was the first time a warrant for a sitting head of state had been issued. Al-Bashir, enraged, decided to respond by banishing several humanitarian aid organizations from Darfur. However, on July 12, 2010, the ICC issued a second arrest warrant for Omar al-Bashir.[92]

87. Holt and Daly, *History of the Sudan*, 149.

88. Holt and Daly, *History of the Sudan*, 150.

89. Holt and Daly, *History of the Sudan*, 163.

90. Hastrup, *War in Darfur*, 2.

91. Hastrup, *War in Darfur*, 2.

92. Berlatsky and Chalk, *Darfur*, 78.

In a referendum held in 2011, the people of South Sudan voted to secede from Sudan and form their own country. As a result, Omar al-Bashir forced all southerners to leave Sudan and return to South Sudan.[93]

In 2018, anti-government protests erupted across Sudan, initially over steep price increases and shortages, but quickly shifting to calls for Omar al-Bashir to step down. Security forces retaliated with a ferocious crackdown, killing twenty-two people. The popular revolt against Bashir intensified, and the Sudanese army decided to arrest Bashir on April 11, seizing power, suspending the country's constitution, and closing its borders and airspace. The thirty years (1989–2019) of the Bashir government era had ended.[94]

Following the fall of Omar al-Bashir, a transitional military government took over and was rejected by the Sudanese who went to the streets demanding civilian rule. After the African Union intervened, a transitional government was formed merging civilian and military representatives. The new leaders had to share power and prepare a transition for a democratic government. Abdallah Hamdok became the interim prime minister of Sudan and began implementing significant reforms to make the country more tolerant, stable, and democratic.[95]

In 2021, Sudan experienced another coup. On October 25, the military deposed the interim prime minister Abdallah Hamdok and took power. On November 21, nearly one month later, Hamdok was reinstated as prime minister after making a deal with the military to resolve the standoff that had resulted in the deaths of dozens of Sudanese protesters. However, on January 2, 2022, the year of the conclusion of this study, Hamdok announced his resignation as Sudan's prime minister. The highest authority in the country became Abdel Fattah al-Burhan, the top military commander.[96]

Darfur: The Fur Homeland

Darfur, also called Western Darfur, is a region in western Sudan. The word *Darfur* means "home of the Fur" in Arabic. In 2003, the Fur homeland entered the international spotlight, becoming well known worldwide due to the eruption of a civil war.

Darfur is a region with a territory roughly the size of France. It covers an area of approximately 170,000 square miles (440,000 square km)[97]

93. Hastrup, *War in Darfur*, 154.
94. Economist Intelligence Unit et al., "Sudan."
95. Economist Intelligence Unit et al., "Sudan."
96. Economist Intelligence Unit et al., "Sudan."
97. Britannica, "Darfur."

and is currently divided into five administrative states: North Darfur, with El Fasher as its capital; West Darfur, with El Geneina as its capital; South Darfur, with Nyala as its capital; Central Darfur, with Zalingei as its capital; and Eastern Darfur, with Ed Daein as its capital.

The landscape of the region is highly diversified:

> Darfur is transversed by several climatic-vegetational zones, ranging from the hot, hyper-arid desert in the north to the woodland savannah with 900 mm of mean annual precipitation in the south. The thornscrub savannah of central Darfur is interrupted by the wetter region of the Jebel Marra massif (3,088 m), which receives 500–1000 mm of mean annual rainfall.[98]

Arabs have long been the larger part of the population in the northern part of Darfur, while Arabs and Fur have long been the more significant populations in the southern part of the region. However, Darfur is home to a variety of ethnic groups.

> The population of Darfur consists of a diverse mix of ethnic groups. The non-Arabs of central Darfur—including the Fur, the Tunjur, the Masalit, the Berti, and the Bergid, among other, smaller groups—are farmers, and the non-Arabs of northern Darfur—principally the Zaghawa and the Bedayat—are nomadic herders.[99]

Darfurians, in general, are more used to nomadic lifestyles, herding cattle, and camels. Most of the non-Arab population of the region tend to be sedentary farmers.[100] Study participants have shared their experiences raising livestock in Darfur. One of them stated that before the war, it was typical for grandparents to present a newborn grandchild with a calf. The child would grow up learning to care for his animal. Also, there was the expectation that the animal would become a source of income at some stage in the child's life. At the appropriate time, parents would instruct the child that the animal needed to breed to reproduce and expand the herd. By the time the child had reached adulthood, a herd would have formed, and the individual Fur would have sufficient animals to sustain himself.

98. Van Ardenne at el., *Explaining Darfur*, 10.

99. Grzyb, *World and Darfur*, 8.

100. Herr, *Darfur Genocide*, xvii.

Geography

Darfur's geography is characterized by a vast and undulating area. Apart from that, Darfur's soil quality varies significantly across its territory:

> The volcanic highlands of the Marrah Mountains dominate the central part of this plain. The Marrah Mountains have an average elevation of 7,200 feet (2,200 metres), with the highest peak, Mount Marrah, rising to 10,131 feet (3,088 metres). Elsewhere the sparsely populated plains of Darfur are relatively featureless and arid, particularly in the north, where they merge into the Libyan Desert. Soils, which are generally stony or sandy, support some seasonal grass and low thorny shrubs with tropical maquis vegetation. The Marrah highlands receive heavier rainfall than other parts of Darfur, and a number of large wadis (seasonal watercourses) rise in the mountains and flow southward across the plains.[101]

On top of the diversity in the soil composition, there is also variation in climate and rainfall. The combination of these characteristics produces a scenario in the region that allows the different people groups who inhabit the area to develop a wide range of economic activities.

> Heavy rainfall in the Marrah highlands permits the intensive cultivation of cereals, rice, and fruits. Crops grown at other locations in the southern part of Darfur include sorghum, millet, sesame, peanuts (groundnuts), other root crops, and vegetables. In the arid north, camels, sheep, and goats are raised. Traditional handicrafts include leatherwork, wood carving, and carpet weaving.[102]

Darfur's History

Darfur is one of Sudan's oldest regions. Historians do not have much information of the region, but they are aware that Darfur's northern residents were related to the predynastic peoples of the Nile River region.[103]

The Fur people have held a prominent position in Darfur throughout the region's history. Today, it is impossible to describe the history of Darfur

101. Britannica, "Darfur."
102. Britannica, "Darfur."
103. Britannica, "Darfur."

without mentioning the Fur and recounting their participation in some of the most significant events that have occurred in the region over the years:

> The early history of Darfur was rather obscure, but at least two states were known to have ruled the region between the thirteenth and sixteenth centuries: the Daju and the Tunjur. After a period of disorder in the sixteenth century, the Kayra clan led by Sulayman Solonge (*Solongdungo*) prevailed until the end of the Fur Sultanate in 1916. Sulayman Solonge (1596–1637) was said to have driven out the Tunjur, united the Fur and non-Fur peoples of Jabal Marra, conquered the area around the mountain, and declared Islam to be the official religion of the kingdom.[104]

Darfur has a history of ethnic conflicts. Some of them result in violence among different people groups: "Ethnic tensions, long simmering between nomadic Arab herders and sedentary Fur and other agriculturalists, began erupting into armed conflict in the late 1980s."[105]

The central government in Khartoum has never made a significant investment or developed a substantial infrastructure in Darfur. This is a long-standing issue that has prompted dissatisfaction among the various people groups in the region: "By 1935, almost two decades after colonial rule started, Darfur still had only one elementary school and two sub-grade 'literary schools' for a school-age population of 500,000."[106]

Over the years, the Darfur population grew frustrated by the lack of attention from Khartoum's leadership, who generally have invested nearly all available resources in the country's more developed areas, particularly the capital.

The Civil War in Darfur

A significant milestone in the history of the Fur people and the Darfur region took place when the civil war started in 2003. The conflicts that have now so destabilized the area began with protests directed to the central government, located in Khartoum:

> The conflict began in 2003 when rebels launched an insurrection to protest what they contended was the Sudanese government's disregard for the western region and its non-Arab population. In response, the government equipped and supported Arab

104. Sidahmed and Sidahmed, *Sudan*, 5.
105. Britannica, "Darfur."
106. Cockett, *Sudan*, 32.

militias—which came to be known as Janjaweed (also Jingaweit or Janjaweed)—to fight against the rebels in Darfur.[107]

Violence escalated quickly and began to destabilize the entire region. Within a year, Darfur was ground zero of a humanitarian disaster. Tens of thousands of people were killed by Sudanese government forces, hundreds of thousands fled to refugee camps in Chad, and many others remained internally displaced.

According to UN estimates, approximately 300,000 people have died since the beginning of the civil war, and the death toll continues to rise. In addition to numerous fatalities, the war has displaced approximately 2.7 million people. Among the forcibly displaced are the internally displaced, asylum seekers, and refugees worldwide.[108]

Since 2003, the Fur people have been living through their darkest years in their whole history. They are one of the Darfurian groups who have been targeted the most by the government-sponsored violence in the region, which has been in a state of humanitarian emergency for nearly twenty years:

> The victims of the Darfur genocide are primarily from three "non-Arab" tribal groups: the Fur, the Zaghawa, and the Massalit. Eyewitness accounts describe how Sudanese government forces and Janjaweed militias rode into Fur, Zaghawa, and Massalit villages on horses and camels, wielding automatic weapons (provided by the Sudanese government) and firing indiscriminately at civilians. Homes, grain stores, and crops were destroyed, while women, children, and the elderly were whipped, raped, tortured, and murdered. These tactics were designed to terrorize victims, forcing them to flee their homelands for displaced persons camps within Darfur or refugee camps in neighboring Chad.[109]

According to official documents from the International Commission of Inquiry on Darfur's *Report to the [United Nations] Secretary-General*, the atrocities committed in Darfur have impacted the lives of the people in several ways. Report 186, a prime example, covers attacks on civilians:

> There are consistent accounts of a recurrent pattern of attacks on villages and settlements, sometimes involving aerial attacks by helicopter gunships or fixed-wing aircraft (Antonov and

---

107. Britannica, "Conflict in Darfur."

108. UN, "Sudan."

109. Herr, *Darfur Genocide*, xviii.

MIG), including bombing and strafing with automatic weapons. However, a majority of the attacks reported are ground assaults by the military, the Janjaweed, or a combination of the two. Hundreds of incidents have been reported involving the killing of civilians, massacres, summary executions, rape and other forms of sexual violence, torture, abduction, looting of property and livestock, as well as deliberate destruction and torching of villages. These incidents have resulted in the massive displacement of large parts of the civilian population within Darfur as well as to neighboring Chad. The reports indicate that the intensity of the attacks and the atrocities committed in any one village spread such a level of fear that populations from surrounding villages that escaped such attacks also fled to areas of relative security.[110]

Numerous American politicians classified the conflict as an attempted genocide led by the government of Sudan. Because of the war crimes and crimes against humanity committed in the region, the ICC issued two prison sentences against the Sudanese President Omar al-Bashir. The charges of his cases are:

> Five counts of crimes against humanity: murder, extermination, forcible transfer, torture, and rape; two counts of war crimes: intentionally directing attacks against a civilian population as such or against individual civilians not taking part in hostilities, and pillaging; three counts of genocide: by killing, by causing serious bodily or mental harm, and by deliberately inflicting on each target group conditions of life calculated to bring about the group's physical destruction, allegedly committed at least between 2003 and 2008 in Darfur, Sudan.[111]

Nevertheless, there is no consensus among international specialists and observers that the war in Darfur can be classified as genocide.[112] For instance, the United Nations has declared the absence of genocidal intentionality from the Sudanese government and always refrained from using the term *genocide* in reference to the atrocities in Darfur. Alternatively, in the *Report to the Secretary-General*, the U.N. Commission confirmed that "two elements of genocide might be deduced from the gross violations of human rights perpetrated by Government forces and the militias under

---

110. Berlatsky and Chalk, *Darfur*, 26.

111. ICC, "Al Bashir Case," para. 2.

112. Mamdani, *Saviors and Survivors*, 5.

their control."[113] However, all analysts agree that the destruction produced by the Sudanese government in Darfur is a humanitarian disaster:

> Regardless of what it is called, the conflict has had, and continues to have, devastating consequences for the Darfur people. By 2008, the United Nations estimated that between 200,000 and 300,000 people had died in Darfur, and 2.7 million more were displaced. In other words, since 2003, half of Darfur's population has either been murdered or fled their homes.[114]

For a period, the Darfur war rallied people worldwide in support of the victims. Massive protests demanded an end to the violence that was going on in the region. Save Darfur, Amnesty International, Human Rights Watch, the United States Holocaust Memorial Museum's Committee on Conscience, and Genocide Watch were among the groups advocating for Darfurians. Additionally, several world celebrities joined the movement, raised their voices, and spoke out in support of the Darfur war victims:

> Celebrity activists have also emerged in full force, including Angelina Jolie's online diary detailing her tour of Darfurian refugee camps on the USHMM website; George Clooney's highly publicized visit to Chad in 2006; and a 2007 Darfur activist guide, *Not on Our Watch*, co-authored by actor Don Cheadle and John Prendergast of the International Crisis Group.[115]

In recent years, though, considerable attention has shifted from Darfur to other parts of the world, particularly after the ICC issued arrest warrants against Omar al-Bashir on March 4, 2009, and on July 12, 2010. Study participants of this research have the perception that the international community presumed that after the ICC sentences, a solution to the violence in Darfur was already underway, which did not occur.

After the government shift in 2019, following the fall of Omar al-Bashir in 2019, there was renewed hope for a complete change in the Darfur situation. However, the bloody conflict remains unabated, as Hastrup highlights: "The vast area of Darfur remains plagued by anarchy, impunity and internal strife between various fractions of formerly allied rebels and different defected militiamen."[116] As a result, Sudan continues to send refugees to several countries in the world, such as Jordan.

---

113. International Commission of Inquiry on Darfur, *Report to the Secretary-General*, 4.

114. Herr, *Darfur Genocide*, 226.

115. Grzyb, *World and Darfur*, 86.

116. Hastrup, *War in Darfur*, 12.

Summary

This chapter has focused on Sudan and Darfur, the country and region, respectively, of the Fur people. The context of the Fur people includes their origins, demographics, language, religion, and history. The civil war, which began in 2003, continues unabated. The ongoing violence in Darfur is the main reason that Fur individuals continue to become asylum seekers and refugees in numerous nations throughout the world, including Jordan, where this research takes place.

The next chapter will focus on Jordan, the context in which a group of Fur asylum seekers and refugees are currently living while they wait to be resettled in a third country. After looking into their past, we will consider their present to explain the circumstances that shape their lives in the environment where this research is being conducted.

4

Understanding the Current Status of the Fur People in Jordan

God is the only one who can make the valley of trouble
a door of hope.

—CATHERINE MARSHALL

Introduction

THE UNITED NATIONS COMMISSIONED an investigation on the civil war in Darfur and published the resulting report on January 25, 2005. The report of the International Commission of Inquiry on Darfur stated "that there is evidence that government-backed Arab militias in Darfur attacked and massacred civilians on the basis of ethnicity."[1] The report confirmed that the Arab militias had been deliberately targeting the Fur, among other people groups, because of their ethnic identity: "It is reported that amongst the African tribes, members of the Zaghawa, Fur and Masaalit tribes, which have a marked concentration of population in some areas, have been particularly targeted."[2]

The facts of this report are still clearly observable today. The Fur individuals currently living in Jordan are war victims. Since 2003, individuals from this people group have been running for their lives, crossing

1. Berlatsky and Chalk, *Darfur*, 24.
2. Berlatsky and Chalk, *Darfur*, 30.

borders, and seeking refuge in a struggle to leave behind discrimination, abuse, and violence.

The purpose of this chapter is to present the living conditions of Fur individuals who currently reside as persons of concern (POC)—asylum seekers or refugees—in Jordan. It introduces Jordanian context, religion, and history to describe the environment Fur asylum seekers and refugees relate to when they arrive in Jordan. The chapter portrays Jordan as a historical haven for refugees. However, it highlights some challenges that refugees, particularly those from Sudan, face in the kingdom. It explains the process Sudanese undergo to become asylum seekers and to be recognized as official refugees. Also, it explores why Fur people migrate to Jordan and presents some historical difficulties Sudanese have encountered on their journey to seek shelter outside Sudan. Next, the chapter discusses their frustrations regarding the international community. Additionally, it examines how their religious worldview has been impacted by the discrimination the Fur have experienced over the years. Furthermore, it demonstrates how Fur asylum seekers and refugees relate to Islam in Jordan and how some of their religious disappointments produce receptiveness to the gospel.

Jordan: The Host Country of the Fur People

The Fur people are one of the refugee communities living in the Hashemite Kingdom of Jordan. Commonly referred to just as Jordan, this Arab kingdom is positioned in Western Asia (or the Middle East) and is strategically located "on the bank of Jordan River, and at the crossroads of Africa, Asia, and Europe."[3]

Jordan has a territory covering about 35,480 square miles (91,880 square kilometers). The kingdom's western border is shared with Israel, its northern border with Syria, its northeast border with Iraq, and its southern and eastern borders with Saudi Arabia.

Though at one time part of the British Empire, Jordan gained independence on May 25, 1946. British control ended following the Second World War, and Jordan was declared independent. King Abdullah I, grandfather of the current king, became the kingdom's first monarch.

The name *Jordan* derives from the name of the Jordan River, while the name *Hashemite* derives from Hashem, a grandson of Qusai and the great-grandfather of Mohammad, the Prophet of Islam. The Hashemites, commonly known as the House of Hashim, are Jordan's royal dynasty. The Hashemites previously controlled the kingdoms of Hejaz (1916–1925),

---

3. Miaschi, "What Languages Are Spoken," para. 1.

Syria (1920), and Iraq (1921–1958). The dynasty had ruled Mecca constantly since the tenth century, frequently as vassals of foreign nations, and was granted the thrones of Hejaz, Syria, Iraq, and Jordan because of their alliance with the British Empire during World War I.[4]

The country's founding took place after the Great Arab Revolution. As Hammad points out, "The history of Jordan began when King Hussein Ben Ali (Hussein I), King of the Arabs in Mecca, decided to declare the Great Arab Revolution against the Ottoman Turks between the years 1916–1917, uniting the forces of the Arabs."[5]

Because Jordan is a constitutional monarchy, the supreme authority is the king, who is solely responsible for maintaining order and enforcing the country's laws. The current head of state and monarch is King Abdullah II, who ascended to the throne upon the death of his father, King Hussein I, on February 7, 1999. The king exercises power over the executive, legislative, and judiciary branches. Also, he appoints the prime minister, who currently is Omar Razzaz and has been serving in this capacity since June 4, 2018.

Jordan's monarchy is founded on a constitution, adopted on January 8, 1952. The constitution establishes a Congress (or National Assembly) made up of a House of Representatives and a Federal Senate. The king appoints the members of the Federal Senate, whereas the members of the House of Representatives are elected. In both cases, the members serve a four-year term.

Jordan is regarded as one of the Middle East's safest Arab countries: it is known worldwide primarily for being a stable place and a secure haven in a region rife with conflict. Jordan is also famous for its hospitality tradition, which dates to ancient times:

> Jordan has a tradition of welcoming visitors: camel caravans plied the legendary King's Highway transporting frankincense in exchange for spices while Nabataean tradesmen, Roman legionnaires, Muslim armies and zealous Crusaders all passed through the land, leaving behind impressive monuments. These monuments, including Roman amphitheatres, Crusader castles and Christian mosaics, have fascinated subsequent travelers in search of antiquity and the origins of faith. The tradition of hospitality to visitors remains to this day.[6]

---

4. Abdullah II, "Hashemites."

5. Hammad, *Jordânia*, 10.

6. Walker and Clammer, *Lonely Planet Jordan*, 7.

Jordan's capital city is Amman, the largest city of the kingdom. In the thirteenth century BC, Amman became the capital of the Ammonites; today, it stands out as a global economic, political, and cultural hub:

> Amman was later a great city of Middle Eastern antiquity, Philadelphia, of the Roman Decapolis, and now serves as one of the region's principal commercial and transportation centres as well as one of the Arab world's major cultural capitals.[7]

As a long-standing cultural center, it's unsurprising that Jordan is accounted for in biblical geography. In the Old Testament, Jordan was home to the ancient biblical kingdoms of Moab, Gilead, and Edom. In the New Testament, Jordan is part of the territory referred to as Perea. Apart from the Jordan River, parts of the Dead Sea are also located in the country's west-central region.

Every year, many tourists pass through Jordan on their way to Israel to learn about the places where biblical characters, such as Abraham, Job, Moses, Ruth, Elijah, John the Baptist, Jesus Christ, and Paul, walked.

The baptism of Jesus took place on this side of the Jordan River (John 1:28), as did several other biblical events. From Mount Nebo, Moses saw the full extent of the promised land (Deut 34:1–4). In Gadara, Jesus delivered the possessed man from the evil spirits (Mark 5:1–13). By the Jordan River, in a place known as Elijah's Hill, the prophet Elijah ascended to heaven (2 Kgs 2:1–11).

Demographics

As of January 2022, Jordan had a population of 10,316,771 people. The country's population is growing at a rate of 1 percent per year. The Jordanian population is expected to continue growing, following a period of fast population growth from 2000 to 2020, which increased the population by more than 5 million people. "The population is expected to peak at 14.15 million people in 2080, after which it will begin to decline slowly, ending the twenty-first century with 13.69 million people."[8]

---

7. Bickerton et al., "Jordan."

8. From 2021 edition of https://worldpopulationreview.com/countries/jordan-population.

Language

Jordan's official language is Arabic, which almost the entire population speaks. English is the primary foreign language in the country and is widely spoken, particularly in the cities. There are language variations in Jordan, but they do not compromise communication among the population: "There are various dialects spoken, with local inflections and accents, but these are mutually intelligible and similar to the type of Levantine Arabic spoken in parts of Palestine, Lebanon, and Syria."[9]

The languages spoken in Jordan allow Sudanese seeking refuge in the kingdom to adjust more easily. Since Arabic and English are the official languages of Sudan, Sudanese freely communicate with people once they enter the country.

Religion

Jordan is a predominantly Muslim country. The Muslim population in Jordan is estimated to be 97.2 percent, while Christians make up most of the remaining percentage.

Almost the entire local Muslim population self-identifies as Sunni. Among Christians, some of the groups represented in Jordan are Greek Orthodox, Greek Catholic, Roman Catholic, and the Syrian Orthodox Patriarchate of Antioch. "Most non-Arab Christians are Armenians, and the majority belong to the Gregorian, or Armenian, Orthodox church, while the rest attend the Armenian Catholic Church. There are several Protestant denominations representing communities whose converts came almost entirely from other Christian sects."[10]

Jordan: A Haven for Refugees

Jordan has served as a refugee host country throughout its long history, responding vigorously to past migration issues and recent migration crises. Only two years after Jordan's independence was declared, in 1946, a complex migration crisis emerged following the creation of the state of Israel. Before that, people were already migrating due to ongoing land disputes. Though, after 1948, the displacement of Palestinians took on much greater proportions. His majesty King Abdullah II speaks of an impressive number

9. Bickerton et al., "Jordan."
10. Bickerton et al., "Jordan."

of Palestinians who needed protection back in those days, stating, "Before, during, and after the 1948 war some 750,000 Palestinian Arab refugees fled the fighting or were evicted from their homes."[11]

In moments, Palestinians had to flee their territory and find shelter beyond their borders; they have long found Jordan to be a nation with open arms. As a result of decades welcoming Palestinian refugees in its territory, "nearly half of Jordanian citizens either are or are descended from Palestinians who found refuge in Jordan following the creation of Israel in 1948, and the Israeli occupation of the West Bank (and Gaza and the Golan Heights) in 1967."[12]

Historically, no other country has hosted more Palestinian refugees than Jordan, a nation that has "the highest ratio of refugees to indigenous population of any country."[13] Some of the most remarkable moments in which Jordan opened its borders to Palestinians happened during the first and second Arab-Israeli wars:

> During the first Arab-Israeli war, Jordan received a large in-flux of refugees and later annexed the West Bank of the Jordan River—a part of pre-1948 Palestine. Within two years, Jordan's population increased from 500,000 to 1.5 million, one-third of them refugees.

> During the second Arab-Israeli war of June 1967, Israel occu-pied the West Bank, sending to the Jordanian East Bank another 400,000 Palestinians who were not deemed refugees but rather internally displaced, as they had not crossed an internationally recognized border. Roughly 175,000 of them were also refugees from the 1948 war."[14]

Palestinian refugees do not fall within the responsibility of UNHCR. Instead, they are overseen by the UNRWA (United Nations Relief and Works Agency for Palestine Refugees in the Near East), created on December 8, 1949, to respond to the Palestinian migration crisis. As of January 2022, the number of Palestinians under UNRWA's mandate was 5.7 million, making Palestinians the second-largest refugee caseload globally, followed by Syrians with 6.7 million.[15]

11. Abdullah II, *Our Last Best Chance*, 10.

12. Davis et al., "Sudanese and Somali Refugees," 6.

13. Chatelard, "Jordan," para. 24.

14. Chatelard, "Jordan," para. 24.

15. See www.unhcr.org/figures-at-a-glance.html.

Throughout decades welcoming refugees in its territory, Jordan welcomed more than just Palestinian nationals: "In addition to receiving Palestinians, Jordan has also hosted forced migrants from other countries in the Middle East, such as Lebanon during the 1975–1991 civil war, and Iraq since the 1991 Gulf War and after the 2003 removal of Saddam Hussein following the Anglo-American military intervention."[16]

During the current migration crisis, Jordan has responded by welcoming astounding numbers of refugees. Despite its tiny size and lack of natural resources, the country is an essential player in the Syrian crisis.

As of early 2022, the country hosted 759,738 active registered persons of concern, with 628,957 living alongside Jordanians in urban areas (82.8 percent). At the same time, Jordan hosts Zaatari refugee camp, the world's largest refugee camp for Syrians. Also, the country has three other refugee camps, Azraq, Mrajeeb Al Fhood or Emirati, and King Abdullah Park (KAP).

The influx of refugees in Jordan is so high that, "in 2015, Jordan was reported to have the second-highest per capita rate of refugees in the world, a rank that the country keeps up to this day. . . . This count and other UNHCR statistics do not include Palestinians."[17]

Welcoming refugees has brought many challenges to Jordan, a small country with limited natural resources; but it has also triggered some economic benefits: "In particular, it has allowed Jordan to receive large amounts of development assistance from the international community to help resettle and integrate the refugees."[18]

Jordan receives annual international aid to help the country mitigate the burden produced by the large population of asylum seekers and refugees living in the country. Over the years, the amount of international assistance has increased. The total amount of international aid Jordan received in 2009 was US $1,375 million, while in 2019, it was US $4,164 million. In a decade, the total amount the international community gave to Jordan more than tripled.[19]

Displaced Fur Becoming Refugees in Jordan

Like other people groups from Sudan, the Fur people have been forced from their homes because of the ongoing war in Darfur. Many victims of war who

16. Chatelard, "Jordan," para. 7.
17. Davis et al., "Sudanese and Somali Refugees," 6.
18. Chatelard, "Jordan," para. 5.
19. Fallah et al., *Moving beyond Humanitarian Assistance*.

cannot leave the country must stay in camps for IDPs as their only option of survival. Unfortunately, the living conditions in the camps in Darfur are unbearable, as Shirley A. Fedorak points out:

> Camps are crowded, and many refugees suffer from acute malnutrition and infectious diseases such as yellow fever and malaria. Tensions run high over access to scarce resources within the camps, there is constant danger of conflicts with neighboring communities, and women and children face sexual violence when they leave the camps in search of firewood. The camps are recruiting grounds for various factions and militias. Loss of traditional family and societal structure, poverty, and trauma have resulted in increased violence in the camps, from rape to extortion.[20]

Frightened by the constant threat of dwelling in a war zone, many Darfurians decided to leave everything behind and run for their lives by crossing borders to seek asylum in countries such as Jordan.

In theory, the Fur individuals who flee their home country in search of international protection precisely fit the profile of a refugee. The internationally accepted definition of a refugee, outlined in the 1951 Geneva Convention, defines a refugee as a person who, "owing to a well-founded fear of persecution for reasons of race, religion, nationality, membership of a particular social group or political opinions, is outside the country of his nationality and is unable or, owing to such fear, is unwilling to avail himself of the protection of that country."[21]

Since the civil war broke out, most of the refugees from Darfur have been crossing into the neighboring country of Chad. By 2020, according to UN estimates, Chad was already hosting approximately 360,000 Sudanese refugees.[22] Though at considerably lower rates, Jordan has also hosted asylum seekers and refugees escaping from the Darfur conflict since 2003.

According to United Nations data, Jordan is home to 5,891 Sudanese who find themselves as people of concern. Among them, the Fur are the predominant people group. Sudanese make up the country's fourth-largest group of refugees, trailing only Syrians, Iraqis, and Yemenis.[23]

Sudanese do not generally enter Jordan as refugees but are instead admitted to the country based on a preapproved visa, such as a medical or visitor visa.

20. Fedorak, *Anthropology Matters*, 72.
21. See "Refugee," in www.iom.int/key-migration-terms.
22. UN, "UNHCR Delivers Much-Needed Aid."
23. UNHCR, "Jordan."

Any Fur individual who enters Jordan and does not intend to return to Sudan because he fears for his life—and wants to receive international protection with UNHCR—must visit a UNHCR registration center before his visa expires. At the UNHCR registration center, the Fur individual will begin a legal process by providing personal and family information and giving the reason he had to leave Sudan. He will present supporting documents and reports to the registration center for analysis. The Fur individual would bring a passport, national identification, driver's license, marriage certificate, birth certificates for any accompanying children, education diplomas, employment records, and medical reports among the documents.[24] This administrative procedure is referred to as refugee status determination (RSD).

> Refugee Status Determination, or RSD, is the legal or administrative process by which governments or UNHCR determine whether a person seeking international protection is considered a refugee under international, regional or national law. RSD is often a vital process in helping refugees realize their rights under international law.[25]

The RSD process can take a significant amount of time to be completed. One male study participant stated that his process is taking more than three years, and he doesn't know when it will be accomplished. A woman who is a member of the Fur community has disclosed that her process is similarly taking more than three years for completion. Though approval can take time, once the RSD process is initiated and while the individual seeking international protection is waiting to be officially recognized as a refugee, he will receive the status of an asylum seeker and the UNHCR will issue an asylum seeker certificate (ASC) in his name. The United Nations defines an asylum seeker as "someone whose request for sanctuary has yet to be processed."[26]

Receiving the Asylum Seeker Status

The ASC states that the individual has a pending refugee claim and is awaiting a decision to confirm his refugee status. The certificate displays information such as the date the document was issued, name, date of birth, nationality, alias, date of expiration, and the description of the person's status:

24. See UNHCR, *UNHCR Service Guide.*

25. See https://www.unhcr.org/refugee-status-determination.html.

26. UNHCR, "Asylum-Seekers," para. 1.

This is to certify that the above-named person is an asylum seeker whose claim for refugee status is being examined by the Office of the United Nations High Commissioner for Refugees.

As an asylum seeker, she is a person of concern to the Office of the United Nations High Commissioner for Refugees, and should, in particular, be protected from forcible return to a country where she claims to face threats to her life or freedom, pending a final decision on her refugee status.

Any assistance accorded to the above-named individual would be most appreciated. This certificate does not entitle the holder to a residency permit or work permit in Jordan. The issuance of such permits is solely within the competence of the Jordanian authorities. Questions regarding the information contained in this document may be directed to the Office of the United Nations High Commissioner for Refugees at the address above.[27]

Possessing the ASC is critical for those seeking international protection because it is a prerequisite for becoming an officially recognized refugee. Also, a Sudanese carrying an ASC is under UNHCR protection and is unlikely to be deported for not holding a residency permit. While he waits for the approval of his refugee status, he must renew his ASC every year.

Receiving the Refugee Status

Upon the conclusion of the RSD process, the UNHCR personnel will determine if the individual requesting international protection is a genuine person of concern (POC). The process is approved if the claim is confirmed, and the individual receives official recognition as a refugee by the UNHCR.

A Sudanese individual who is formally recognized as a refugee obtains an identification document called the UNHCR refugee certificate (RC). This document attests that the individual has received a favorable decision confirming his refugee status. The certificate also displays information such as the date the document was issued, name, date of birth, nationality, alias, date of expiration, and the description of the person's status:

This is to certify that the above-named person has, on the basis of available information, been recognized as a refugee by the United Nations High Commissioner for Refugees, pursuant to its mandate.

27. Transcribed from an actual UNHCR asylum seeker certificate.

As a refugee, she is a person of concern to the Office of the United Nations High Commissioner for Refugees, and should, in particular, be protected from forcible return to a country where she would face threats to her life or freedom. Any assistance accorded to the above-named individual would be most appreciated.

This certificate does not entitle the holder to a residency permit or work permit in Jordan. The issuance of such permits is solely within the competence of the Jordanian authorities.

Questions regarding the information contained in this document may be directed to the Office of the United Nations High Commissioner for Refugees at the address above.[28]

The ASC and the RC include a list of accompanying family members. Their picture and personal information are displayed in a separate field on the document.

The details of this complicated and time-consuming process are important to understand because they impact the daily life and outlook of Fur refugees in Jordan.

Reasons for Fur Individuals Coming to Jordan

Fur asylum seekers and refugees are people who have moved beyond the borders of their country to flee from the war and secure their lives. All the participants in the study fall into this category. Therefore, they are not migrant workers (or economic migrants)—a term referring to people seeking an opportunity to improve their standard of living—but forcibly displaced people, individuals who have crossed their borders "as a result of persecution, conflict, generalized violence or human rights violations."[29]

Hundreds of thousands of Fur individuals have relocated to Chad, Kenya, Uganda, or Egypt. Study participants could have done so, but they chose Jordan as their shelter because they believed becoming a refugee and living as an exile in the kingdom would be more manageable.

The number of arrivals of Darfuri Sudanese in Jordan has been on the rise since the civil war began. However, it has consistently increased during the waves of political unrest and continuous violence in Sudan:

> 30 percent of the Sudanese who are currently registered with UNHCR arrived before 2011, during the height of the civil war

---

28. Transcribed from an actual UNHCR refugee certificate.

29. UNHCR, *UNHCR Global Trends 2014*, 2.

in Darfur. There was another increase in arrivals in 2013 and 2014 following the separation of South Sudan, the collapse in the Sudanese economy, the escalation of conflict in the peripheries, and the government's crackdown on political opposition (Sudan had its own Arab Spring in 2011 and 2012).[30]

After entering the kingdom, Sudanese in need of protection do not move to a refugee camp but stay in urban areas. For them, being relocated to a refugee camp is not an option. Furthermore, at this point, they are not yet officially recognized as refugees by the local authorities and by the UNHCR.

Amman is the preferred city for Sudanese entering Jordan. The overall assumption is that the capital city, although more expensive than any other Jordanian city, can offer them better access to the UNHCR offices and better living conditions, such as employment, education, and health care. This understanding applies to Sudanese and most refugees living in Jordan. For this reason, Amman hosts the largest population of refugees in the country, 274,017 (36.1 percent).[31]

Challenges That Fur Individuals Face in Jordan

Nearly all Sudanese arriving in Jordan have endured violence, abuse, and loss. They experience an initial feeling of joy for leaving the war zone and coming to a country where they can find protection. Participants show pictures of their arrival at the airport in Amman. The photos capture expressions of joy, excitement, and relief. However, as they embrace the reality that they are now displaced, living in exile, and dealing with challenges they don't know how to overcome, their perceptions begin to shift, as Alayrian asserts: "This seldom lasts. The uncertainties of the asylum-seeking process add to the pressures they must live with and this insecurity may become a major distressing factor and cause mental illness."[32]

An essential aspect that causes pressures on the Fur asylum seekers and refugees in Jordan is that the socioeconomic situation they find in Jordan is not satisfactory. Participants indicated that financial struggle is the main factor compromising their quality of life. The next chapter will further discuss this crucial aspect of the Fur refugee experience.

One of the first challenges that Fur in need of protection face is to receive official refugee status. "Syrians are granted *prima facie* refugee status

---

30. Johnston et al., *Realizing the Rights*, 7–8.

31. UNHCR, "Jordan."

32. Alayarian, *Resilience, Suffering and Creativity*, xviii.

and must register with both the government and the UNHCR, whereas others—Iraqis, Somalis and Sudanese—are required to undergo Refugee Status Determination on a case-by-case basis."[33]

Moreover, participants consider themselves members of a vulnerable community and have expressed dissatisfaction with the lack of assistance provided to their people. They argue that they cannot handle the living cost in Jordan without financial aid:

> They have expenses that those living in camps do not have, such as rent and utilities. They may also have to pay to access and travel to services. On average, urban refugees of all nationalities spend half or more of their monthly expenditures on rent, contributing to their housing being insecure. To cope, they accrue debt and eat lower quality foods.[34]

The cash assistance that the UNHCR gives to Sudanese refugees is intended to help them pay for rent, monthly utility bills, and health expenses, among other things. According to study participants, the amount is limited, varies, and doesn't come every month. However, when it comes, it is an essential help.

A challenge Sudanese face is that they cannot receive cash assistance from the UNHCR immediately after they arrive in Jordan or during the time they are registered as asylum seekers. They "are not eligible for monthly cash assistance from UNHCR until they complete the RSD process and are recognized as refugees."[35]

This situation leaves Sudanese with only two survival-challenging alternatives. They are forced to beg for humanitarian aid among people, NGOs, and houses of worship or earn money from an illegal labor activity since they do not have access to legal employment.

Getting an illegal job in Jordan is not an easy thing. Employers know they can be penalized for allowing a refugee to work illegally for them, and they don't want to take the risk: "Employers who hire workers without a residency permit are subject to fines of between 50 to 75 JD per irregular status worker."[36]

When refugees find someone willing to give them a job, they usually work for long hours and receive much lower wages than a local employee. If they do not receive the agreed-upon payment, they just keep quiet because

---

33. Davis et al., "Sudanese and Somali Refugees," 2.
34. Johnston et al., *Realizing the Rights*, 10.
35. Mennonite Central Committee, *On Basis of Nationality*, 8.
36. Johnston et al., *Realizing the Rights*, 24.

"those working irregularly are unlikely to assert their rights as employees out of fear of being reported."[37]

UNHCR suggests that there are three long-term solutions for those living in a situation of refuge: 1) Voluntary repatriation: the return of asylum seekers and refugees to their country of origin; 2) Local integration: the incorporation of asylum seekers and refugees into the foreign country in which they find themselves; and 3) Resettlement: relocation to a new country that "has agreed to admit them as refugees with permanent residence status."[38]

The Fur asylum seekers and refugees in Jordan cannot envision long-term solutions becoming a reality for them any time soon. How are they going to have a future, since the civil war continues to take the lives of civilians in Darfur, local integration has not been offered by the Jordanian government, and fewer than 1 percent of refugees are resettled each year?[39]

Transnationalism

As displaced Fur people migrate to Jordan, their culture suffers a considerable transformation. As they make efforts to adjust to their new living context, their cultural identity and worldview begin to change. This doesn't happen because they have given up their culture. Even if the Fur people do their best to keep their culture of origin, as they live in a new context, their culture is affected. In anthropological literature, this process of cultural transformation is called transnationalism. Schiller defines *transnationalism* or *transnational migration* as "the process by which immigrants forge and sustain simultaneous multi-stranded social relations that link together their societies of origin and settlement."[40]

An area of study called *transnational anthropology* focuses on immigrants, considering that their "daily lives depend on multiple and constant interconnections across international borders and whose public identities are configured in relationship to more than one nation-state."[41]

Transnationalism can be a very stressful experience for displaced people, particularly when it involves learning a new language. However, when they migrate to a context that is closer to their original cultural and linguistic context, it becomes easier for them to adjust, as Alayarian asserts:

37. Johnston et al., *Realizing the Rights*, 23.
38. UNHCR, *Resettlement Handbook*, 28.
39. UNHCR, *Resettlement Handbook*, 28.
40. Schiller et al., "From Immigrant to Transmigrant," 48.
41. Schiller et al., "From Immigrant to Transmigrant," 48.

There are fewer mental health problems where the immigrants form a significant proportion of the local population, and where they are not subject to excessive pressure to adopt the language and customs of the host country. Some refugees may try to adopt the new culture too quickly, and reject aspects of their own culture. This rapid adaptation may not be healthy psychologically, if the loss of the familiar culture has not been worked through, and the change may prove artificial and transient.[42]

Migrating to a new cultural context will always be a challenging experience and require a great amount of effort on the side of the migrant. Even if they move to a very welcoming context, they will still struggle and feel emotionally vulnerable.

Fur asylum seekers and refugees living in Jordan form a new cultural identity as they synthesize worldview elements that they bring with them and new ones they specifically find in their new country. Therefore, with time, Fur individuals who live in Jordan will be different in some ways from Fur individuals who live in any other context around the world.

The following chapter will examine cultural customs and practices of the Fur people living in Jordan and will reveal several examples of transnationalism, such as preferring not to go to the mosque and thus being less communally focused.

The Hierarchy of International Assistance

Participants have also expressed dissatisfaction with the hierarchy of international assistance provided to refugees, confirming what previous studies and advocacy papers have noted on this theme: "Those from countries other than Syria have less access to services and often fewer legal rights."[43]

Claims of unfair treatment are not idle complaints. Sudanese are treated differently from other people groups needing protection, and as a result, they lack access to a wide range of services. It is not a victimization attempt or a manipulation of reality to bring more attention to Sudanese needs. The different treatment given to refugees based on their nationalities is a fact: "While the humanitarian community espouses the principle that assistance should be provided on the basis of need alone, in Jordan access to assistance is often conditioned on nationality."[44]

42. Alayarian, *Resilience, Suffering and Creativity*, xix.

43. Davis et al., "Sudanese and Somali Refugees," 3.

44. Mennonite Central Committee, *On Basis of Nationality*, 4.

The distinction made based on the nationality of the refugee regarding assistance is often referred to by Sudanese living in Jordan as discriminatory treatment. However, the reality is different from what they think should be the proper approach:

> The most vulnerable Iraqi and Other refugees, namely those that fall below the vulnerability threshold to receive UNHCR cash assistance, receive much less cash/voucher assistance from UN agencies than Syrians who fall below the same vulnerability threshold. This is because in addition to UNHCR cash assistance, Syrians also receive either a 10 or 20 JD voucher from WFP and many Syrians receive a 20 JD per child cash grant from UNICEF. Iraqis and Other POCs are excluded from these programs. UNHCR attempts to compensate for this by providing Iraqi and Other refugees a higher amount of cash assistance than Syrians but in most cases Iraqi and Other refugees still receive less total assistance.[45]

The difference between the treatment given to the Sudanese refugees and the Syrian refugees, for instance, produces a sense of discrimination among the Sudanese refugee community in Jordan. However, the UNHCR personnel in the country are not responsible for this situation. UNHCR Jordan has recognized the issue and expressed a desire to promote what they call the "One Refugee" approach:

> UNHCR Jordan, together with partners, have adopted and continue to advocate for the "One Refugee" approach for all persons of concern, Syrian and non-Syrian alike, in all sectors and services in Jordan. This approach seeks to reduce and ultimately eliminate differences in rights and services based on nationality, in Government, UNHCR, and NGO approaches to protection and assistance.[46]

The so-called "differences in rights and services based on nationality" did not originate in Jordan. They are a result of international agreements that have been signed and must be observed by the people dealing face to face with the victims of the current migration crisis:

> Refugees are defined by their national origin as a result of agreements struck between the UNHCR and governments, as well as government policies. Thus, in the case of Jordan, refugee and asylum-seeking populations experience differential

45. Mennonite Central Committee, *On Basis of Nationality*, 5.
46. UNHCR, "Jordan," 2.

access to services as well as differences in how they obtain refugee status."[47]

A critical observation to make at this point is that, while Jordan has been historically a place of refuge for POCs, it is not a signatory of the main conventions relating to the status of refugees and is not obligated to adopt general standards regarding refugees.

> Jordan is not a State party to the *1951 Convention relating to the Status of Refugees* or its *1967 Protocol*, nor is there any national legislation for the protection of asylum-seekers and refugees. In the absence of any specific legislation, the Law on the Residence of Foreigners remains applicable to asylum-seekers and refugees. Jordan is also not a party to the *1954 Convention relating to the Status of Stateless Persons* and the *1961 Convention on the Reduction of Statelessness.*[48]

The conditions offered to refugees in Jordan are much different from those in other countries. For instance, is almost to the opposite of the conditions provided in the UK: "Refugee status gives a person five years of permission to remain in the UK, with permission to work and study, and access to the NHS and benefits. Refugees have the right to seek family reunion with family members left behind."[49] In Jordan, none of these conditions are available, which makes the life of a refugee a fight for daily struggle.

Since Jordan is not a signatory of the Refugee Convention of 1951 or its subsequent 1967 Protocol, the bases for dealing with victims of migration in Jordan are the country's constitution and some other international agreements signed between the kingdom and the UNHCR:

> The 1998 MOU between UNHCR and the Government, amended in 2014, outlines the major principles of international protection, the definition of a refugee, and confirms the principle of non-refoulement. It provides the legal basis for the stay of asylum seekers in Jordan pending refugee determination by UNHCR and of mandated refugees for a limited period after recognition while a durable solution is sought. As there is no possibility of local integration in Jordan, UNHCR must either resettle or assist refugees to voluntarily repatriate.[50]

---

47. Davis et al., "Sudanese and Somali Refugees," 6.
48. UNHCR, *Universal Periodic Review: Jordan*, 1.
49. Lenegan and McKinney. "What Is the Difference," para. 20.
50. Johnston et al., *Realizing the Rights*, 14–15.

Another significant issue faced by the Sudanese community in Jordan is the lack of legal residency and employment. The ASC and the RC that they receive make it clear that the documents are not the equivalent of a residency permit or a work permit. Therefore, the ASC and the RC do not provide legal residency and employment. The same regulation does not apply for Syrians because they can obtain work permits under the Jordan Compact.

> The Jordan Compact was an agreement reached at the February 2016 London donor conference in which Jordan agreed to loosen restrictions on the acquisition of work permits by Syrian refugees within certain sectors of Jordan's job market. In exchange, Jordan was to receive financial assistance and more inclusive rules of origin regulations to open Jordan's manufacturing industry's access to European markets. Prior to the Jordan Compact, refugees were not technically barred from acquiring work permits, but quotas on foreign workers and prohibitive requirements such as high fees, which in practice were often paid by employees rather than by employers, limited the number of Syrians who actually received permits.[51]

Once Sudanese land in Jordan and their entry visa expires, they become illegal immigrants and can be imprisoned if they are caught working and even deported. Therefore, to enjoy some measure of protection under Jordanian legislation, they must register with UNHCR for an asylum seeker or refugee status while they still have a valid visa:

> Unlike the special procedures that have been introduced to regularize Syrians' presence in Jordan, annual residency for Iraqis, Yemenis, Sudanese, and Somalis remain regulated by the standard (and restrictive) conditions of the Law on Residence and Foreigners' Affairs. The regulations are dealt with by the Public Security Directorate (PSD), which falls under the authority of the Ministry of Interior (MOI). A foreigner who falls under this legislation can be "legally present" up to three months after arriving in Jordan (one month initially and then for an additional two months if they apply for an extension) and can request a further three-month extension. After this, they are not legally present unless they pay overstay fines and/or receive a one-year residency. Foreigners who are not "legally present" in Jordan

---

51. Mennonite Central Committee, *On Basis of Nationality*, 16.

can be arrested and legally deported unless they are registered with UNHCR as an asylum seeker or refugee.[52]

There is a critical implication for Sudanese becoming illegal immigrants in Jordan. Suppose a Sudanese individual decides to leave the country, either to move to a third country or to return to Sudan. In that case, he must pay 1.5 Jordanian dinars (US $ 2.12) per day for the whole time he stayed illegally in the kingdom.

> The lack of formal legal status under Jordanian law leads to the accrual of fines of 1.5 JD a day for overstaying an entry visa, even for refugees registered with UNHCR and possessing an Asylum Seekers Certificate (ASC). This fine is contrary to the Memorandum of Understanding signed by the Government of Jordan and UNHCR in 1998 which states that "to facilitate voluntary repatriation or resettlement in a third country it was agreed to exempt refugees from overstay and departure fees."[53]

Sudanese in Jordan have reported that the only time they are excused from paying this penalty is when they leave the country for resettlement under the auspices of the UNHCR. In all other circumstances, however, if they depart the country without paying the overstay fines, they will be forbidden from reentering Jordan for five years.

The financial burden to cope with life in Jordan is heavy on Sudanese. Fur individuals describe it as an everyday battle for their survival. The next chapter will deal with the issue of living conditions in Amman, the most expensive Arab city in the Middle East.[54]

Sudanese Deportation

Although most study participants receive some humanitarian aid from UNHCR, they express distrust and resentment toward the institution. They make a point of stating that they do not feel represented by the institution but rather discriminated against. To justify this perception, one male participant cited an incident in 2015. The Jordanian authorities deported over five hundred Sudanese asylum seekers by sending them back to Sudan. The deportations had tremendous implications for the protesters since the Sudanese refugees from Darfur fear returning to Sudan. The Sudanese government sees them as potential soldiers of the rebel forces: "The majority

---

52. Johnston et al., *Realizing the Rights*, 15.

53. Johnston et al., *Realizing the Rights*, 15.

54. Aljadid, "Amman Ranked Most Expensive."

of the Sudanese in Jordan are from ethnic groups originating from the conflict-affected 'peripheries' of Sudan who stand in opposition to the Sudanese government (Darfur in Western Sudan, the Nuba Mountains near the southern border, and Eastern Sudan)."[55]

The official reason for the deportation of Sudanese was their peaceful protest at the UNHCR headquarters for obtaining "recognition of their rights as refugees and asylum seekers, and to receive better treatment from the agency."[56]

There were also complaints about the length of time for recognition of their status and right for assistance. The registration processes, which had once been quick, were taking more than a year—and, in some cases, longer than two years.

In 2014, Sudanese had peacefully protested for the same reason, but the police persuaded them to end the protest. In late 2015, however, Sudanese staged a sit-in outside the office of the UNHCR in Khalda, and this time, the police could not convince them to leave.

> The police arrived in force in the early hours of a mid-December morning. They dismantled the camp and transported some 800 protesters and others—men, women and children—to a holding facility close to Queen Alia International Airport. In the ensuing days, the Jordanian authorities, assisted by Sudanese government representatives, deported the majority of these people to Sudan. Nuclear families were split up between countries. More than 100 of those deported were detained and questioned upon arrival in Khartoum. Several reported harassment and intimidation at the hands of the Sudanese authorities from whom they had originally fled. Some had their documents seized and are now on the run. The whereabouts of others are unknown.[57]

Based on the information provided by the local media, the BBC reported that when police sprayed tear gas against them for refusing to board a plane, three Sudanese died as a result. The incident produced great desolation among the Sudanese community in Jordan.[58]

Currently, Sudanese in Jordan are still perplexed as to why the UNHCR failed to protect the individuals who peacefully protested and were later deported or killed. Some participants said they believe the institution

---

55. Johnston et al., *Realizing the Rights*, 50.
56. Johnston et al., *Realizing the Rights*, 50.
57. Davis et al., "Sudanese and Somali Refugees," 2.
58. BBC, "Jordan Deports Hundreds."

bears significant responsibility for how the Jordanian authorities dealt with the case.

Participants have also expressed their lack of trust in their own embassy staff members in Jordan. They are convinced that the Sudanese embassy collaborated with Jordanian authorities in the deportation event. This sentiment has been expressed by the Sudanese community in Jordan in previous studies: "It reportedly assisted the Jordanian government in deporting asylum seekers and refugees in 2015, and community members report incidences of harassment by embassy staff. This has compromised the ability of the Sudanese asylum seekers and refugees to access consular services."[59]

Discussing this event in particular, study participants have expressed that they do not feel protected and perceive unjust treatments by the humanitarian community toward them. In general, they believe the root of the problem is racial.

One study, which examined the issues the Sudanese refugees have been facing in different contexts, argues that there is a hierarchy of aid that affects the assistance refugees receive:

> The stated reason behind the Sudanese protests in all of these countries—lack of access to services for refugees—points to a larger pattern in responses to refugees in the Middle East. That pattern shows a hierarchy of policies and agreements based on the national origin or citizenship of the persons, rather than their status as refugees or asylum seekers."[60]

The study points out four elements that were identified as part of this hierarchy: size, race, time, and awareness:

> The first element, size, addresses the large refugee populations that have arrived in countries of first asylum—Palestinians in 1948 and 1967, Sahrawis in 1975–1976, Iraqis after 2005 and now Syrians. Because the movements are so large, they become the target of funding and programs (which is not to say the responses are adequate). Refugees who do not fit that citizenship-based designation are often left without emergency care or assistance.[61]

Sudanese often engage with people, particularly in the Middle East, who have a sense of superiority. This attitude affects the access to services

59. Johnston et al., *Realizing the Rights*, 50.
60. Davis et al., "Sudanese and Somali Refugees," 3.
61. Davis et al., "Sudanese and Somali Refugees," 3.

they have the right to receive. Sudanese end up receiving less or nothing at all because they are often looked down upon.

> The second element, race, is tied to the African-ness of Sudanese and Somali refugees and the assumptions about civilizational underdevelopment and inferiority that accompany how they are seen in the Middle East. Such inexcusable views reflect the legacy of an Arab nationalism that deemed Semitic Arab-ness superior to other types, particularly those that are both Arab and African, even though both Sudan and Somalia have long been members of the Arab League. These assumptions are also the residue of older experiences with former African slaves or soldiers, who are most often seen as "other" due to their skin color.[62]

The civil war in Darfur and the subsequent displacement of the Darfuri Sudanese began about two decades ago, producing a humanitarian disaster. However, some people prefer to focus on helping refugees from more recent calamities. These people think it is not the time to focus on Sudanese and therefore overlook this group of refugees:

> The third element is time. And while not particular to the Middle East, the region has endured major population movements as a result of wars in the last 15 years (Iraqis, Syrians and now the ignored Yemenis). The urgent fact that, today, Turkey, Lebanon, Jordan, Egypt and Iraq are the hosts of 4.8 million Syrian refugees simultaneously obscures hundreds of thousands if not millions of others who are victims of conflicts going back many decades and live in situations of protracted displacement.[63]

The horrors of the war in Darfur and the displacement of Sudanese no longer get much attention in the international media and public opinion. Once their suffering is not on the radar, they don't attract much attention and funding:

> The fourth and final element is awareness. Sudanese and Somali refugees in the Middle East are only a small percentage of the many Sudanese and Somali refugees in the world, the vast majority of whom fled south or west to other African countries. Because these people are not a single large concentration in the Middle East (except in Yemen), relatively little is known of the conflicts in their countries or the reasons for their flight.[64]

62. Davis et al., "Sudanese and Somali Refugees," 3.
63. Davis et al., "Sudanese and Somali Refugees," 3.
64. Davis et al., "Sudanese and Somali Refugees," 3.

For different reasons, the Sudanese refugees don't receive the resources they need and feel discriminated against by the international community. A common question they ask is this: "Why are people not willing to help us?"

Violence against Sudanese

Darfurians have experienced violence in more places than just Sudan. Recent history shows that in their journey of seeking refuge beyond their borders, they have also encountered harsh treatment in other countries. For instance, "in Egypt in 2005, a peaceful sit-in of Sudanese outside UN-HCR offices in Cairo turned deadly when Egyptian police attacked the group, killing at least 28 protesters."[65] Another similar case also happened in the Middle East: "In 2012 in Lebanon, 13 Sudanese refugees and asylum seekers who mounted a two-month hunger strike outside UNHCR offices were reportedly arrested and detained."[66]

Sudanese have also experienced deportation in Israel. In 2007, asylum seekers from Sudan's Darfur region and other African countries were expelled after entering the country illegally:

> Authorities announced that they had expelled 48 of more than 2,000 African refugees who have entered illegally from Egypt in recent weeks. Officials said they would allow 500 Darfurians among them to remain, but would deport everyone else back to Egypt and accept no more illegal migrants from Darfur or other places.[67]

In general, Sudanese interpret all these events as discriminatory. They feel there is a racial element behind them. They believe if they were refugees from a different context, other than Africa, they would receive a different treatment worldwide. They think that, in the eyes of the world, their lives do not have the same value as other people's lives.

A History of Discrimination

Many Darfurians blame the prejudice perpetrated by Arabs against non-Arabs as an explanation for the ongoing conflict in Darfur. Furthermore, from the beginning of the hostilities, non-Arabs in Darfur have underlined

---

65. Davis et al., "Sudanese and Somali Refugees," 2.

66. Davis et al., "Sudanese and Somali Refugees," 3.

67. Berlatsky and Chalk, *Darfur*, 39–40.

the issue of discrimination. The UN Security Council, in a meeting on July 30, 2004, that assessed the situation in Darfur, voiced the people's opinion on this issue:

> To suppress a rebel uprising begun in early 2003, the Government began a "campaign of terror" against innocent civilians. Government aircraft bombed villages and, exploiting an ancient rivalry between Arab African herdsmen and groups of largely black African farmers, armed the Janjaweed militia and unleashed them against black civilians.[68]

Numerous war reports also substantiate the discriminatory allegations. In one of them, Halima Bashir, a doctor from a Darfuri village, witnessed war crimes and discrimination against her people and herself:

> The Arab militia known as the Janjaweed had held some 40 of the children hostage for two hours, forcing them to watch as their friends were raped, beating them in the head with sticks or rifle butts if they tried to resist and yelling at them that Sudan was for Arabs, not black dogs and slaves.[69]

Documentation of crimes perpetrated in Darfur endorses the discriminatory nature of conflict-related occurrences. The most comprehensive record, *Documenting Atrocities in Darfur*, includes over 1100 interviews with Darfur conflict victims. It was collected in July and August 2004 by the Coalition for International Justice and the US State Department's Atrocities Documentation Project and contains the following:

> During an attack in western Darfur (near Masteri) in November 2003, a Massalit woman was raped by ten soldiers who said that the government "sent them to kill and rape and clean their land."[70]

> During a ground attack in western Darfur (near Seleya) in November 2003, a Eregnan man reported hearing, "we will kill all men and rape women. We want to change the color. Every woman will deliver red. Arabs are the husbands of those women."[71]

> A Massalit woman in west Darfur (near El Geneina) in December 2003 saw Arabs take eight male babies by their feet and slam them into the ground until they died; the Janjaweed

---

68. Security Council, "Security Council Demands," para. 70.
69. Berlatsky and Chalk, *Darfur*, 115.
70. Interview 287, in Totten and Markusen, *Genocide in Darfur*, 147.
71. Interview 533, in Totten and Markusen, *Genocide in Darfur*, 147.

told women being raped, "We rape you to make a free baby, not a slave like you."[72]

A Fur male reported that in December 2003, a few months before his village in West Darfur (near El Geneina) was attacked, Janjaweed raped his daughter and two other girls (ages 14, 15, and 16) and said, "We will take your women and make them ours. We will change the race."[73]

A Massalit woman in South Darfur (near Garsila) had her village attacked in June 2004 by GoS and Janjaweed. Despite being four months pregnant, she fled, but was caught running by five men. They beat her with a whip, causing her to lose her baby. The attackers said, "Black prostitute, whore, you are dirty blacks."[74]

Darfur's racial tensions are a historical concern, and they began considerably earlier than the current civil conflict, which started in 2003. To offer just one example, in 1987, the Arabs released a statement titled "Manifesto of Racial Superiority," which sparked a war among the region's various groups:

In 1987, they published a manifesto of racial superiority, and clashes broke out between Arabs and Fur. About 3,000 people, mostly Fur, were killed, and hundreds of villages and nomadic camps were burned before a peace agreement was signed in 1989. More fighting in the 1990s entrenched the divisions between Arabs and non-Arabs, pitting the Arab pastoralists against the Fur, Zaghawa, and Massaleit farmers. In these disputes, Sudan's central government, seated in Khartoum, often supported the Arabs politically and sometimes provided arms.[75]

Several pieces of evidence confirm the claim that the Fur people, together with other people groups from their homeland, face deadly discrimination in their home country. Fur asylum seekers and refugees residing in Jordan openly express frustration that discrimination is not only a past reality. In the following chapter, along with the results sections, Sudanese will better describe the present discrimination they face.

---

72. Interview 489, in Totten and Markusen, *Genocide in Darfur*, 147.

73. Interview 575, in Totten and Markusen, *Genocide in Darfur*, 147.

74. Interview 1056, in Totten and Markusen, *Genocide in Darfur*, 148.

75. Berlatsky and Chalk, *Darfur*, 98.

Religious Consequences of the Darfur Conflict

The Fur people's religiosity has been dramatically influenced by the war in Darfur because the groups involved in the conflict, both the perpetrators and the victims, practice Islam. Today, the dissatisfaction expressed by the Fur community in Jordan with members of the Sudanese government is so widespread that they strongly question the religiosity of the members of the government. "How can they claim to be Muslims and kill other Muslims? Is that what Islam is?" they ask.

A male participant shared that Fur people have always done what the Muslim government demanded and presented evidence of their devotion to Islam. They even fought in favor of the government during the war against the South (today, South Sudan). At the time, they learned from the Khartoum administration that the conflict had a religious bias. Consequently, many Fur parents encouraged their children to kill people from other faiths and die in the war, if necessary. Under the promise of a place in heaven, they wanted to help establish an entirely Islamic nation in Sudan. Nowadays, many of these people have a different understanding of the war and feel used and deceived: "The government in Khartoum told us that to become real Muslims, we had to kill the infidels. Today, despite being Muslims, government forces kill us as they did to the Sudanese in the South in the past. We are Muslims. Are we also infidels?"

In response to this scenario of disillusionment, many Darfurians have sought a religious alternative. Before the war started, people in Darfur had no exposure to biblical Christianity. The tribes in the region were considered 100 percent Muslim and were proud of their faith. After the war broke out in the area, there has been much diffusion of the Christian faith and people in Darfur now have better access to the gospel.

As a result of the civil war in Darfur, Christianity is growing among Darfurians. Experiences of religious conversions have been taking place both in and around the Darfur region and even among Darfurian refugees outside the country. On Sudanese land, the number of people declaring the Christian faith is becoming public even though the Sudanese government is exerting pressure and promoting persecution against new converts. The high price of religious persecution these converts are paying, sometimes with death, indicates that their religious conversion represents a genuine experience.[76]

---

76. Barnabas Aid, "Christian Converts from Islam."

Summary

This chapter has presented the specific context where the Fur asylum seekers and refugees, participants of this study, live: Amman, Jordan's capital city. Additionally, it has provided insight into how their host-context influences their lives.

Since its foundation in 1946, Jordan has been a haven for refugees and an essential partner of the international community regarding several migration crises. In the past twenty years, the country has welcomed both Sudanese who needed protection and people in similar circumstances from other countries.

In Jordan, Fur people benefit by being in a country in which they already speak the language and follow the majority religion. However, African refugees, notably Sudanese, face several obstacles as they seek international protection in the kingdom, such as lack of proper assistance and legal employment.

Sudanese in Jordan express a widespread mistrust in institutions because they feel discriminated against, even by the UNHCR. One root problem is the different treatment they receive compared to Syrian refugees, and this scenario makes them feel they are less important in the world's eyes. Also, they still express resentment for the incident in 2015 with Jordanian police, which resulted in deportations and killings. Sudanese were peacefully protesting for better access to the services UNHCR provides to asylum seekers and refugees. People who survived the horrors of the war in Sudan ended up dying in Jordan at the hands of those they thought would protect them.

The war has impacted their spiritual worldview, producing discontent with Islam since their executioners also follow the same religion. Consequently, some in Darfur and worldwide are embracing the Christian faith.

While relevant literature has been foundational for approaching the main topics, the chapter also explored the viewpoints of Fur asylum seekers and refugees, often referring to what they think about the discussed issues.

The focus of chapter 4 is an ethnographic study grounded on a survey with participants from the Fur tribe living in Jordan. Based on their own description of the Fur culture, it will provide an account of the Fur ways of life manifested in a context where they are asylum seekers and refugees.

5

Describing the Culture
of the Fur People

*God is the only one who can make
the valley of trouble a door of hope.*

—Catherine Marshall

Introduction

The voices and experiences of the Fur asylum seekers and refugees living
in Jordan give insight into their hearts, minds, and felt needs. For many,
their decision to move to Jordan is based on a hope for the future. One
participant said, "What can I expect from life? My opportunity is over. Now,
I must invest everything in my children."

The analysis of their ways of life in this specific context is essential to
respond to the research question I propose: *What are the best approaches for
evangelism and discipleship to be employed in the process of planting a church
among Fur asylum seekers and refugees in Jordan?*

This chapter uses interdisciplinary research to build a broader understanding of a specific people group, the Fur people of Sudan. For this study,
their ways of life were examined in a determined period, 2019 to 2022, in a
particular location, Amman, Jordan.

Data was collected through a series of ethnographic interviews and
is examined based on three philosophical categories of study: ontology
(study of existence, being, becoming, and reality), epistemology (study of

the nature, origin, and limits of human knowledge), and axiology (study of principles and values).

The content of this chapter will also address the supporting research questions of this study: *What is the spiritual worldview of the Fur people? How do the Fur people in Jordan currently regard Islam? Which challenges that the Fur people face as asylum seekers and refugees in Jordan should be addressed during the pre-evangelism process? In a gospel presentation, which themes will make the most sense to Fur asylum seekers and refugees in Jordan? Which themes need to be discussed first in the discipleship process with Fur individuals?*

The chapter will present several challenges that shape the life of the Fur people in Jordan. Also, it will suggest that improving living conditions for Fur asylum seekers and refugees in the country would help to mitigate some of the difficulties they face. However, other adversities would persist, because some of the struggles refugees experience here would still be an issue anywhere in the world. This happens for one reason: "In the host country, refugees have lost their social world and are likely find themselves separated from their familiar way of life, beliefs, and occupation."[1]

Moreover, this chapter will identify five main themes that emerged during the interviews—themes that reflect central issues impacting their lives. Throughout this research, the five topics will serve as the foundation upon which I design a contextualization project for Fur asylum seekers and refugees living in Jordan.

The survey participants were selected by a Fur community member as people who could provide the best information. The interviews were conducted in person with a translator and cultural consultant assisting in the process. To protect personal identities, names and some characteristics have been changed. Further information on the methodology is available in Appendix D.

Characteristics of the Participants

The study was carried out with members of the Fur tribe. Their ethnic identity is Fur, and their context of origin is Darfur, the former Islamic sultanate of Darfur in the western area of the Republic of the Sudan.

All participants declare themselves to be Muslims or followers of the religion of Islam. They are registered with the UNHCR and hold either asylum seeker or refugee status. The participants are based in Amman, Jordan, and live close to downtown Amman. They reside in the neighborhoods of

1. Alayarian, *Resilience, Suffering and Creativity*, xviii.

Jabal Akhdar, Jabal Nadif, Jabal Webdeh, and Wehdad. They all have lived in Jordan for more than two years.

All the participants came to Jordan directly from Sudan, without ever living in any other country as refugees. Additionally, they don't have extended family members other than the nuclear family living with them in Jordan. It's important to note that within this cultural context, friends from the same ethnic group that participants have met after arriving in the country are frequently referred to as family members.

Meeting the Fur People

The answers registered in the following section were collected in face-to-face interactions with members of the Fur tribe in Jordan with the purpose of studying their culture in this specific context. Therefore, they contain firsthand knowledge gained through field experience to identify the best approaches for evangelism and discipleship to be employed in the process of planting a church among Fur asylum seekers and refugees in Jordan.

Family

For the Fur people, family plays an essential role in people's lives. In their perspective, the family and the community are more important than the individual. As in many collectivist cultures, the individual does not live for himself. In the Fur culture, a person exists primarily for the benefit of her family and the tribe.

Family provides a sense of identity, sustains the culture, and serves as the main factor that keeps the community together. Most study participants highlighted that there is no life if there is no family. In the words of a male participant: "My family is the most important thing in my life, and I cannot live without them. Maybe I should say that they are my life."

Although they value family, Fur families in Jordan number few. All participants agreed that married couples must have children. However, the maximum number of children found among participants was three in one family, and the other two families had a maximum of two children.

Participants pointed out that before the war started, Fur families were large. Some parents had upwards of ten, twelve, or fourteen children in Darfur. This scenario was confirmed in the words of a participant: "My father had three wives, and I have more than twenty siblings." But in Jordan, they have fewer children because they feel pressured by their limited conditions produced by the lack of resources and opportunities. "There is no future for my children unless we get resettled in a third country."

In Fur families living in this setting, the husband generally works outside the house to provide for his family while the wife takes care of the house and educates their children. There are exceptions, though, because many Sudanese men struggle to find a job in Jordan: "The job situation here is very hard. In one week, sometimes I work two days or three days. I spend most of my time in the house because I cannot find a job."

As a result, some wives have been proactive in looking for paid activities to help support their families financially. Sewing and artisan crafts are common activities. Many Fur women have been trained in self-sustaining activities to learn how to make products to earn money. "Sometimes I get so tired because I have to cook, wash, clean, watch the children, and work to make some money for my family," said one of the females among the group.

Marriage

Although there are exceptions, men generally marry women from the Fur tribe. However, since most of the Sudanese refugees arriving in Jordan are young males, Fur men struggle to find single women of the same ethnicity to marry. A study participant explained the background of this phenomenon: "Most of the Fur refugees here are young males because they are viewed as a threat by the government. The Khartoum administration assumes they will join the rebel groups and fight against the government's forces. So, the young men are a target in Darfur, and several of them feel they have no choice but to leave our homeland."

Since the Sudanese asylum seekers and refugees do not have residency permits to live in Jordan, they cannot fulfill the civil procedures for registering a marriage. Consequently, if they find a wife from a different nationality, they may not be able to have their marriage legally recognized unless the wife is a Jordanian citizen. Though they may face issues registering a transnational marriage, they express openness to marrying women from different countries. For example, a participant mentioned a Sudanese man who got married to a Palestinian woman in Jordan. Another participant shared with excitement about a few cases where Sudanese men proposed to European and South American girls, although he expressed disappointment when concluding that they never got married. Then, a participant explained their view on transnational marriage and how difficult it has been for Fur men to marry a foreign woman in Jordan: "We prefer marrying women from our tribe, but we are open to marrying women from any nationality, but here it is so difficult to find a girl willing to marry a Fur man. Most non-Sudanese women do not want to marry a Sudanese man."

Finding a Spouse

Although living overseas, Sudanese in Jordan can have marriage certificates issued in Sudan, which opens a possibility for the Fur to marry and build families. So, when young Fur men feel ready to get married, they contact their family members in Sudan and ask them for help arranging a wedding. One of the participants explained in more detail how this works: "Our family members in Darfur look for a wife for us. Once they have identified a suitable girl, they make a marriage agreement with her family, pay the dowry, and organize the wedding. The two families celebrate the wedding, having just the bride at the ceremony. After the wedding, our family members send the wife to us on an airplane, and we meet her here at the airport in Jordan."

Another participant also shared his experience of marrying someone from a distance: "I have been married for two years. My wedding took place in Darfur, Sudan. My father was the one who chose the bride for me. Then, the two families got together, made all the arrangements, and performed the wedding ceremony without my presence. Once the wedding was made official, they sent my wife to Jordan. I know that this scenario is difficult for people to understand in other cultures, but things happen like this in our situation. There are no Fur single women here that we can marry. So, we need our family to send them from Sudan."

Fur men feel relieved that they can find a way to get married even if it requires not attending their own weddings or meeting their spouses after days, weeks, or months. Also, managing to maintain the intraethnic marriage tradition is particularly meaningful to them: "My family was responsible for finding a wife for me. They found a nice girl, paid for the dowry, and celebrated the wedding. Later, they sent my wife from Sudan to Jordan, and here we started our relationship as a married couple. I was so glad that even though I was living outside my country, I could still succeed in marrying a woman of my tribe."

Nevertheless, during the interviews, a single man narrated one case in which this remote matrimonial procedure did not work. He got married to a Fur girl who was living in Darfur. Following the wedding, she traveled to Jordan, but her admission into the country was rejected at the airport in Amman, even though she had a valid medical visa. She went back to Sudan and attempted to join her husband in Jordan two more times but was unsuccessful. The couple remained married for five years, but husband and wife could never meet each other in person. Since they could never meet and consummate their marriage, they opted to annul their marriage.

Study participants shared that Fur women who live in Sudan and marry a husband who lives in Jordan usually deal with conflicting emotions. They feel excited about getting married, leaving the war zone, and building a family. However, they also feel sad about leaving their family, friends, and homeland behind. When such Fur women come to Jordan, in the beginning, they experience a lot of excitement for the new life they are building. Over time, as they begin to face the challenges in their new living context, disappointment sets in. In this regard, a participant shared: "Several women come from Sudan to meet their husbands here. After some months, they get particularly disappointed with life here. In some cases, they request their husbands to return to Sudan. I know two Sudanese women who got so disappointed that they divorced their husbands and returned to Sudan."

Marriage within the Family

Consanguineous marriages (or cousin marriages) are a common practice among the participants of this study. Three of them stated that they had married one of their first cousins. "Sometimes, our family members in Sudan choose a wife for us among our own relatives. It is easier to marry a relative than someone outside the family. In this way, if there is any problem in the marriage, the family can solve it without having to look for an outside solution with people who they don't really know."

In addition to choosing the wife, the groom's family is usually responsible for paying the dowry to the bride's family. Marrying someone who is a family member is typically less expensive. The value is negotiated by an intermediary and paid before the wedding day. Upon mutual agreement, the payment can be made in cash, goods, and animals. Agreeing to pay a generous amount is an expression that the bride has great value, as one participant described: "A family of a girl who has higher formal education or speaks multiple languages, for example, will require more money for the dowry. Any quality that points out that she knows how to take excellent care of her house and educate her children well will add value to her dowry."

According to academic literature, the practice of levirate marriage, which is the customary marriage to an elder brother's widow, used to be particularly common in the Fur culture. However, I have not found a single case of levirate marriage among the Fur in Jordan. One participant shared that this tradition is dwindling, and it is becoming optional rather than a requirement, because women now have a voice and are heard in the Fur marriage process: "It is her decision. If she becomes a widow, she can marry her husband's brother or look for a husband outside of her husband's family."

All couples represented in the interviews had in common the fact that the husband was older than the wife. The most significant age difference found among them was seven years: "We were married while we were still in Sudan. I was thirty-seven, and she was thirty years old when we got married."

One of the male participants shared a theological reason why the husband must always be older than the woman: "First God created Adam, then Eve. Therefore, this indicates that, in a marriage, the husband must have been born before the wife." According to another male participant, while this is a good pattern, it is not always a rule: "Prophet Mohammed married Khadija, a woman who was older than him. I suppose it isn't wrong to find an older wife, though it is better if we marry a younger woman."

Female Genital Mutilation (FGM)

In Sudan, several ethnic groups practice female genital mutilation (FGM). Depending on the type of female genital mutilation observed by the participants, the practice can take various forms. The procedure generally entails the partial or complete removal of external female genitalia. FGM is also known as female genital cutting and female circumcision.

Female genital mutilation has traditionally been practiced among the Fur people on girls between the ages of ten and fourteen, prior to puberty. The FGM ceremony is performed as a rite of passage for females to mark their transition from girlhood to womanhood, and it is preceded by a celebration attended by female family members, friends, and close neighbors. Participants reported that the cultural justification for genital mutilation is to restrain women's sexual impulse.

Female genital mutilation is internationally condemned as a form of violence. FGM is extremely harmful to girls and women and constitutes a violation of their human rights. It produces lifelong consequences and causes complications during pregnancy and childbirth.

Prior to the outbreak of the current Darfur conflict, most Fur girls were subjected to female genital mutilation. However, study participants noted that this practice has been gradually declining among the Fur people over the last two decades. Additionally, they added that families with girls in Jordan do not follow this practice. "In this country, we don't have our traditional practitioners to do the cutting," one participant said, implying that FGM was abandoned because the Fur community in Jordan was unable to maintain the practice. Another one claimed, though, that female genital mutilation is an old and wrong practice, suggesting that FGM had to cease regardless of how transnationalism affects them in their global migration process.

Polygamy

According to the Sudanese in this study, polygamy is widespread in Fur culture, and their religion ratifies this practice. They pointed out that according to the Qur'an, the husband can have up to four wives if he demonstrates fairness in dealing with all of them. They were referring to Sura 4:3, which says, "Marry women of your choice, two or three or four; but if ye fear that ye shall not be able to deal justly (with them), then only one, or (a captive) that your right hand possesses."

In general, Fur society views a husband with more than one wife as a man economically successful due to his ability to support multiple wives or families. Study participants also commented that sometimes the first wife asks the husband to find a second wife. Generally, this happens because she wants another woman to help her with household chores. Moreover, in some instances, the first wife chooses the woman her husband will marry as a second, third, or fourth wife. "In some families among our people, the first wife chooses the others. In this way, she gets the chance to choose a woman that she likes."

Although they consider polygamy culturally and religiously appropriate, none of the study participants practice it. One male participant shared his views about this: "As a Muslim, the Islamic law gives me the right to marry multiple wives. But, I have only one wife and don't want to look for another one. Regardless of what she thinks, this is a personal decision. As a refugee, having a second wife would be a burden. How can I support another wife and children in my current situation? Also, having a second family may complicate our application process for resettlement with the UNHCR. Polygamy is illegal in several countries where refugees are resettled. Our chances of being accepted for resettlement are less likely if we are polygamous."

A male participant commented on his decision to remain married to only one wife: "I only have one wife, and I am satisfied. Although it is culturally appropriate for me to marry other wives, my wife doesn't want me to have another one, and it's okay with me like that. My father had three wives, and I realize that it is particularly complicated to have several wives and live with equity with all of them, as the Qur'an prescribes. And if the husband commits an injustice, then problems with wives and children arise. Having just one wife is good."

The absence of polygamy among the Fur in Jordan does not necessarily lead them to extramarital affairs. Infidelity between husbands and wives is not a common practice among the Fur community in Jordan, even though it can occur in some marriages. In general, Fur partners have a reputation for being faithful to their spouses.

Traditions are of the utmost importance among the Fur, but they also understand the need to accommodate cultural changes and adjust to life circumstances. Additionally, Fur individuals, both males and females, benefit from the cultural change. They believe that a husband with fewer wives and children can focus on the needs of their household, resulting in a better quality of life for them. Also, according to one participant, there is less tension in life when a couple is monogamous: "My father had three wives, so I understand what it's like to be polygamous. The jealousy among the wives causes frequent fights among them and their children." Polygamy is one of the aspects of the Fur culture that is changing among the younger generations, particularly amid their refugee community in Jordan.

Children

For the Fur people, their children represent both the present and future. The Fur parents living in Jordan expressed that the war took away their opportunity to accomplish great things in life. In their understanding, only their children will have an opportunity to build a professional career and achieve success in the upcoming years.

Parents also believe that if they provide enough formal education and good living conditions for their children to grow well, they will be rewarded. In the future, when parents cannot work because of health conditions or age limitations, for instance, their children will take care of them. A father participant noted: "I will do everything I can for my children now. Later, when I cannot take care of myself, they will do everything they can for me. Among our people, this is how life is supposed to be."

Nutrition is a common concern Fur parents raise regarding their children. Due to their inadequate economic circumstances, it is difficult for parents to provide their children with a proper healthy diet. Some children require certain foods and vitamins due to health conditions. Because their parents cannot afford to buy them frequently, they ask for help in the community and tend to rely on donations. Feeding their children is a struggle for Sudanese, as one of the female participants narrated: "In Jordan, fruits and vegetables are costly. We do our best to offer the best food for our children, but there are times when we have nothing to feed them."

Another area in which the Fur parents often express apprehension is that of the future spouses of their children. They see intercultural marriage as a threat to the perpetuation of their ethnicity. However, there is not much they can do since it is a situation outside their control. This is one of the examples of transnationalism mentioned in chapter 4, in which the transnational identity of the Fur people is developing and producing significant cultural changes. In this regard, one participant commented: "The refugee condition in which we live affects our identity as a people. If our children start to marry people who are not from our tribe, our ethnic group will not perpetuate itself." When asked to what extent it would be realistic to expect his children to marry someone from his people group, he added: "Since they were born here and we are not living among our people, it will be so difficult for them to marry a Fur person. Our circumstances are complicated, and I guess human beings must adapt to the scenarios that life imposes on them."

Another participant also expressed that it will not be easy to preserve the custom of marrying his children to a spouse from the same tribe: "It is difficult to think with whom our children will marry. They were born and grew up far from our original cultural context. So, they have a different mentality than ours. Can I expect them to marry someone from my tribe? Maybe, but it will not be easy. I think I will let them marry a spouse of their choice."

One cultural aspect found among the Fur in Darfur that is preserved even in this context is that children live with their parents until marriage, regardless of their age. However, parents expect that when their children marry and move away from the family house, they will reside in proximity and nurture family ties.

Formal Education

The Fur people highly value formal education. Whenever they refer to their children's needs, they mention schooling and highlight their efforts to provide good education to their children. A parent participant stated in this regard: "One of my priorities in life is the education of my children, and making sure they are attending school is my main concern."

A significant obstacle concerning formal education is that the school system in Jordan costs money. Study participants mentioned during the interviews that until 2019, some school fees were waived. Now, either the UNHCR or the Sudanese must pay the fees. Most refugee parents struggle to pay school expenses for their children because they cannot afford the costs: "We do not have the money to pay for the school fees. Sometimes we must pay the registration and then tuition for four or six months in advance. We also must cover expenses with textbooks and school supplies. Unfortunately, we cannot afford all these costs. As we are not legally allowed to work, we depend on humanitarian aid even for paying for healthcare and school services." Consequently, Sudanese school-age children often stay out of school.

Besides the challenge of cost, the annual registration for Sudanese in primary and secondary school is a complex process, with the bureaucratic steps varying widely from one year to another. Parents remarked that school registration periods are generally loaded with tension and characterized by transportation expenses, since they are often sent from one place to another to get one more signature or stamp in their paperwork.

Additionally, participants reported that some public schools limit the number of refugees that can register, as a participant described: "I tried to register my son in one school, and the administration said they were not taking more refugees because each class had reached a cap of twenty percent for refugee children."

One serious challenge that affects Fur children in Jordan, particularly those attending school, is bullying. All the parent participants expressed concern about this topic. One of them reported: "Our children often face bullying in school. They are discriminated against, called chocolate, and hit by other children because they are Sudanese. Sometimes, they also suffer physical violence on their way home from school. People call them names, make fun of them, and slap them."

In 2017, UNICEF coordinated a study detailing violence against refugees in Jordanian schools.[2] Following that, several documents were written to spotlight the issue, demonstrating how this violence affects Sudanese refugee children. In one of these accounts, a Sudanese mother corroborates what the study's participants have stated:

> My daughter gets beaten up in school. A student chooses a black girl every day to beat. It was my daughter's turn. The principal punished my own daughter. Violence happens in the schools and schools do not take it seriously. I had been to the UN to complain about my daughter facing violence in the school after another student's father threatened her and used physical

2. Thompson Coon et al., *Knowledge for Children*.

violence. But the UN did not do anything. All that happened was that the father got a chance to say that he did not want his daughter to study with black people.[3]

Keeping children motivated to succeed in school is another responsibility of parents of Sudanese children, as one participant commented: "There are moments when my children would rather stay at home than go to school. I understand how difficult it is for them to overcome the obstacles they face in the school setting, but they must complete their education. As a result, we constantly encourage them not to give up."

Community Structure

Although Sudanese, in general, have a strong sense of community, due to their condition of being displaced in a second country, they have lost the fundamentals of their community structure. They generally lack personal, cultural, and socioeconomic links that would enable them to form social networks with Jordan's host community. For those who are married and have kids, the nuclear family is the only component of the system they have left.

The Fur people in Jordan try to help each other and build relationships with people beyond the members of the tribe, but there are no solid institutions or social structures to support them. When asked about support from their embassy in Jordan, a participant said: "We cannot trust them. They work for the government in Sudan, not for the Sudanese people here in Jordan."

The Fur people also do not feel welcome in most social settings, not even in their worship places. Several of them expressed their preference to pray at home because they also feel discriminated against in the mosques. As a result, only a small number of the participants attend Islamic worship services. One participant reported an episode to highlight the issue: "When I go to pray at the mosque, often people come to me to ask me questions. On one occasion, after the prayer, I noticed that some people were looking at me. One of them came and asked if I was a Muslim. Well, why do you ask someone that question if you have seen the person performing the prayer ritual with you? How could I be a follower of another religion if I had just observed one of the five pillars of Islam inside of a mosque? However, do you know why he asked me that question? Because we look strange to them. It is hard for some Arabs to believe that black Africans are true Muslims."

3. Johnston et al., *Realizing the Rights*, 33.

Another participant also shared an incident that happened in a mosque in Jordan that he thinks was discriminatory: "One of the Sudanese here has a father who is a sheik [*sheikh*]. His father came from Sudan to Jordan for health treatment purposes. While he was here, he began to visit a mosque in the neighborhood where he was staying. As a sheik, he introduced himself to the imam of that mosque and asked if he could lead the prayers one day. The imam told him that he could not lead the prayers without explaining why. When my friend's father asked if there was a specific reason for the negative answer, the imam said the Sudanese man could not lead the prayers because he was a foreigner. However, sheiks from Saudi Arabia, Syria, Iraq, and other Muslim countries always visit the local mosques, and they are allowed to lead the prayers."

While mosques have been less than welcoming, community development centers are among the institutions that have been supportive to Sudanese by offering them services and helping to build a sense of community. In these environments, Fur individuals engage in different physical and educational activities. They also learn essential skills for self-sufficient living and participate in events that help to reinforce their cultural identity. Six participants stated that they regularly engage in activities in community centers. Besides learning new skills, they frequent the centers to keep in contact with people who help them establish a network of friends here.

In general, community development centers do not focus on Sudanese alone but broadly serve the refugees and the local community. Sudanese view the interaction with people from other nationalities in the centers as a positive aspect. A female participant highlighted: "I like joining a classroom with refugees from other countries and even with Jordanians. We build new relationships and learn from each other."

Hospitality

One outstanding characteristic of the Fur culture is hospitality. When entering a Fur home in Jordan, a visitor will soon realize how hospitable the Fur people are, even to visitors they meet for the first time.

Inside the home, the visitor will notice—by the smell or the smoke—that the Fur people make use of incense. They burn incense for purifying and cleansing their houses. Fur individuals tend to make more use of incense when receiving visitors. One study participant said: "The incense makes the environment more welcoming by removing bad smells from the rooms and perfuming the air."

The use of incense also carries a religious element. Some Fur individuals believe the incense protects them from evil spirits and other bad influences such as evil eyes. Another study participant explained the use of incense by saying: "It produces good vibrations in a house." The use of incense is more common in Fur houses where a family lives, though. Single men living alone tend not to use incense. They say, "Incense is a woman's business."

A visitor will probably notice another cultural aspect when visiting a Fur home: men and women typically do not sit together. They usually form two separate groups as they sit around the living room. Depending on the family tradition and the space available in the house, the women may be assigned to a separate room. Also, physical contact—which usually includes handshakes, hugs, and kisses—is shared among hosts and visitors only of the same gender.

When entering a Fur home in Jordan, the visitor will likely find a single bed in the living room, in addition to a sofa, chairs, and other furniture. Often, people are curious about this. The bed in the living room means one simple thing: it is a sign of hospitality that the Fur people bring from Sudan. The bed is there for the visitor in case he wishes to take some rest after a meal, enjoy a nap in the afternoon, or even spend the night. The Fur usually feel honored if a visitor asks to lie on that bed: "The bed extends hospitality to you. If you receive it, you are honoring us. You are confirming that you are a friend," said a married participant.

Another way the Fur people express their hospitality is by feeding their visitors well. Always, visiting the Fur homes in Jordan involves sitting around a table. Fur hosts serve the visitor a long list of things, including mineral water, hibiscus juice, coffee, tea, fruits (such as dates, apples, and bananas), snacks, and the main meal. One of their traditional dishes is called *assida*. It is made of wheat flour dough cooked only in water and served with a sauce, including tomato, okra, lamb, and seasoning. The Fur people in Jordan commonly eat *assida* on special days and Fridays. Friday, a weekly holiday, is often a community event, as they invite Sudanese friends and neighbors to join them.

Toward the end of a visit, as the visitor communicates his desire to leave the Fur home, the hosts will probably try to convince him to stay, which is also a sign of hospitality. The general rule is that he can leave after drinking the coffee served after the dessert. However, often the hosts invite the visitor to stay overnight.

Authority Structure

According to the Fur people, God is the supreme authority in their lives, and he is responsible for all the good things that occur in the universe. Fur individuals believe that the practice of religion is the best way to please God. Due to their Sufi influences, they believe in a transcendent and immanent God. One participant commented: "God is in heaven, but God is also on earth. He can be found anywhere. I know that I will always be able to count on God wherever I go."

Although Fur participants criticized the government of Sudan for promoting the civil war in Darfur, they have shown much respect for the Jordanian authorities. Since they live in Jordan, they understand that the country has authority over their lives; as one participant commented: "We don't live in our country, and this is a disadvantage. Everything we do here, we must do according to the norms of the Jordanian government."

Two participants had a picture of King Abdullah II in their house. One of them said: "King Abdullah II is a great leader, much respected, and responsible for maintaining peace in Jordan, not like Bashir who fights his own people in Sudan."

Another authority they recognize over their lives is the UNHCR. A participant commented: "The UNHCR is like a government for us. The people working for the UNHCR are the ones who tell us to go here and there. They have power over our lives, and they can decide our future." According to one participant, the UNHCR is so significant to Sudanese that they fear missing a call from its personnel: "The main reason why I have a cellphone is to keep in touch with the UNHCR people. If I go to a place that doesn't have good phone coverage, I leave my phone with a friend. If the UNHCR people call me, he will answer them for me. In this way, I will not miss any calls from them."

Religious authority is also crucial for the Fur in Jordan, but they respect the sheiks from their own people more than the local sheiks. Participants stated that they were not aware of any Sudanese sheiks in their community at the time the interviews took place. So, on special occasions and ceremonies, they had to call a person of authority or a leader among the Sudanese community to lead the event. Trying to justify this behavior, a study participant said: "We prefer to deal with our own leaders because they already know our culture and speak our mother tongue. In my understanding, it is better to do things in this way."

Within the Fur family, the husband is recognized as the higher authority. Therefore, he is responsible for making the most significant decisions affecting his wife and children. Even when the wife has higher formal education, is more skilled in communicating, and contributes more financially to support the family, the husband still has more authority. A female participant responded in this regard: "I do not make decisions by myself. Before I decide something important, I must ask permission from my husband. If I say right and he says left, I go left. I do what he tells me to do."

People more advanced in age are also considered people of authority and are highly respected by the Fur. A participant shared his view on that: "What a gray-haired man says, the others will follow, even if they don't agree, but just out of respect for the authority that an experienced man has."

Origin of the Universe

Having Islam as common ground, study participants unanimously declared that the universe's origin is in God, the Creator of everything in the world, including material and spiritual things. A study participant expressed: "God created everything that exists. Without God, there would be no people, no animals, no rivers, no spirits, and nothing else would exist."

Fur individuals indicated that this understanding makes the most sense for them, as they do not believe in any other reasonable explanation for the universe's origin. One of the female participants pondered: "Apart from God, who could have created human beings, animals, and trees?"

Participants stated that their knowledge of origins had been initially passed on to them by their parents and later by Islamic leaders. A participant provided more background: "As Muslims, we grew up learning from our parents, imams, and religious teachers that there is a God [Allah] who is the Creator of everything that exists."

While still talking on the issue of origins, another participant pointed out that knowledge, in general, is based on the cross-generational teachings that the Fur people receive. A single male participant commented: "From one generation to another, our people learn to discern what is right and wrong. We learn about God, Islam, our culture, other people, and the whole world around us. We learn as children, and when we grow up, we make our choices based on the knowledge we build."

Power

According to the Fur people's understanding, God is the source of all power in the universe. Also, God has control over everything and everyone. Participants pointed out that God sometimes uses his power to discipline and judge humanity. When commenting on the coronavirus pandemic, they highlighted that God has control over the virus. A participant added, "The divine permission for the virus to spread and produce a pandemic may have been given to make people repent and turn to God."

The Fur people believe that powerful people are those who have money and influence. A male participant commented on that by saying: "If you have money, you can have almost everything in life. The same is true if you have influence. If you have much influence, you can go everywhere and meet everyone. As you can see, this is power. So, you don't have to be the president of a country to have power. If you want power, all you need to do is to be one of his closest friends."

Participants have also referred to the spiritual world as a source of power that influences earthly life. One participant shared that he relates to the spiritual world to seek protection and healing. According to another one, some practices require the use of the Qur'an or the blood of an animal: "In Sudan, many people wear necklaces or armlets with qur'anic verses to protect themselves from illness and evil attacks. Additionally, when we purchase something, we make a sacrifice. For instance, when we purchase a car, we slaughter an animal. Then we place our right hand on the blood of the animal and then on the car, pleading for divine protection so that we never have a car accident."

Another participant shared: "If a wife wants to exert control over her husband or increase his love for her, for example, she goes to the holy man. After listening to the woman's account of the problem, he prescribes a special tea for her husband. Typically, the holy man will instruct the wife to give her husband a special tea. What makes it unique is that the water utilized to prepare the tea was used previously to wash a piece of wood with qur'anic verses carved into it. So, it possesses spiritual power to influence the husband's behavior."

This subject involves a significant component of transnationalism. Due to the Fur people's displacement in Jordan, they lack a holy man to consult and obtain guidance on dealing with the evil spirits. This results in a sense of disorientation in the Fur people's interactions with the spiritual world. In attempting to address their daily concerns, people tend to act independently: "Because we do not have a holy man here, we don't reproduce the same practices we observe in Sudan. We tend to do simple things to protect ourselves. For example, we place the Qur'an next to a baby's pillow to protect him from attacks of the evil spirits."

Destiny

As Muslims, participants believe in life after death. They all agree that destiny holds two places for people, and the two ultimate destinations are paradise (*jannah*) and hell (*jahannam*), as described in the Qur'an. According to the Islamic teachings they have received, paradise is the place of physical and spiritual pleasure for people who have done good deeds and who will find favor before God on the day of judgment. On the contrary, hell is the place of physical and spiritual suffering for people who have not done well enough and who, as a punishment, will face the wrath of God for all eternity.

Participants understand that many people are not taking all the necessary steps to get to paradise. Because of that, they fear what the future holds for them. As one participant said: "People are afraid to die because they don't know where they are going, and they don't know the way to get there. In a certain sense, this is normal. We are distressed about traveling to an unknown place. We fear arriving at an airport that we have never visited, we are hesitant to go where we don't know anyone and nobody knows us."

Study participants highlighted that although religious obedience is essential to take them to paradise, they are not sure if paradise is their ultimate destination. One of them said: "We have no assurance of where we are going after death. Even if we are good Muslims, it is up to God to decide our destiny. We must do our prayers and everything else to go to paradise. We have hope in God, but only he knows who will go there and who will not. God willing, we will go to paradise."

The Problem of Humanity and Its Solution

Participants believe that practicing religion and abstaining from bad behavior is the correct solution to humanity's problem: "The problem of humanity is sin. Human beings, in general, must change the way they live their lives for the world to be a better place."

Referring once again to the coronavirus pandemic, one of them mentioned: "In these times of COVID-19 with so many people sick and dying, God is calling our attention. He wants us to turn away from sin and experience a better life."

The sin that several participants condemned most is that of discrimination. Fur individuals demonstrated strong opposition to this sin and often reaffirmed the condition of equality that must be among all human beings, without any distinction.

When another participant was asked to explain the origins of the pandemic situation, he connected it to racial discrimination. Through his religious lens, he sees the spread of coronavirus as a heavenly instrument to help people worldwide understand that they are equal and to dispel any feeling of superiority: "The coronavirus is proving that humans are the same in everything. The virus does not choose a place, color, race, social status, or religion, and it is a divine punishment to show humanity that we are all equal before men and in the eyes of God."

Study participants reported being victims of discrimination, harassment, and physical violence by people in their neighborhoods and workplaces. Most participants were unwilling to report such hate crimes to the police because they believed they had no rights. In the few cases when they called the police or reported an incident to the UNHCR, participants felt ignored. One participant offered this example: "The owner of my apartment came to me to receive the rent. It was past due, but unfortunately, I did not have the money to pay him. I explained my situation, but he got mad at me, which I understand—though he shouted at me and slapped my face. Then, he told me that if I did not pay him within a week, he would send people to kick me out of the apartment and kill me eventually. I did not report this physical aggression and threat to the police because I knew nothing would happen to him, and he could become even more aggressive toward me."

Decision-Making

According to what participants shared in their interviews, Fur individuals seem to share similar beliefs, ethics, and values. However, the way they make their decisions differs widely. Some of them make decisions by considering the consequences and evaluating the results, as one of the participants narrated: "If I am facing a difficult situation or experiencing suffering in a particular area of my life, this can be a sign that I must change something wrong that I am doing. So, many times I make decisions in response to the obstacles I encounter in my daily life."

Others make their decisions based on listening to people they trust, as one of the husbands commented regarding his wife. He presented her as having an essential role in the major decisions he makes in life: "I make decisions after listening to my wife. Usually, I don't tell the details of my life to other people, just to her. When something that requires a decision comes up, I talk to my wife, reflect about the implications of my decision, and decide according to what I think is right."

Another participant shared that he makes decisions based on previous personal experiences: "We learn from experience. That's how I know when I'm doing what's right and wrong. Based on this perception, I make my decisions. For example, if I put the television in the wrong place and it falls to the floor and breaks, it is a sign that I have made a bad choice. If I put it in the right place and nothing wrong happens, I conclude that it was a good choice. Also, if a thief comes into the house and takes the television because I left the door open during the night, I am partly responsible for the mistake. So, next time, I will decide differently."

Remarkably, the concept of fatalism, common among Muslim people groups, was not discussed by the participants. Instead of framing life's events as if they were predetermined or presenting their conditions as powerless, participants emphasized the importance of taking responsibility for making decisions that impact their lives.

Ethics and Values

In general, the Fur people are event-oriented thinkers. They are not driven by time but by events. What matters most to them is not to arrive on time at a specific occasion but to meet the people attending the event. Thus, arriving up to one hour late for an appointment between Sudanese is culturally acceptable, even here in Jordan.

The Fur highly value hospitality and generosity. They show great joy when receiving guests and strive to make them feel welcomed. When hosting a visit, it is common for them to offer the visitors the best food and drink they can get.

Among the Fur, religious practice is considered a sign of virtuous behavior. Therefore, a person with a good reputation is generally someone who obeys the precepts of his religion. Although not all participants attend a mosque, they do the Islamic prayers at home or in any place they find themselves during the prayer times. Some participants feel more comfortable praying at home, as one shared: "Honestly, I prefer to do my prayers at home. I don't feel welcomed at the mosques here."

The Fur people value respect for laws, religion, authorities, parents, and older people. "To respect the laws of the country and those who exercise authority gives people a good reputation before men and great merit before God."

Sudanese do not believe that engaging in illegal employment in Jordan is necessarily disrespectful, unethical, or sinful. The Fur people understand that although it is against the law, employment is a right for people in desperate circumstances like theirs; it is a matter of life or death. For the Fur people, subsistence depends on any money that they can earn. They argue that God-given life is more crucial than human-written law. Therefore, if one of those two must be violated, it must be the law. An asylum seeker participant who receives no cash assistance from the UN-HCR commented on that: "I swear to God, if I do not work here and make money for my basic needs, I perish. Why leave Darfur to perish here? God knows we need to work."

When in public, whether working or not, Fur men typically dress in slacks or jeans and dress shirts. At home, however, it is common for them to wear a white tunic and an Islamic cap over the head. Women dress traditionally, with colorful clothing that covers the entire body. At all times, women wear headscarves. Their most common dress is the *tob*, a traditional Sudanese dress commonly found among Darfurians. It consists of a piece of colored fabric approximately four meters long that wraps around the body.

The Fur women understand that it is unethical for women to expose their bodies to people outside their family. They believe a woman's beauty should be displayed only to her husband. However, among their family members and close friends, they can uncover their heads and arms.

Affection is usually shown among people of the same gender. It is acceptable in the culture for men to hold hands in public, though this practice is disappearing because of the social and physical distancing due to COVID-19. Therefore, there is little physical contact between men and women, and not even a handshake is commonly seen among them. However, people of the same gender can shake hands and exchange hugs and kisses on the cheeks.

Civil War in Darfur

The participants expressed that before the war, life in Darfur had many limitations, such as a lack of development, a scarcity of investment, and restricted access to public services such as infrastructure maintenance, education, and healthcare. Despite these shortcomings, life was quiet, simple, and peaceful. One study participant shared: "Life in Darfur was not easy, but we had enough to survive. In our village, no one would bother us. My father had a piece of land, and my brothers and I were responsible for taking care of our animals. Then the war came, and everything was gone. My village was filled with death and destruction." Another participant commented: "Before the war, my life was wonderful. My sisters would help my mother cook for my family, and I would play with my brothers. It was when the war broke out that everything changed." Another participant added: "I cannot complain about the life I had in Darfur. I loved the weather, the mountains, and the trees. Everything was fine for me until the war came. It was when Omar al-Bashir sent the Janjaweed to kill our people that our biggest problems started."

Finally, one of the participants said: "Life was very good in Darfur, but the war destroyed everything there. There are no more people in my village, no more houses, and even no more trees. The Janjaweed killed the people and burned everything. They are cruel people who don't respect life and the nature God created."

Participants have also expressed that the war was an unethical and dehumanizing event on the government's side. A participant said: "No one in my village was fighting for the rebel groups, and we had nothing to do with the war. Still, the government forces were killing my people. Do they fear God? Do they respect human beings? No, their hearts are like stones. Who is teaching them about life? All they know is killing babies, raping women, and killing men. They killed all my family, and I am lucky to still be alive."

The war forced the Fur and other ethnic groups in the Darfur region to live with a relentless reality. Armed conflicts and constant attacks by the Arab militias known as Janjaweed decimated and displaced the people, bringing destruction and disappointment in their wake. One participant reported: "The war started because Bashir had no respect for our people. He sent the Janjaweed to attack us because of some reactions from people in Darfur against his government. The conflict resulted in attacks on villages, rape, and the death of innocents. We are Muslims, those who attacked us too. However, they did not take this into account."

Fur asylum seekers and refugees display a strong sense of cultural identity, which the current regime has been striving to eradicate through a variety of efforts, including the prohibition of them from speaking their mother tongue, as a participant commented: "After the war started, the government forces began telling us that we were not allowed to speak the Fur language. We lost everything in the war, and they even wanted to take our culture and language from us."

A study participant shared a personal account of the war from 2003 when his village in Darfur was attacked by Janjaweed militias. "I still remember the day the Janjaweed came to my village. They usually come riding their horses and holding their guns. They surrounded my village, set fire to the houses, and murdered everyone they found, including my mother and younger brother. My father, eight brothers, and I survived the attack because we were in the field, caring for the family's animals when the militiamen carried out the attack. After receiving the news that our village was on fire and my mother and brother were killed, my father told my brothers and me that we had to leave the field and run for our lives. We were so afraid of the Janjaweed that we did not return to our village, not even to bury our loved ones. We went straight to Kassab, a camp for IDPs in northern Darfur." Today, seventeen years later, this study participant lives as a refugee in Jordan, awaiting approval for his resettlement process.

The war experience in Darfur has produced much suffering in the lives of the people who inhabit the region. Some witnessed the Janjaweed militias killing their parents and family members, while others became refugees when they were still children. One participant shared his personal war account: "They killed my mother in front of me. They shot her on her left side, and she fell before my eyes. My mother was pregnant at the time, expecting a baby girl. Unfortunately, she didn't resist the gunshot and passed away, but neighbors were able to take the baby from my mother. The baby was born prematurely and was treated with camel and goat milk. Praise God, the baby survived, and she is alive up to this very day."

Participants have expressed that those who manage to survive the conflicts in Darfur tend to feel traumatized by the conflict experience because the war leaves its imprint on their bodies and souls. None of the participants had visible signs of war on their bodies. However, they reported that people who escape the attacks in their villages in Darfur are frequently left with severe injuries. Men often have their bodies mutilated, and women are sexually assaulted.

The suffering the victims of war undergo often impacts their souls, producing traumatic consequences that affect their relationships with people and even with the world around them, as Friesen asserts: "As evil spreads through any community or group, it leaves behind signs such as trauma, but even more insidiously, it brings about the disappearance of relationships, trust and love."[4]

Hinshelwood presents the terrible emotional effects of violence in the human experience:

> The threat of persecution, torture, and death is aimed at a complete destabilization. The result is a complex of anxieties that add up to far more than simple suffering. They have a unique status, to which only serious illness can compare. The total destabilization is a plague of internal locusts attacking us through our insecurities, vulnerabilities, doubts, and fears. But, they do not come from inside. They are not a phantasy construction from the conflicts and prohibitions of the unconscious and a harsh

4. Friesen, *Living from the Heart*, x.

superego. They intrude from outside us, where we are least able to control ourselves. Against them, we have less defence than the terrors from within. They come as a chilling reminder that the real world can be as bad as anything that can be imagined.[5]

One can commonly find the disturbing effects of violence in the lives of forcibly displaced people. A study participant shared a traumatic war experience from his childhood that corroborates Hinshelwood's words: "The Janjaweed men came to my village on horses. Three of them entered my house and took my mother. I was watching them from a distance, and they saw me. They began to talk to me and said they wanted to show me something. I was so afraid, but I knew they could shoot me if I tried to run away. So, I decided to walk in their direction. When I came very close, they asked me to watch what they would do to my mother. Next, they raped her in front of me. I could do nothing but watch and cry. They did this to humiliate her and traumatize me for the rest of my life. They knew well what they were doing because I can recall every detail of what happened, and every time I see a horse, I want to run away."

Seeking Refuge

The Fur people never intended to be displaced from their original context. Because of the civil war that took place in Darfur, they were forced to abandon their original setting and seek refuge beyond its borders. They made such a radical decision to safeguard their existence because their lives were at risk due to the spread of violence in Darfur. A participant explained the scenario that made him leave his country: "Deaths and rapes continue to happen in Darfur, even in the camps. How can you live in a situation like this? I love my people and my land, but I had no other option but to leave everything behind. The circumstances in Darfur forced me to escape and look for a place where people are not trying to kill me."

Another participant shared how both the war and its aftermath were responsible for casting him into the exile he experiences today: "I was in poor health and could not continue living under the same circumstances that I was living in Darfur. So, I began looking for the first opportunity to escape, and when I found one, I ran away."

One young male participant reported: "I fled Sudan because I had no choice. As a young man, I posed a threat to government security forces. In their perspective, I had the potential to join the rebels and fight them. I

---

5. Hinshelwood, "Foreword," xiii–xiv.

never intended to join the war, but the government security forces understood they had to kill me before I could fight them."

The participants said they decided to take refuge in Jordan following advice from people in Sudan who knew about places that Sudanese could find refuge: "When the war broke out in my village, several people from my family were killed, and I was taken to a camp for IDPs inside Darfur. Life conditions there were distressing, and my life was still in danger. Then, I decided to flee the war in Darfur. When discussing with friends about places to go, some of them told me about Jordan. I had no idea what life would look like here, but it sounded like a good option to me, and I began the process to come here."

Unfortunately, not everyone who lives in a conflict-torn area has the option of fleeing the situation. Many people who are forced out of their homes become displaced within the area where armed conflicts occur. Frequently, they end up being killed. A single participant brought attention to this terrible reality that affects people in Darfur: "My sister did not have a chance to leave Darfur. Sadly, she was killed with her husband and children. I also lost two cousins who were also killed when their village was attacked. In addition, I lost many friends in the war. The people working for Bashir have decimated my people."

Living in Exile

Jordan is the context where the study participants found refuge after they were forcibly displaced from Darfur. They like the freedom of living in an urban setting rather than in a refugee camp; however, they struggle to support themselves due to the high cost of living, as one participant pointed out: "Life in Jordan is difficult. The currency is more valued than the dollar. The cost of living is high, and we have difficulties supporting ourselves."

Due to the land-limited expansion potential of Amman, apartments have become the most common type of housing. Fur asylum seekers and refugees typically rent one- to two-bedroom apartments or rooms inside apartments. One of the interviews took place in an apartment in which two families live together.

One significant limitation that the Fur people face in Jordan is that they cannot enjoy the same legal rights as the nationals, the foreigners on resident visas, and even the other refugees. Because they do not have a residency permit in the country, they cannot work, open a bank account, or apply for a driver's license, among other things.

Participants have expressed how exile represents a challenging reality. One of them commented about the complexity of the situation: "Some people say that Sudanese here are doing well because we no longer face the war in Darfur. This opinion reveals a simplistic look at our situation. In general, people don't know the day-to-day adversities we face here in Jordan. The truth is that we are still on a journey of daily survival."

Another significant limitation for the Fur people living in this context is that the local authorities have banned people such as Sudanese asylum seekers and refugees from accessing legal labor. They do so to protect the nationals' right to employment. However, this condition leaves the Fur attempting to survive on only one source of income: humanitarian aid. Unlike people who hold refugee status who are eligible to receive some humanitarian money, asylum seekers do not receive any financial assistance from the UNHCR and therefore are forced to find other forms of survival.

Regarding financial assistance, study participants noted that there is no guarantee that individuals with refugee status and financial assistance eligibility will receive any cash assistance. In Jordan, the cash assistance for refugees takes several forms: 1) some refugees receive no financial help at all; 2) some receive assistance twice a year (the winter cash assistance), in October and November; and 3) some receive the assistance monthly. According to a single male participant who receives monthly assistance, the amount he receives is twenty-three Jordanian dinars (thirty-three US dollars), which is not enough to meet his basic needs. This sum equals about one-sixth of his monthly rent payment.

Many Sudanese in Jordan engage in illegal employment as their final recourse to survive: "As refugees, we know that we are not allowed to work, but we must work. Otherwise, how can we feed ourselves? However, we always go to work fearing the police. If the police officials catch us working, they can arrest and even deport us."

Additionally, in Jordan, services such as education and healthcare are not subsidized. Therefore, if Sudanese asylum seekers and refugees do not have financial resources, they cannot access these services. Even more challenging is the fluctuation of the assistance that some refugees receive from the UNHCR: "The humanitarian aid I receive is not regular. It arrives according to each person's luck."

In general, Fur individuals struggle to maintain even illegal employment. Discussing the hardship to acquire a job, another person commented: "I have been living here for seven years, and one of the main difficulties is that I don't have a job. Sometimes, I do some work for two or three days in the construction industry, but that's it. Then I need to go in search of a new activity. So, I wake up early, go out, and ask people for work. I live like that, fighting day by day."

The two female participants did not have jobs, although they have both developed informal activities to help support the family. All the males had illegal jobs or were looking for one in areas like construction, market sales, and manual labor.

Refugees and asylum seekers who have illegal jobs fear being arrested and deported. During one of the interviews, a Fur community member passing by gave a personal testimony in this regard: "Seven months ago, the police caught me working illegally and arrested me. I spent two months in jail. Before releasing me, the police officers said they would deport me if they caught me again. But what can I do? I must work, or I have nothing to eat. Nevertheless, I fear being arrested again and deported."

Challenges like dangerous conditions and exploitation at work are realities that the Fur people in Jordan face due to working illegally. Most Fur individuals who can find illegal jobs tend to work for many hours and receive a minimum payment. However, what disturbs them the most is not being paid in full at the end of a work period, which occurs often. According to the participants, there is nothing they can do about it. One of them shared: "If the boss says he doesn't have money to pay us, we must wait. We can do nothing else since we do not have permission to work. If we complain to the police, we will be the ones taken to jail." According to participants, some local employees delay payment of salaries on purpose to take advantage of Sudanese.

A young male participant shared his conflict when dealing with adversities in his current living context: "When I left my family in Sudan, I thought I was moving to another country to find a better life. Well, life here is better. But at times, the circumstances are so difficult that we compare life here with the one we had in the camp for IDPs in Darfur. In those moments, I desire to return to my country, despite the risk of dying in the war. However, I need to be strong and patient."

Despite the adversities, survey participants also highlight positive aspects of life in Jordan. One of the participants said: "The most positive aspect of life here is security. We may be victims of violence, but we are unlikely to be shot by machine guns. Here, people may curse and even hit you, but they don't shoot you as they do in our region in Sudan."

Racial Discrimination

In their current living context, Fur asylum seekers and refugees face a great deal of discrimination. Participants often shared personal experiences or made comments regarding this subject. One of the comments was: "I recognize that discrimination happens everywhere, as it is a human heart problem. However, since the Arabs discriminated against us in Sudan and we are discriminated against here in Jordan, I feel that the problem of prejudice among Arabs is even greater than among other peoples." Another participant added: "I have the impression that the people here don't like us."

For Sudanese living in Jordan, racial discrimination is not a new reality. In 2014, the UNHCR conducted a consultation with refugees in the country, in which Sudanese confirmed the discriminatory treatment they receive: "What set the Sudanese feedback apart were widespread reports of discrimination on the basis of their color."[6]

One participant presented a religious aspect that explains the discriminatory attitude that Sudanese suffer: "Muslim Arabs discriminate so much because they believe they are superior to other peoples. This discriminatory attitude stems from the understanding that they are descendants of Prophet Muhammad. Consequently, they believe that this puts them in a position of superiority over other peoples."

Discrimination also affects the lives of Fur children. Parents who fear for their children's safety shared some measures they have taken to protect them: "I don't leave my children playing on the streets because they are always mistreated and bullied when playing outside. Because of our condition as refugees, we can do nothing if they suffer any kind of violence. The local legal system will never be on our side."

Another parent also shared: "My daughters would come home from school by themselves, but one day a person beat them on their way home from school. Now, we don't let them walk alone anymore. To protect our children from violence, we go or send a Sudanese, a community member, to pick them up from school."

When sharing about the racial discrimination they suffer, one participant shared an incident in which he was a victim of physical violence. He believes the occurrence was directly related to marginalization and racial discrimination: "Recently, we as a family had to leave the apartment where we used to live. We left because I had a serious issue with the apartment owner. On a Friday night, I was leaving the building when the apartment owner came in my direction. He began shouting and telling me that I could not go

6. Sibson, *Jordan*, 3.

out. I was going to be with friends, and I argued with him that I needed to meet people outside. He came closer to me and hit me with a slap in the face. I noticed that he was drunk, and to avoid more problems, I went back to my apartment, but the man was mad and called on a group of Palestinians to harass me. Hours later, the group came to my apartment and attacked my family and me. We went to the police station and registered a case, but the Palestinians told their version, and the police took no action. Despite the violence my family and I suffered, the case was closed."

Some participants speculate about the possibility of overcoming racial discrimination once they are resettled in a third country. During the interviews, Sudanese mentioned a few countries, such as Australia, New Zealand, and Canada, where they believe discrimination would not be an issue. The Fur people long for a context in which they can live without being discriminated against by other groups in society. "I hope to live in an environment where I will be treated equally to everyone and where the authorities will not apply the law based on the color of my skin," one participant said.

When discussing prejudice, one of the participants made the point that not all Jordanians are biased: "Not all people here are prejudiced or treat us in a discriminatory way. There are good and bad people everywhere, and here it is not different."

Future Perspectives

The long-lasting violence in Darfur has had an impact on the future perspectives of the Fur people living in Jordan. As the civil war continues in western Sudan, despite the fall of the Bashir regime, Fur individuals don't see any indication of improvement in Sudan or believe in a peaceful solution for the near future of the country.

If there were peace in Sudan, returning home would be their first option, as a participant expressed: "If Sudan were a safe nation, I would go back home. Why would I be seeking resettlement and being separated from my family if I had the option of returning to my home country?" However, considering the current violence in Darfur, another participant voiced frustration with the prospect of a shift in the war situation in Sudan: "Sincerely, I have no hope that living conditions will improve in Sudan or that I will have any future in my country. The Janjaweed militias continue to kill my people in Darfur, and the violence happening right now in the region is even worse than when the war started. I don't see any good change in the situation there on the horizon."

The Fur participants in this study are aware that there is no current possibility of local integration in Jordan or a voluntary return to Sudan. They describe their existing situation as being in limbo, as they cannot return to their country of origin due to the war, nor can they move forward in a resettlement process until a third state has agreed to admit them. A participant commented on his surprise at having to wait for a long time to be resettled: "I imagined that I would be in this refugee condition here for two or three years. Though, seven years have passed, and the worst thing for me is not knowing how much time is still left for this wait to end."

Looking into the future, the members of the Fur community in Jordan see resettlement as a priority, as one participant expressed: "The most important thing for me at the moment is to get out of this refugee situation and be resettled somewhere." Although some of them have been waiting for a long time, they have not given up their dream of finding a better life through resettlement. A study participant made a comment in that regard: "Despite living here for fifteen years, I still hope to be resettled one day."

Nevertheless, a recurrent word used by the participants was *uncertainty*. Fur asylum seekers and refugees express distress for not knowing when they will get out of their exile: "I have been here for seven years, and UNHCR does not make any predictions about my resettlement process. I keep asking them when I will be resettled, but they know nothing about my future and give me no hope."

A young participant shared how complex it is to deal with a future clouded by so much hesitation: "When I think about the future, I have a sense of uncertainty. Honestly, I have no idea what the future has in store for me. One day, will I see the family members I left in Sudan? I don't know. The feeling I have is that I am on a long journey, walking day and night, looking ahead and not knowing where I am going and when I will arrive at the destination."

While they peer into a future they cannot predict, Fur refugees expressed much dissatisfaction with the lengthy wait for resettlement, which can last a long time: "There are Sudanese refugees who have been here for over ten years and have never had the opportunity to be resettled. What is the problem? Are we unheard and unseen? Why doesn't anyone care about the situation faced by the Sudanese refugees?"

A male participant expressed his dissatisfaction with the prolonged period he has been waiting for a decision regarding his future: "Nowadays, it is not easy for me to talk about the future. I have been waiting for seven years for a resettlement opportunity. This long wait is now suffocating my dream of a better future. It is frustrating to live not knowing when I will leave this situation. The UNHCR staff only keep telling me that I must wait. But they don't say for how long. How much longer will I have to wait? While I wait, my worst nightmare is when I think that not all refugees will get a chance of resettlement. Well, it's better not to even think about this. Otherwise, I will let die the little hope of a better life that I still carry in my heart."

Another participant also expressed his surprise for the long time having to wait to be resettled: "When I left Sudan and became a refugee, I thought that this condition of refuge would end in a short amount of time. However, I have been stuck here for seven years. I am doing my best to wait patiently for a solution, but I am starting to wonder if there will ever be one for me. The reality is that I find myself in a complicated situation. I cannot return to Sudan because the war is still going on. Also, I cannot move forward because no country is receiving me in a resettlement process. I have no idea when I will overcome this situation, and I feel I am wasting my life."

All participants expressed a desire to be resettled, regardless of the country willing to host them. One of the participants made a straightforward comment on his willingness to be resettled anywhere: "I have no preference for a country to be resettled, and I am willing to go to any country that opens its doors." Two participants had specific preferences, and one of them stated his preferences by saying: "As for the future, I dream of being resettled in Australia or Canada. However, I will be pleased when any country opens its doors to me."

The Sudanese people are very anxious to escape their refugee situation. Participants shared their expectations for moving to a country where they can rebuild their lives: "I need to go to a place where I can work legally, make my own money for living, and let my children have a normal life."

Another participant shared how he hopes that future resettlement will become an opportunity that will favor his children: "Returning to Sudan is not something I have been planning since I left Darfur. The war continues to devastate our villages, and the scenario is one of widespread violence. What I hope is to be resettled in a third country so that at least my children will have an opportunity to have a future."

Fur refugees are tired of waiting for a definitive solution to their situation, since they do not have an estimated time for their resettlement. It is a challenging situation for them, particularly for those with children, to live with limited circumstances while they wait for a future that seems so distant.

Trying to explore how life will look like when they get a chance to be resettled in a third country, a participant shared a wish that reveals a sense of empathy regarding his people: "When I am resettled and living a new life, my concern will be to help my people. I will do my best to alleviate the suffering of those living as refugees worldwide. Only those who have been through this situation know how difficult it is."

Five Main Themes

Analyzing the content of the interviews, I identified five significant themes that resonated in the answers given by the participants. They were referred to frequently and illustrate patterns and trends affecting the lives of the Fur people in Jordan. The five key themes are: discrimination, war, displacement, exile, and suffering.

Discrimination

Throughout the interviews, I noted that all the participants were placing a tremendous emphasis on the theme of discrimination. This focus proved surprising to me because there was no direct question covering this specific subject in the survey questionnaire.

Discrimination emerged as a feature through the interviews because it is a reality that has historically affected the Fur people. It has been present in their relationship with other people before the civil war started in Darfur and has been following the Fur through various contexts. Fur individuals long for a place where they will be welcomed, respected, and treated similarly to everybody else.

War

The content of the interviews clarifies how the civil war that broke out in Darfur brought much harm into the lives of the Fur people. Even though years have passed since they first left Sudan, they are still highly affected by what they experienced in Darfur, and fallout from the war spills into different areas of their lives.

For Fur individuals who were born before 2003, the war is central to how they process their experiences. They divide their lives into two distinct moments: before and after the war. The ones who were born after 2003, however, have faced the reality of the conflict since the first days of their lives.

Having been forcibly displaced from their homeland, Darfur, the Fur left Sudan to run away from the war and find peace in a foreign land. The ones who came to Jordan believe that they have not yet arrived at their final stop; instead, they feel that they are on a path on their way to another destination. They look forward to a place where they will be allowed to rebuild their lives and live in peace.

Displacement

The Fur people who have participated in this study narrated how difficult it has been for them to be forced out of their homes, villages, regions, and country because of the civil war. The interviews expose their grief for having to leave behind their homeland, their memories, and family members in a desperate attempt to save their lives.

At this stage in their pilgrimage as asylum seekers and refugees, one of the realities they face is that they do not have the freedom to decide when and where they are going next. They can leave Jordan and be relocated to a third country only when the UNHCR request for their resettlement is accepted by a government willing to resettle them.

Exile

Participants expressed gratitude for the opportunity to move to Jordan in their attempt to be resettled outside of Sudan. Also, they communicated different challenges they face living in a second country that will not integrate them, in which legal employment is not an option, and where they struggle to access public services.

The circumstances of the Fur people's exile experience in Jordan create uncertainty regarding their future as they don't know if or when they will receive an opportunity to be resettled in a third country and rebuild their lives. Also, the fear of going back to Sudan puts a lot of pressure on them, and they believe that their only option in life is to be approved for resettlement under the UNHCR.

Suffering

The Fur people in the context of this study have experienced tremendous suffering in life since the war started in Sudan. The people's suffering continued as they left the war zone, making suffering a past and present reality in their lives.

I observed that when participants were narrating their experiences of suffering, they often expressed how their sufferings have produced trauma in their lives and how emotionally wounded they have been. The Trauma Healing Institute helpfully defines trauma as "a wound of the heart and mind that causes deep suffering."[7]

Summary

This chapter has provided an opportunity for the Fur people to present their ways of life, allowing me to hear directly from the people and examine their worldview.

When Jesus preached the gospel, he would always present his message considering relevant issues or themes that are relevant to people interacting with him. For instance, sitting by a well, the Messiah talked about a spring of living water to a woman handling an empty water jar (John 4:1–15). Based on Jesus's example, this study advocates that when preaching the gospel and discipling Fur asylum seekers and refugees, there is a need to understand the themes that are relevant to them.

The Fur participants in this chapter have shared information that, when analyzed, pointed to five emerging themes that are relevant to them. The five key themes are: discrimination, war, displacement, exile, and suffering. In the next chapter, I will address the five main themes in depth while building a contextualization project for evangelism and discipleship of Fur asylum seekers and refugees based on each one.

7. See https://www.traumahealingbasics.org.

6

Proposing a Contextualized Approach of Evangelism and Discipleship

Hope is called the anchor of the soul (Hebrews 6:19) be-
cause it gives stability to the Christian life. But hope is not
simply a "wish" (I wish that such-and-such would take
place); rather, it is that which latches on to the certainty of
the promises of the future that God has made.

—RC SPROUL

Introduction

THIS CHAPTER OUTLINES CONTEXTUALIZATION concepts and theological principles to be implemented in the subsequent contextualization project by incorporating the research findings from the previous chapter. The research outcomes revealed five themes that emerged from the interviews: discrimination, war, displacement, exile, and suffering. These five themes represent the Fur people's most discussed issues as they examine their condition living as asylum seekers and refugees in Jordan. Therefore, they are addressed in the contextualization project.

Three questions have inspired this study and especially this chapter: *What are the themes most often discussed among the Fur asylum seekers and refugees in Jordan? How does the Bible address these themes? Finally, how can*

Christians effectively communicate biblical teachings to the Fur asylum seekers and refugees in Jordan in response to the discussed themes?

The contextualization project is based on a model developed by Dr. David Cashin and described in his book *The Seven Essential Questions of Life*. Throughout the research process, I closely followed the method structure, which includes the following sections: Cultural Exegesis, Biblical Exegesis, Principle and Application, Implementation and Communication, Apologetics Issue, and Evaluation.

The purpose of the contextualization project is to foster evangelism and discipleship among Fur asylum seekers and refugees. The project sections are designed to help individuals develop a personal relationship with God, grow as Jesus's disciples, overcome suffering, persevere in the faith even when facing religious persecution, and avoid syncretism. Additionally, the project proposes fruitful practices for Christian workers to employ in reproducing the faith among the Fur community in Jordan and elsewhere.

Contextualization

Various definitions or proposals of contextualization are used in missiological literature within the evangelical tradition. Kato provides a definition of contextualization that resonates with this study: "We understand the term to mean making concepts or ideals relevant in a given situation."[1] Nichols similarly defines the concept while making specific reference to the transmission of the gospel: "[Contextualization is] the translation of the unchanging content of the Gospel of the kingdom into verbal form meaningful to the peoples in their separate cultural and within their particular existential situations."[2]

Moreau gives another helpful definition of contextualization that reverberates with the purpose of this study: "Contextualization is a process where followers of Jesus adapt the forms, content, and praxis of the Christian faith to communicate it effectively to the minds and hearts of the people within their cultural background."[3]

Although the term *contextualization* has a variety of definitions, it is frequently used to refer to the process of communicating the gospel to people of different contexts by overcoming such obstacles such as social, cultural, and linguistic barriers so that the receiver can completely comprehend and respond appropriately.

1. Kato, "Gospel, Cultural Context," 1217.
2. Nicholls, "Theological Education and Evangelization," 647.
3. Moreau, *Contextualization in World Missions*, 36.

While defining contextualization remains a work in progress, Dowsett points out that the concept of contextualization is not new in the world of missions but is a practice that has been prevalent throughout Christian history:

> Contextualization is not a theory or a method or a 20th century passing fad. No, it is the dynamic living out of biblical truth in the here-and-now, so that faithfulness and relevance, truth and life, continuity and freshness—all the amazing contours of God-made-visible in and through his people—are held in God-derived balance with each other. Down through the centuries and all around the world, wherever the gospel has taken root and been genuinely incarnated in this culture or that, contextualization has taken place. The term may be modern. The practice is as ancient as God's people.[4]

Contextualization also entails the messenger adapting himself to the cultural context and characteristics of the people he wishes to reach to deliver the gospel more effectively. A frequently cited biblical passage that exemplifies this principle is 1 Cor 9:20–23:

> To the Jews I became like a Jew, to win the Jews. To those under the law I became like one under the law (though I myself am not under the law), so as to win those under the law. To those not having the law I became like one not having the law (though I am not free from God's law but am under Christ's law), so as to win those not having the law. To the weak I became weak, to win the weak. I have become all things to all people so that by all possible means I might save some. I do all this for the sake of the gospel, that I may share in its blessings.

When attempting to communicate the gospel in the most effective manner possible, the messenger must consider the culture of those interacting with the message. The culture of the people must be as equally relevant to the messenger as it is to the people he is attempting to reach, as Brown states that "no custom is 'odd' to the people who practice it."[5] Also, when contextualizing the gospel or making the message understandable to a specific people group, Kraft stresses that the goal is "doing whatever is necessary to make sure Christianity is expressed in ways that are appropriate to the context of the receiving group."[6]

---

4. Dowsett, "Dry Bones in West," 455.

5. Van Pelt, *Bantu Customs*, 17.

6. Kraft, *Appropriate Christianity*, 4.

Considering how the gospel relates to culture, the biblical texts do not prescribe the attitude of canceling, suppressing, or harming cultures. The gospel recognizes, preserves, and enriches cultures as part of its redemptive work and mission. The International Congress on World Evangelization that was held in Lausanne, Switzerland, in 1974, proposes in its covenant how cultures are affected by the gospel:

> The development of strategies for world evangelization calls for imaginative pioneering methods. Under God, the result will be the rise of churches deeply rooted in Christ and closely related to their culture. Culture must always be tested and judged by Scripture. Because men and women are God's creatures, some of their culture is rich in beauty and goodness. Because they are fallen, all of it is tainted with sin and some of it is demonic. The gospel does not presuppose the superiority of any culture to another, but evaluates all cultures according to its own criteria of truth and righteousness, and insists on moral absolutes in every culture.[7]

Although contextualization in the evangelical tradition has to do with considering cultures to communicate the good news of Jesus, Campbell asserts that the gospel must be liberated from the control of any single culture to spread across cultures.[8] Arguing that the gospel is not limited to the cultural expressions of a particular people, he adds: "The gospel is not Eastern nor Western, Jewish nor Gentile. The gospel is Jesus. This is the genius of the gospel. Jesus knows no cultural boundaries. When the gospel becomes in-culturated or over-contextualized, it becomes less than the good news."[9]

Because the gospel and the church are not tied to a particular culture but can be planted as seeds and flourish in any culture, Engen states that they "are not foreign plants that have been slightly modified to be able to grow in foreign soil. Rather, this gospel is a new hybrid seed with new and different characteristics that allow it to flourish as an indigenous plant."[10]

Reflecting on the effect of the gospel on different cultures, Lidorio affirms:

> I believe that there are six key functions of the Gospel in relation to culture. The Gospel is Supracultural—it contains the complete truth about men and their society, revealed in the Scriptures (2 Tm 3:16); Multicultural—it brings people from all nations around Jesus (Rev 5:9); Crosscultural—it should be sent

7. Stott et al., "Lausanne Covenant," §10, para. 11.

8. Campbell, "Releasing the Gospel," 167.

9. Campbell, "Releasing the Gospel," 167.

10. Moreau, *Contextualization in World Missions*, 36.

from one culture to another (Act 1:8); Cultural—it is revealed throughout the history of humankind (Jo 1:14); Intercultural— it promotes dialogue and understanding between different languages and cultures (Cl 3:11); Contracultural—it confronts people in their own culture, producing real, personal and eternal transformation (Act 26:18).[11]

Missiologists and Christian anthropologists interpret the incarnation of Jesus Christ as an illustration of the gospel message taking on physical form to be transmitted to human beings. According to this understanding, the gospel is not a message without a body. On the contrary, in Jesus, it takes a body, a culture, a language, and so on. As a result, the gospel is presented in a way that humans can grasp what the divine was expressing. According to Karl Barth, "The Word did not simply become any 'flesh.' It became Jewish flesh."[12]

When it comes to transforming people's ways of life, contextualization must balance the tension between adapting the gospel to the culture while preserving the message's meaning. A balanced approach is necessary to adhere to the Scriptures and avoid syncretism, which Fleming defines as the "incorporation of non-Christian elements into the Christian faith resulting in the formation of a new entity which is no longer Christian."[13] Also, Payne writes, "In these situations the Christians identify themselves as Christians, but their worldview remains unchanged."[14] Therefore, the most widely accepted definitions of contextualization in the evangelical world are those that not only consider culture but also reaffirm the centrality of Scripture, as the authors of the Willowbank Report assert: "Despite a lack of agreement on an exact definition of contextualization, missiologists favor the concept when supported by Biblical truth."[15]

Since the gospel is culturally translatable, one can infer that it has been contextualized when its proclamation retains the message's original meaning. Another significant sign of contextualization is if the gospel has been effectively understood by the listeners to the extent that they realize that the biblical teaching is relevant to them and their context. On the contrary, when the listeners cannot comprehend the gospel meaning and believe it is irrelevant to them or their cultural context, the gospel has likely not been contextualized.

11. Lidorio, "Gospel and Culture," para. 5.

12. K. Barth, "Christian Life," 1956–57.

13. Prince, "Contextualisation of the Gospel," 23–24.

14. Payne and Terry, *Developing a Strategy*, 161.

15. Rheenen, *Contextualization and Syncretism*, 4.

The study emphasizes the contextual theologizing of emerging themes that express the realities faced by Fur asylum seekers and refugees living in Jordan. The cultural contextualization of Islamic customs, forms, or meanings is outside the scope of this study. I assume that the gospel message is communicated satisfactorily and has excellent potential to lead the people to a personal relationship with Jesus when relevant themes are identified and explored from a biblical worldview.

The contextualization project proposed in this chapter will be primarily concerned with the exegesis of the Scripture. This resonates with what Peters defends. In his opinion, contextualization must be based on the proper exegesis of the biblical texts to be legitimate.[16]

Contextual Theology

The objectives of this chapter's contextualization project on evangelism and discipleship are threefold: 1) to effectively communicate the gospel to the target people, 2) to promote a church-planting movement among them, and 3) to facilitate the process of developing a contextual theology with them.

I understand that if these objectives are met, the Fur community in Jordan will consequently experience a significant impact, as Harlan expresses how transforming this process can be: "Theology is a bridge between the Bible and the context so that the Word of God can speak and powerfully impact the community."[17]

Rather than performing all the work, someone who wants to reach the Fur people with the gospel will need to collaborate with the participants at each step of the process and act as a facilitator, including at the stage of constructing a contextual theology, as Harlan suggests: "Instead of only teaching theology, missionaries should act as facilitators in the constructing of local theology."[18]

Contextual theology is critical in the process of church planting because it promotes genuine transformation among the people and places a strong emphasis on the Bible as the word of God and ultimate authority. Additionally, it protects believers against fraudulent teachings that often take them away from the gospel of Jesus Christ to a different gospel (Gal 1:6). Gusman asserts, "Bad theology is developed when its source is not the Scripture, when it is not guided by the Holy Spirit, when it is not centered on Christ, or when it is not done by and oriented to Christians who

16. Peters, "Issues Confronting Evangelical Missions," 169.

17. Harlan, "De-Westernizing Doctrine," 160.

18. Harlan, "De-Westernizing Doctrine," 160.

bring their experience and struggles to the Scripture to affect the world in which they live."[19]

Contextual theology consists of a process built with the people and mainly by the people. Bevans understands, "Contextual Theology is a way of doing theology that considers, or puts together in a mutually critical dialogue, the experience of the past recorded in Scripture and the experience of the present on a particular context."[20] Contextual theology is relevant to the people involved in the process as it transforms their living context:

> The contextualization of the Gospel and Christian theology then calls for a discerning of the times, involvement in one's particular situation, and participation in the ongoing mission of the church wherever it is situated. It brings the text (Bible) into a dynamic interaction with the context (life-situation). From this interaction, a life-situation or contextual theology emerges.[21]

For this study, contextual theology is to help Fur individuals learn how to apply the Bible to their lives considering their current living context. Basically, it is to enable the teachings of the Scripture to become alive and applicable to individuals.

Contextualizing the Themes

The study's research was based on the Fur people's culture as expressed in Jordan. In chapter 5, when I was doing a detailed analysis of the interview content, five major themes emerged from the responses offered by the participants.

Why is it necessary to identify emergent themes within a group of individuals, and how are they pertinent to a gospel presentation? When Jesus preached the gospel, he demonstrated an understanding of the living context of his listeners and conveyed his message in a way that made sense to them. For example, when presenting the gospel to the Samaritan woman (John 4:1–26), Jesus spoke to a woman by a well with an empty water jar about a spring of living water: "Everyone who drinks this water will be thirsty again, but whoever drinks the water I give them will never thirst. Indeed, the water I give them will become in them a spring of water welling up to eternal life" (John 4:13–14).

19. Segura-Guzmán, "Practice of Theology," 77.
20. Bevans, *Essays in Contextual Theology*, 106.
21. Tano, *Theology in Philippine Setting*, 10.

If the Lord were on the east side of the Jordan River and came across a group of asylum seekers and refugees from the Fur tribe, he would almost certainly use pertinent themes and comprehensible language to communicate the gospel to them.

Therefore, in determining how to present the gospel in a way that is understandable to Fur asylum seekers and refugees in Jordan, it is critical to identify ways in which the message of the cross can reach their hearts. When analyzing the Fur culture based on this context, I conclude that contextualization for this ethnic group should contemplate five emerging themes: discrimination, war, displacement, exile, and suffering.

God, in his very nature and attributes, addresses each of these themes as the ultimate source of human goodness: "Every good and perfect gift is from above, coming down from the Father of the heavenly lights, who does not change like shifting shadows" (Jas 1:17). Examining the meaning of the names of God used in the Old Testament, it becomes clear that Sudanese from Darfur can find an answer to their issues in God:

- For the ones discriminated against and abused, "The Lord Is Our Righteousness" (Jehovah Tsidkenu)

- For those who are victims of war and are searching for peace, "The Lord Is Our Peace" (Jehovah Shalom)

- For those who have been forced out of their homes and are displaced, "The Lord Is There" (Jehovah Shammah), providing shelter and being their place of refuge in each step of their journey

- For those in their exile fighting to survive and hoping to find a place to begin a new life, "The Lord Will Provide" (Jehovah Jireh) a hope and a future for them

- For those who have experienced much suffering in life and are seeking healing to their bodies, souls, and spirits, "The Lord That Heals" (Jehovah Rapha) is waiting for them with arms wide open

First Theme: Discrimination

Fur asylum seekers and refugees face a great deal of prejudice. Discrimination has been a critical obstacle in their lives, both in Sudan, their previous living context, and in Jordan, their existing living context. Study participants feel that the civil war in Darfur is founded in racial discrimination against black Africans. Also, they believe that discrimination is to blame for some of the adversities they face amid Jordanian society, such as rejection, marginalization, and violence.

During the interviews, the word *discrimination* appeared several times, and the participants described a variety of experiences relating to it. All the participants stated their dissatisfaction with discrimination in one form or another. They long for a place where everyone is treated equally before the law and receives equal levels of respect.

Cultural Exegesis

During the interviews, participants stated their exhaustion and justified this condition by citing the hectic lifestyles they lead. The discrimination they have faced at various periods has impacted them in various ways. They yearn to live in a society in which different groups of people can coexist peacefully without being judged based on their skin color, ethnicity, or other factors. They dream of a future in a country of resettlement where they will be treated equally and have the chance to start a new life.

It is significant that participants believe that discrimination is a problem that originates in the human heart. As Muslims, they are used to the Islamic teachings that contradict the doctrine of original sin and the concept that human beings have sinful hearts. According to Mohamed, an Islamic scholar, the common idea in Islam is that people sin because of external forces: "Every child is born in a state of *fitrah*, and social environment causes the individual to deviate from this state."[22]

However, the study participants' understanding of the root of racial discrimination echoes biblical teachings that assert that humans have a wicked nature, "a body ruled by sin" (Rom 6:6), which is the basis of all wrongdoing, including discrimination (1 John 5:17).

Biblical Exegesis

As part of the process of biblical exegesis as it relates to the theme of discrimination, Eph 2:14–16 will be employed to establish a contextualized approach for evangelism and discipleship among Fur asylum seekers and refugees:

> For he himself is our peace, who has made the two groups one and has destroyed the barrier, the dividing wall of hostility, by setting aside in his flesh the law with its commands and

22. Mohamed, *Fitrah*, 41.

regulations. His purpose was to create in himself one new humanity out of the two, thus making peace, and in one body to reconcile both of them to God through the cross, by which he put to death their hostility.

He is our peace. The pronoun *he* is employed in this context to refer directly to the person of Jesus Christ, the Messiah and the Shepherd of the sheep (Heb 12:24). As the mediator of a new covenant (Heb 12:24) and through his work (death, burial, and resurrection), Jesus sealed peace between God (holy) and men (sinners), and between Jews (people who have a covenant with God through Abraham) and gentiles (nonmembers of the Jewish community of faith).

The Scriptures assert that in Jesus, we can have peace—"I have told you these things, so that in me you may have peace" (John 16:33)—because *he* is our peace, the Prince of Peace (Isa 9:6), the peace of God that transcends all understanding (Phil 4:7).

He made the two groups one. The Jewish worldview would divide humanity into two groups: Jews and gentiles. Also, it would place the Jews in a superior position to the point of rejecting the gentiles: "The Jews felt so strongly about their moral and racial purity that they made a point of keeping outsiders away."[23] Erickson adds his analyses of the perception that the Jews had of the gentiles:

> One of the deepest yearnings of the human soul is to belong. We instinctively draw circles that include ourselves and exclude others, giving us coveted membership in a group others wish they belonged to. There can be no "inner ring," in C. S. Lewis's terms, unless there are despised outsiders. The Jewish nation, God's "inner ring" in their own view, drew the circle at the law, epitomized in marks of Jewishness. Jews stigmatized Gentiles as the "uncircumcised," often in self-exaltation (2:11). Without the despised Gentiles, Jews would have failed to be distinctive in their own nationalist perspective.[24]

However, Christ worked to transform the identity of these two groups, bringing them together through the cross so that both people would become one and begin to share the same spiritual blessings. Through his works, Jesus Christ eradicated any possibility of a position of privilege, discriminatory distinction, and place of superiority among them. Because of the grace found in Jesus, those (from both groups) who are reconciled with God are

23. Knowles, *Bible Guide*, 615.

24. Erickson, *Commentary on Ephesians*, 23.

called "children of God" (1 John 3:1). In Christ, there is no separation between Jews and gentiles, as they are members of the same body and part of the same faith family: "This mystery is that through the gospel the Gentiles are heirs together with Israel, members together of one body, and sharers together in the promise in Christ Jesus" (Eph 3:6).

He destroyed the barrier, the dividing wall of hostility. Jesus tore down the wall of animosity that had separated Jews and gentiles for thousands of years. He destroyed all the factors that created a wall between Jews and gentiles and regulated their access to God.

Through Christ, the hostility between Jews and gentiles is ended, and humanity is seen without this duality. Although exclusion emanates from the sinful heart of humankind, there is no separation or exclusion in Christ. All who believe are one: "There is neither Jew nor Gentile, neither slave nor free, nor is there male and female, for you are all one in Christ Jesus. If you belong to Christ, then you are Abraham's seed, and heirs according to the promise" (Gal 3:28–29).

He set aside in his flesh the law with its commands and regulations. Although Jesus fulfilled the law of Moses (Matt 5:17), Christ overthrew the previous paradigm of spirituality, which was based on the law. Two crucial characteristics distinguished his work. It served as a substitutive and inclusive work. Considering our guilt, Christ took upon himself our sinful nature, our transgressions, and our iniquities (Isa 53:4–6). So, at the cross, Jesus took the place of sinners by acting as a substitute and dying for them. At the same time, sinners were attracted to his body (John 12:32) and became partakers of his death (Gal 2:20), burial (Rom 6:4), and resurrection (Eph 2:6). Consequently, Christ transformed us into a new creation (2 Cor 5:17) and gave us a new heart and a new spirit (Ezek 36:26). So, those who are born-again believers are "dead to sin but alive to God" (Rom 6:11).

His purpose was to create in himself one new humanity out of the two. Christ transforms those who believe, regardless of their background, into a new creation. They all become members of the same spiritual family and embrace a context of human relationships based on the values of the kingdom of God (Eph 4:17–32). Thus, Jews who consider themselves superior to the gentiles need to understand that both groups share the same spiritual blessings. Gentiles who feel inferior must believe that God loves them and that, in the kingdom of God, they are members of a single family of faith in which all members are brothers and sisters.

Analysis of this verse confirms God's purpose to eradicate all sorts of discrimination, difference, and hostility among humankind. Also, it shows that "God does not show favoritism" (Rom 2:11) and requires his people not to show partiality or favoritism (Lev 19:15). Therefore, whoever discriminates or shows favoritism is sinning: "But if you show favoritism, you sin and are convicted by the law as lawbreakers" (Jas 2:9).

He reconciled in one body both of them to God through the cross. The children of God have experienced reconciliation and unity with God. As for the Jews and gentiles, Christ "took both for himself and reconciled them."[25] All believers are one through Jesus: "All this is from God, who reconciled us to himself through Christ" (2 Cor 5:18).

He put to death their hostility. The enmity that existed between Jews and gentiles has been destroyed. They are now more than friends. By faith in Jesus, Jews and gentiles are brothers and sisters. Through the work of the Messiah, peace between antagonistic peoples is a possibility and becomes a reality, as Markus Barth comments: "Jews and Gentiles, who always had been segregated in hostility, are now 'reconciled' to one another and to God."[26]

Principle and Application

Breaking down the phrase "destroyed the barrier, the dividing wall of hostility," two principles can be applied to evangelism and discipleship among the Fur asylum seekers and refugees in Jordan.

Principle 1—Evangelism Approach: When the apostle Paul wrote the Letter to the Ephesians, his primary audience was a group of Christians from the churches he had planted in and around Ephesus (Acts 19). Although Paul wrote Eph 2:14–16 to assist Jews and gentile believers in overcoming their division, hostility, and animosity, the scope of God's ultimate plan for all of humanity is continually demonstrated throughout the epistle. Consequently, Paul's description of Christ's identity, attributes, and work can be applied to discipling those who are already believers and inviting non-Christians into a new way of relating to God and other people.

Because God loved humankind that were lost in their sin, he sent Jesus Christ into the world (John 3:16) to carry out the work of the cross, burial, and resurrection (1 Cor 15:3–5) so that humanity would be rescued and those who believe would become his children: "So in Christ Jesus you are all children of God through faith" (Gal 3:26). Therefore, Jesus became our peace, and through his work, all discrimination, difference, and hostility between groups are canceled out, because the Messiah rescued the sinners and made them members of the family of God.

---

25. Jamieson et al., *Commentary Critical and Explanatory*, 346.
26. M. Barth, *Ephesians*, 266.

Those who put their faith in Jesus will have transformed hearts and belong to a spiritual family that congregates all peoples without any distinction and experiences God's abundant love: "If anyone acknowledges that Jesus is the Son of God, God lives in them and they in God. And so we know and rely on the love God has for us. God is love. Whoever lives in love lives in God, and God in them" (1 John 4:15–16). Consequently, through the forgiveness of their sins, they will appear before God on the day of judgment with much confidence to spend the eternity with God: "This is how love is made complete among us so that we will have confidence on the day of judgment: In this world we are like Jesus" (1 John 4:17).

Principle 2—Discipleship Approach: Christ's disciples need to understand their new spiritual identity as a member of God's family. It is from this identity, based on the principles and values of the kingdom of God (Rom 14:17), that a daily personal relationship will develop. The new creation (2 Cor 5:17) needs to be aware that God does not show favoritism (Acts 10:34) and that in God's eyes, no one is more or less important. God sees only children among his people, all equally loved: "So in Christ Jesus you are all children of God through faith, for all of you who were baptized into Christ have clothed yourselves with Christ. There is neither Jew nor Gentile, neither slave nor free, nor is there male and female, for you are all one in Christ Jesus" (Gal 3:26–28).

Bearing in mind the possibility of a church planting movement among the Fur people in Jordan, new believers need to be encouraged to create a healthy environment for fellowship, thus allowing the development of relationships that overcome all types of rivalry and discrimination. Additionally, they must also demonstrate a willingness to receive members from other ethnic communities in their fellowship groups. Likely, members of other Darfurian tribes (Masalit, Zaghawa, Daju, and others) will be willing to join them.

Regarding believers from outside of the Fur community working with Fur individuals, a fruitful practice proposed to address the theme of discrimination is to nurture positive relationships with Fur individuals based on biblical equality, respect, and love, allowing them to experience a relationship that recognizes God's image in all human beings.

Implementation and Communication

Considering the possibility that members of the Fur people in Jordan will believe in the gospel, the following are proposals for attitudes that disciplers should encourage the new believers to adopt throughout their discipleship process.

Continue to reflect on the concept of our unity in Christ in your regular study of the Holy Scriptures. Study individually and with other disciples a selection of biblical texts such as Rom 12:5, which talks about how God has positioned all the believers around the world as members of the same body: "In Christ, we, though many, form one body, and each member belongs to all the others."

Expand your understanding of man's sinful nature, which is continuously antagonistic to God and leads to death (Rom 8:6–7). What are some other sins that you consider as evil as discrimination? Is it true that we are sinners because we sin, or do we sin because we are sinners? What is a fair view of humankind's internal struggles and external forces? When the apostle Paul wrote 2 Cor 7:5, what exactly was he communicating? The Scriptures state, "For, when we came into Macedonia, we had no rest, but we were harassed at every turn; conflicts on the outside, fears within."

Encourage Jordanian Christians to be constantly welcoming and loving to refugees and foreigners. Talk to Muslims about caring for the poor, needy, vulnerable, and foreigners. Create opportunities for Jordanian Christians to interact with Sudanese asylum seekers and refugees to exchange love, care, and empathy. For example, organize refugee service activities and invite local Christians to participate.

Reject any attitude of prejudice among other believers and in society in general. Build healthy relationships based on the example of Jesus Christ, who never discriminated against people. Keep in mind that love, care, and kindness are mighty tools, even more when used in relationships with those who are victims of prejudice, rejection, and exclusion. Remind Christians and Muslims that all humans have the same father and mother in the flesh, since they are all descendants of Adam and Eve. Therefore, if all people are part of one offspring, they are brothers and sisters.

Go beyond denouncing the sin of racial discrimination. Discuss with other believers how the Scriptures are opposed to all kinds of racism and prejudice, including that which affects, for example, women's lives in this context. Endeavor to appropriately report any case of racial discrimination to local authorities and international organizations.

Apologetics Issue

Theological Controversy 1: How can I believe that the Bible is teaching the truth about Jesus? The religion of Islam teaches that the Bible has been corrupted and that God sent the Qur'an as a final revelation to correct the problem of the corruption of previous sacred texts (Sura 29:46).

Apologetic Response: The claim that the Bible has been corrupted has come up in multiple interactions with Fur individuals in Jordan. In most cases, they brought up this issue after inquiring of me about my religious beliefs. When they learned that he believed the Bible to be the inspired word of God, they began to present the controversy of the corruption of the Bible. They make this claim because according to Islam, the four sacred texts (books) that God revealed are the Law (or *Torah*), the Psalms (or *Zabur*), the Gospel (or *Injil*), and the Qur'an. Some qur'anic verses that mention parts of the Judeo-Christian Scriptures are:

- The Law: "It was We who revealed the Law (to Moses); therein was Guidance and Light" (Sura 5:442).

- The Psalms: "We did bestow on some Prophets more (and other) gifts than on others: and We gave to David (the gift of) the Psalms" (Sura 17:55).

- The Gospel: "It is He who sent down to thee (step by step), in truth, the Book, confirming what went before it; and He sent down the Law (of Moses) and the Gospel (of Jesus) before this, as a guide to mankind" (Sura 3:3).

Also, the Qur'an says that there is no distinction between the revelations of God given to different prophets throughout history (Sura 5:46). Therefore, according to Islamic writings, to reject the Scriptures that were revealed before Muhammad is to depart from the truth: "You who believe, believe in God and His Messenger and in the Scripture, He sent down to His Messenger, as well as what He sent down before. Anyone who does not believe in God, His angels, His Scriptures, His messengers, and the Last Day has gone far, far astray" (Sura 4:136).

The Bible is a reliable source. Christians believe that "all Scripture is inspired by God" (2 Tim 3:16), and the Qur'an prescribes that the revelation given to the apostles must be recognized and accepted by Muslims, together with all the other revelations (Sura 4:163–65). The Qur'an acknowledges biblical individuals such as Abraham, Ishmael, Isaac, and Jacob. In addition, Moses and Jesus are mentioned as prophets who received God's revelation, according to Sura 2:136.

The Qur'an says on different occasions that no one can change the words of Allah, as in Sura 6:34: "There is none to change the words of Allah." Therefore, the Qur'an does not endorse the idea that the text of the Bible has been corrupted or must be discarded.

Since the Qur'an refers to the Bible as a book revealed by God, believing that the Bible has been corrupted would have significant implications for Muslims, as Gerhard Nehls argues:

> If the Bible was corrupted before or at the time of Muhammad, the Qur'an would hardly have spoken of the Bible in such a positive manner. Had the Bible been changed or corrupted afterwards, the many existing old manuscripts that predate Muhammad by hundreds of years would have given proof of that fact.[27]

The Bible has been supported by thousands of archaeological finds for each book of the Bible. Aside from that, "for the New Testament over 5,898 Greek New Testament manuscripts have been cataloged, 10,000 Latin manuscripts, and an additional 9,300 other manuscripts in such languages as Syriac, Slavic, Gothic, Ethiopic, Coptic, and Armenian."[28]

The Dead Sea Scrolls (also known as the Qumran Cave scrolls) are considered one of the most important finds in the history of modern archaeology. They were found at the Qumran Caves in what was then Mandatory Palestine, near Ein Feshkha in the West Bank, on the northern shore of the Dead Sea, and contain an amazing material, as Attard comments:

> In 1947, the Dead Sea Scrolls were discovered; among them were several manuscripts of portions of the Bible dating back prior to the time of Jesus. Specifically, there was found among them a complete manuscript of Isaiah in classical Hebrew, radiocarbon-dated earlier than 100 CE. On comparing it to our current Masoretic text, their agreement was fantastic: thus, it restored confidence in the replicating process of the Old Testament.[29]

Most of the scrolls are held by the state of Israel at the Israel Museum in Jerusalem, although some are displayed at the Jordan Museum in Amman. Fur asylum seekers and refugees residing in Jordan are welcome to go to the Jordan Museum and see some of the Dead Sea Scrolls for themselves.

Theological Controversy 2: How can Jesus be the Prince of Peace as in Isa 9:6, if in Matt 10:34 Jesus said, "I did not come to bring peace"?

Apologetic Response: This issue was not discussed with the Fur people, yet it was included in this section because it has such a potential to create confusion and mislead the people when they begin to read the Bible for the first time. Also, bibliographic research has shown that this issue has

---

27. Nehls, *Dear Abdallah*, 9.

28. Andrews, *New Testament Documents*, 29.

29. Attard, *Is the Bible Infallible?*, 28.

been used by Muslim debaters to discredit the Bible.[30] Since the Fur people do not want to be associated with war, it is essential to explain that Jesus's statement "I did not come to bring peace" does not exist in isolation. The whole passage from Matt 10:34 says: "Do not suppose that I have come to bring peace to the earth. I did not come to bring peace, but a sword" (Matt 10:34). Although the text presents a seeming paradox regarding other biblical texts that talk about Jesus as a peacemaker, it can be explained in the context of the biblical teachings.

First, it is critical to consider that Jesus never promoted an armed conflict or a rebellion or used a sword. In fact, at Gethsemane, when Peter wielded the sword against one of the soldiers for seizing and arresting Jesus, the Lord objected to Peter's reaction: "Then Simon Peter, who had a sword, drew it and struck the high priest's servant, cutting off his right ear. (The servant's name was Malchus.) Jesus commanded Peter, 'Put your sword away! Shall I not drink the cup the Father has given me?'" (John 18:10–11). And Jesus "touched the man's ear and healed him" (Luke 22:51).

Jesus was a peace ambassador: "He came and preached peace to you who were far away and peace to those who were near" (Eph 2:17). In the Beatitude section of the Sermon on the Mount, Jesus highlighted to his disciples the blessing of becoming peacemakers: "Blessed are the peacemakers, for they will be called children of God" (Matt 5:9). Additionally, Jesus taught his disciples to love their enemies and pray for their persecutors: "But I tell you, love your enemies and pray for those who persecute you" (Matt 5:44).

The war that the Gospel of Matthew is talking about is not a reference to the violence that Jesus and his disciples would promote against people. Instead, it is an allusion to the violence the world would promote against Jesus and his disciples: "You will be hated by everyone because of me" (Matt 10:22). Hatred and violence against Jesus's disciples have been a reality over the centuries. Sittser shares about the experience of the early Christians in this regard: "The early Christian martyrs were victims of such hate, not perpetrators. They absorbed violence; they did not inflict it. They were called to martyrdom."[31]

Why would the world intend to fight against Jesus and his disciples? Because people in the world who are not under the lordship of Jesus are under the control of Satan, and the evil one hates them: "We know that we are children of God, and that the whole world is under the control of the evil one" (1 John 5:19). Therefore, there is a battle in progress between good and evil, God and Satan. Consequently, the world hates Jesus as he

---

30. N. Qureshi, *No God but One*, 141–43.

31. Sittser, *Water from Deep Well*, 28.

openly testifies that its works are evil (John 7:7), and whoever joins Jesus in testifying against the world will also be hated, persecuted, and killed: "Remember what I told you: 'A servant is not greater than his master.' If they persecuted me, they will persecute you also" (John 15:20). The clamorous demands of the people to crucify Jesus (Luke 23:23) and the historical persecution against Jesus's disciples have proven the teachings of the New Testament to be accurate. Smither asserts: "Many early Christians in the first three centuries verbally shared their faith during their arrest and court proceedings. These testimonies have been captured in accounts such as the acts of the martyrs (*acta*) or martyrdoms (*passio*), which were preserved and transmitted by the early church."[32]

Another tension Jesus brings to the world is that he requires that anyone who follows him makes the Messiah the priority of his life: "Anyone who loves their father or mother more than me is not worthy of me; anyone who loves their son or daughter more than me is not worthy of me" (Matt 10:37). A Christocentric lifestyle sometimes causes conflict among families, friends, neighbors, among others:

> Conflict and disagreement will arise between those who choose to follow Christ and those who do not. In saying this, Jesus was not encouraging disobedience to parents or conflict at home. Rather, he was showing that his presence demands a decision. Because some will follow Christ and some will not, conflict will inevitably arise. As his followers take their crosses and follow him, their different values, morals, goals, and purposes will set them apart.[33]

Confessing Christ as Lord and refusing to worship political authorities have caused the death of numerous believers throughout Christian history. Martyrdom, dying for the faith, is not only Jesus's legacy but also a heritage that Christians today receive from many disciples who preceded them. At different times, Christians have been persecuted and killed just for publicly confessing their faith, as Smither points out:

> Many early Christians in the first three centuries verbally shared their faith during their arrest and court proceedings. These testimonies have been captured in accounts such as the acts of the martyrs (*acta*) or martyrdoms (*passio*), which were preserved and transmitted by the early church. On one level, verbal witness included the simple confession of being a Christian. In the famous martyrdom account of Polycarp of Smyrna (d. 155),

32. Smither, *Christian Martyrdom*, 31.

33. Osborne and Comfort, *Matthew*, 213.

the bishop defended his refusal to make the pagan sacrifice by stating, "For eighty and six years I have been his servant, and he has done me no wrong, and how can I blaspheme my king who saved me?" The governor prosecuted him based on his testimony: "Polycarp has confessed that he is a Christian."[34]

Jesus is the Prince of Peace, who came to bring peace to the world. However, because evil powers operating in the universe are actively striving against the establishment of Jesus's kingdom, the Lord's peace produces strife.

Evaluation

1. How does this contextualization project avoid encouraging syncretism among the Fur people?

The project will avoid syncretism by helping Sudanese develop a biblical understanding of the work of Christ (1 Cor 15:1–5) and how it addresses discrimination as opposed to the teachings they received and interactions they had in their cultural or religious environment that perpetrated the heavy prejudice they have experienced.

As they study the Scriptures, they will learn to think critically about their beliefs and life context. They will apply biblical principles to daily practices rooted in their cultural context and will gradually begin to transform their community and the surrounding society by the power of the Holy Spirit.

2. How does this contextualization project constructively engage the Fur people's worldview?

The project constructively engages the Fur people's worldview by addressing the sin of discrimination that directly impacts the lives of the Fur asylum seekers and refugees in this context. This type of approach can act as an encouraging tool for the Fur people to open their ears to hear the gospel of Jesus Christ—probably for the first time—in a way that makes sense to them. As soon as they embrace the message and become believers, they will be encouraged to apply the Scriptures to this and other themes that affect different areas of their lives and generate concerns in their daily lives.

34. Smither, *Christian Martyrdom*, 30–31.

3. How does this contextualization project challenge the Fur people toward (specific) personal change?

Helping men, women, and children to understand that they are loved by God will naturally bring about change by reaffirming that they do not need to live based on what society thinks but on what God says about them and by equipping them to transform society, helping those living under the yoke of discrimination to look at the cross and to trust Jesus to experience a new life (Eph 2:5), have it to the full (John 10:10), and, consequently, experience an eternal life with God (John 3:16).

Second Theme: War

The war in Darfur is the primary catalyst that brought the Fur individuals to Jordan. It was responsible for destroying their villages, killing their family members, forcing them to leave their country, and placing them in the circumstances where they currently live as asylum seekers or refugees. Whenever they look back to Darfur, everything they see is framed by the war, as Hastrup comments: "The entire area has been fundamentally, and probably irreversibly, changed as entire communities have been forced to flee and millions of people have lived and continue to live in a prolonged state of emergency."[35]

In addition to the material losses, the war has affected the Fur physically, emotionally, and spiritually. It brought much destruction to their past, unutterable suffering to their present, and a great deal of uncertainty about their immediate future. The war forced the study participants to leave their homeland in absolute despair for peace.

Cultural Exegesis

War has caused widespread devastation in Sudan. It continues to play an essential role in the lives of the Fur people since it affects their homeland and threatens the lives of their family members. Even though Sudan has a lengthy history of violence, and the Fur asylum seekers and refugees living in Jordan were born in a country with conflicts in various regions, they do not consider living in war a normal aspect of human lives.

According to the voices of the Fur community in Jordan, the ethnic, tribal, and religious violence in Darfur cannot result in any social, economic,

35. Hastrup, *War in Darfur*, 3.

or political development for the country. On the contrary, they think that the continuation of the civil conflict in Darfur could potentially demolish the infrastructure of the surviving parts of the region.

Although they cannot predict an end to the conflict anytime soon, they believe peace in the region will be possible only through a nonviolent resolution. If they had thought that war could bring peace to Darfur, they could have joined the rebel forces and fought against the Khartoum government, but they chose not to do so. They are peace-seekers, which explains why they decided to leave their home country.

The fact that Muslims are represented on both sides of the conflict in Darfur causes great concern to the Fur people. They are perplexed as to why fellow Muslims would conspire to eliminate one another. They feel that the spiritual link among Muslims produced by the concept of an Islamic nation or community (*ummah*) represented by "a group of people from diverse backgrounds, ancestry, locations and nationalities"[36] must not include African Muslims. They question how the Qur'an is applied in this regard, considering verses like Sura 3:110: "You are the best community (UMMAH) raised up for (the benefit of) humanity; enjoining what is right and forbidding what is wrong and believing in God."

The Fur asylum seekers and refugees wish for peace in Darfur, Sudan, and the rest of the world. Even though they face discrimination, marginalization, and even physical violence, they live as peacemakers. Without realizing what they are doing, they are following the biblical instruction to "make every effort to live in peace with everyone" (Heb 12:14).

The Fur people's desire to experience peace in the world and to "live in harmony with one another" (Rom 12:16) can be a contributing factor to lead them to seek and find in Jesus Christ, "the peace of God, which transcends all understanding," that can guard their hearts and minds (Phil 4:7). Following the biblical teachings, may the Fur community in Jordan reap the harvest of righteousness as it has been promised: "Peacemakers who sow in peace reap a harvest of righteousness" (Jas 3:18).

Biblical Exegesis

As part of the process of biblical exegesis as it relates to the theme of war, John 14:27 will be employed to establish a contextualized approach for evangelism and discipleship among Fur asylum seekers and refugees.

36. Stacey, "Concept of Ummah," para. 3.

Peace I leave with you; my peace I give you. I do not give to you as the world gives. Do not let your hearts be troubled and do not be afraid.

Peace I leave with you. These are the words of the Lord Jesus Christ. In the context of this text, he addresses his disciples and presents them with two future realities. The first is his upcoming assumption into heaven, and the second is the subsequent dwelling of the Holy Spirit on earth after that. Amid these realities, Jesus leaves peace with his disciples.

As in Eph 2:14, where Jesus is presented as "our peace," the verse here corroborates that Jesus came to bring peace to the world. War has been an enduring characteristic of human history, yet it was not God's intended purpose for humanity. Because sin brought corruption to earth (Gen 3:11), human hearts have turned away from God, resulting in fights and war: "What causes fights and quarrels among you? Don't they come from your desires that battle within you?" (Jas 4:1).

My peace. Jesus gives his disciples his peace, a different kind of peace that cannot be found anywhere else in the world but only in Jesus. His peace puts us at peace with God and with people. Since Adam and Eve sinned against God in Eden's garden (Gen 3:6), humanity turned away from the Creator. Therefore, sin created animosity between man and God (Col 1:21) and consequently between man and man (Mic 7:5–6).

In the Old Testament, the word *shalom* or "peace of God" was used often to communicate peace, justice, harmony, integrity, prosperity, well-being, and tranquility. Therefore, shalom is a broad concept, as Nicholas Wolterstorff states: "To dwell in shalom is to *enjoy* living before God, to *enjoy* living in one's physical surroundings, to *enjoy* living with one's fellows, to *enjoy* life with oneself" (original emphases).[37]

The peace of Jesus restores our relationship with God and frees us from all condemnation (Rom 8:1). It also transforms and reconciles people who have declared war on others and restores relationships (Luke 15:17–32).

I give you. What is the best way to experience Jesus's peace? Jesus stated to his disciples that he was willing to grant them his peace. Even though Jesus was speaking to a specific group of believers, his peace is available to everyone without distinction because God "rewards those who earnestly seek him" (Heb 11:6). Jesus doesn't privilege any group in society or any people group over the earth (Acts 15:8–10). Anyone from anywhere in the world who comes to him by faith and asks for his peace will receive: "Ask and it will be given to you; seek and you will find; knock and the door will be opened to you" (Matt 7:7). Because of God's grace, a

---

37. Wolterstorff, *Until Justice and Peace*, 69–70.

heavenly favor, we are not required to pay for it. The peace of God brings salvation, and it is a divine gift to humanity: "For it is by grace you have been saved, through faith—and this is not from yourselves, it is the gift of God—not by works, so that no one can boast" (Eph 2:8–9). Acceptance is not merely passive: it is something we must be willing to do. If we desire heavenly peace, we must come to Jesus in prayer and ask for it. Jesus will give it to us in fulfillment of his promise.

I do not give to you as the world gives. The absence of war is the most widely held definition of peace in the world. The biblical concept of peace, on the other hand, encompasses far more than this. For this reason, Jesus distinguishes between the two perceptions of peace in this verse.

> The concept of peace in the Bible is different in many ways from modern ideas of peace. Peace as the absence of strife, war or bloodshed, so often sought by humanity at any cost, is far removed from the focus of the biblical teaching. The biblical concept of peace is one in which God's authority and power over his created order are seen to dominate his relations with his world, including both the material and the human spheres.[38]

Biblical theology also teaches that peace is a state of being that can be attained only by the presence of Jesus in the believer through the Holy Spirit (Gal 5:22; Rom 14:17). Even amid war, a person who has been filled with the peace of Jesus can remain calm and unperturbed, like Daniel's three friends who remained untouched by flames when they were thrown into the blazing furnace (Dan 3:19–25).

The peace we find in the world (absence of war) may be accomplished through peace treaties between hostile parties. Still, these accords can result in collateral consequences such as unfairness, loss, and even subjugation for a segment of those involved in the process. Also, such peace may be fleeting or illusory: "'Peace, peace,' they say, when there is no peace" (Jer 6:14).

People in many parts of the world feel they need to fight to gain the right to live in peace with their neighbors. When it comes to God, because Jesus has already paid the price on the cross with his blood (Eph 1:7), the Messiah is able to give us peace through faith in him and without any compromise attached (Isa 53:5).

Do not let your hearts be troubled and do not be afraid. War and many other circumstances can disturb human hearts, cause fear, and produce trauma in those who are subjected to them. However, the Messiah, the one who can give people inner peace, is encouraging his disciples not to let their hearts be troubled and afraid. Since, in the context, Jesus is promising to

---

38. Porter, "Peace," 682.

leave them, they could feel troubled and fearful before the reality of not having their Master with them. In John 14:27, Jesus is instructing the disciples to rely on the peace that he was leaving with them to overcome these challenges. The disciples needed to learn that the peace of Jesus in action can help them overcome troubled and fearful hearts, as Henry explains:

> It is our Savior who says, Let not your heart be troubled. All comforts come from God, and our sweetest comforts are in him. He speaks peace to souls by granting the free remission of sins; and he comforts them by the enlivening influences of the Holy Spirit, and by the rich mercies of his grace. He is able to bind up the broken-hearted, to heal the most painful wounds, and also to give hope and joy under the heaviest sorrows. The favors God bestows on us, are not only to make us cheerful, but also that we may be useful to others. He sends comforts enough to support such as simply trust in and serve him. If we should be brought so low as to despair even of life, yet we may then trust God, who can bring back even from death.[39]

Principle and Application

Breaking down the phrase "my peace I give you," two principles can be applied to evangelism and discipleship among the Fur asylum seekers and refugees in Jordan.

Principle 1—Evangelism Approach: In the referred passage, Jesus was teaching disciples about the kingdom of God while also preparing their hearts for his departure. At the time, Jesus was still revealing himself to the disciples and working to win their hearts. A few verses before, Jesus had told them: "I am the way, and the truth, and the life" (John 14:6). The words of Jesus in this passage were not delivered to a church audience as they were in Rev 3:1–23, for instance. In John 14:27, Jesus is speaking to those who had not yet believed him in as their Savior and Lord. Therefore, this passage can be applied to individuals who would like to become disciples of Jesus Christ and experience the peace that he provides to those who place their faith in him.

According to the biblical teachings, only in Jesus Christ can a person find God's peace. To experience peace, she must enter a relationship with Jesus through faith in the work done by the Messiah in his crucifixion, burial, and resurrection.

---

39. *Short Comments*, 889.

The prophets prophesied about Jesus as the one who would be a Prince of Peace: "For to us a child is born, to us a son is given, and the government will be on his shoulders. And he will be called Wonderful Counselor, Mighty God, Everlasting Father, Prince of Peace" (Isa 9:6).

The God of the universe cares for us, and he has taken the initiative to bring us back into a personal relationship with him. Showing an incomparable love, "He sent His Son, Jesus, to be both the sacrifice that would make us eternally clean before God and the scapegoat who would bear our shame and sin upon himself, removing it forever. This is God's provision and the only way of redemption for every person."[40] Stott adds to this description of God's proactive love and care for humankind:

> Many people visualize a God who sits comfortably on a distant throne, remote, aloof, uninterested, and indifferent to the needs of mortals, until, it may be, they can badger him into taking action on their behalf. Such a view is wholly false. The Bible reveals a God who, long before it even occurs to man to turn to him, while man is still lost in darkness and sunk in sin, takes the initiative, rises from his throne, lays aside his glory, and stoops to seek until he finds him.[41]

Christians never use the Islamic expression "May God honor Him and grant Him peace" (*sallallahu alaihi wa sallam*) or wish peace upon Jesus. Why? Because according to the Bible, no one can deliver peace to Jesus but only receive the peace that he can provide to the world.

The ones who believe in Jesus will receive the peace that God gives his children: "Therefore, since we have been justified through faith, we have peace with God through our Lord Jesus Christ, through whom we have gained access by faith into this grace in which we now stand. And we boast in the hope of the glory of God" (Rom 5:1–2). Consequently, the believer will experience a new and eternal life with God: "For God so loved the world that he gave his one and only Son, that whoever believes in him shall not perish but have eternal life" (John 3:16). The one who came from heaven to earth and went from earth to heaven knows the way to our country in heaven and can take the ones who believe to eternity (1 John 5:11).

Principle 2—Discipleship Approach: The ones who follow Jesus must have their eyes fixed in their Lord, "the pioneer and perfecter of faith" (Heb 12:2); then they will experience daily peace and express the peace to the world because "the LORD blesses his people with peace" (Ps 29:11).

---

40. Frank, *Covered Glory*, 115.

41. Stott, *Basic Christianity*, 1.

The peace of Jesus speaks to our troubled hearts and dispels our fears. New disciples need to understand that the peace of God and personal transformation in every area are to be experienced in a daily journey with Christ, and they come through a personal relationship with God. This relationship can be maintained by distinct practices found in Scripture that promote spiritual growth among believers in the gospel of Jesus Christ. Dallas Willard numbers fifteen practices and organizes them into two groups: 1) Disciplines of Abstinence: solitude, silence, fasting, frugality, chastity, secrecy, sacrifice; and 2) Disciplines of Engagement: study, worship, celebration, service, prayer, fellowship, confession, submission.[42] Richard Foster, on the other hand, numbers twelve practices and arranges them into three groups: 1) Inward Disciplines: meditation, prayer, fasting, and study; 2) Outward Disciplines: simplicity, solitude, submission, and service; and 3) Corporate Disciplines: confession, worship, guidance, and celebration.[43]

The peace of God needs to be shared with others through meaningful relationships. We are called to live in this world with our "feet fitted with the readiness that comes from the gospel of peace" (Eph 6:15) and proclaim the good news from heaven to those around us as God's messengers: "How beautiful are the feet of those who bring good news!" (Rom 10:15).

The disciple should pray for peace around the world, in Sudan, and in Jordan in particular: "Also, seek the peace and prosperity of the city to which I have carried you into exile. Pray to the LORD for it, because if it prospers, you too will prosper" (Jer 29:7).

Bearing in mind the possibility of a church planting movement among the Fur, new believers need to be encouraged to continue promoting peace through their relationships, growing in understanding of the biblical concept of peace, and serving as peacemakers in Jordan and wherever God leads them: "If it is possible, as far as it depends on you, live at peace with everyone" (Rom 12:18).

Regarding believers from outside of the Fur community working with Fur individuals, a fruitful practice proposed to address the theme of war is to pray with Fur individuals for peace in Sudan and throughout the world, creating a culture of prayer and encouraging them to enter a relationship with the Prince of Peace.

42. Willard, *Spirit of the Disciplines.*
43. Foster, *Celebration of Discipline.*

Implementation and Communication

Considering the possibility that members of the Fur people in Jordan will believe in the gospel, the following are proposals for attitudes that disciplers should encourage the new believers to adopt throughout their discipleship process.

Continue to explore biblical teachings about peace to broaden your understanding of God's peace. Ask the Lord to show you the areas of your life that still need to be touched by God's peace. List your fears and ask God for his peace to take them away. Meditate on verses like Isa 26:3 and ask God how you can apply the truth about peace expressed in this text to your life: "You will keep in perfect peace those whose minds are steadfast, because they trust in you."

Expand the concept of the word *peace* in the Scriptures. Study the meanings of the word as used in the Old and New Testaments. Also, compare the aspects of the "peace of God" found in Jesus with the characteristics of the fruit of the Spirit: "But the fruit of the Spirit is love, joy, peace, forbearance, kindness, goodness, faithfulness, gentleness and self-control. Against such things there is no law" (Gal 5:22–23). What are the aspects or characteristics that are still missing in your life?

Encourage other people to talk about the meaning of peace by asking non-Christians what they understand about peace and inquiring of believers about areas of their lives in which they need to experience peace. If you feel comfortable, share lessons you have learned from the war and your perspective on God's peace. Talk to Jordanians about the blessing of living in a country where there is no war and mobilize the believers you know to pray for peace in Sudan.

Reject signs of violence around you by denouncing the sinful behavior of the perpetrators, encouraging people to report the violence they suffer, and looking for help to protect those who have been attacked. Resist the desire to ignore or bury your memories, fears, and hatreds. Ask the Holy Spirit to search your own heart and redeem your thoughts: "Search me, God, and know my heart; test me and know my anxious thoughts. See if there is any offensive way in me, and lead me in the way everlasting" (Ps 139:23–24).

Go beyond by promoting God's peace in your current living context and begin fostering peace in Sudan. As much as possible, communicate with Sudanese in Darfur, talk about the reconciliation that God's peace can bring, and share that war is not God's intended plan for humanity. Explain that Jesus is coming to judge the world, and those who practice injustice among the nations will be judged and condemned (Matt 25:31–32). God's peace is to be experienced and shared, as Guelich says of "those who, experiencing the shalom of God, become his agents establishing his peace in the world."[44]

Apologetics Issue

Theological Controversy 1: How can I accept the teaching that Jesus is God's peace, since this condition highlights his role as a mediator between men and God? As a Muslim, I do not believe that we need a mediator because I don't believe that our relationships with God have been broken (Sura 32:4). Instead, I enter paradise by being rewarded by God after doing my good deeds.

Apologetic Response: During a conversation with a member of the Fur community, the need for a mediator between man and God was brought up as an issue. He emphasized that we do not need a mediator and that we can approach God based only on our own efforts. Consequently, he argued that the lack of dependence on a mediator represents freedom, since it allows people to have a direct relationship with God. Expressing a lack of understanding on the topic from a biblical viewpoint, he gave a negative example to express why he thinks we do not need a mediator. He claimed that the Sudanese government has been attempting to mediate their relationship with God as a means of exercising control over their lives. He concluded that because this teaching carries a potentially risky situation, it is safer to reject the concept entirely.

In an effort to present to Sudanese friends the human need of Jesus to act as their mediator, explain that the sin Adam and Eve committed in the garden of Eden (Gen 3:1–7) not only caused their expulsion from the garden, according to the Bible (Gen 3:23–24) and even to the Qur'an (Sura 20:123), but has also produced a spiritual separation between humankind and God: "But your iniquities have separated you from your God; your sins have hidden his face from you, so that he will not hear" (Isa 59:2). Despite this, knowing that Adam and Eve could not be justified for their sin by their own effort and good deeds, God spoke to Adam and Eve in Eden and promised to send someone from the seed of the woman who would shed his blood while crushing the power of the serpent: "And I will put enmity between you and the woman, and between your offspring and hers; he will crush your head, and you will strike his heel" (Gen 3:15). Therefore, our relationship with God can be restored only through the work of a mediator who can offer himself as a ransom for humankind, free us from the power of the serpent, and restore our relationship with God: "For there is one God

---

44. Guelich, *Sermon on the Mount*, 90.

and one mediator between God and mankind, the man Christ Jesus, who gave himself as a ransom for all people" (1 Tim 2:5–6).

A person who violates human law becomes guilty and needs to go before a judge. For instance, if someone steals money from a bank, he has broken the law and will be imprisoned for that action regardless of whether he repents, asks for forgiveness, or returns the money. Similarly, when we sin, we break God's law, become guilty, and will be held accountable before heaven. According to the Holy Scriptures, God will not forgive our sins because we have good behavior or do good deeds. Why? Because our good actions will not cover or erase the evil we have done: "All of us have become like one who is unclean, and all our righteous acts are like filthy rags; we all shrivel up like a leaf, and like the wind our sins sweep us away" (Isa 64:6). The only way we can find forgiveness for our sins is through the way God has established in the garden of Eden. Our sins are forgiven through the shedding of the blood of the Messiah: "And by that will, we have been made holy through the sacrifice of the body of Jesus Christ once for all" (Heb 10:10).

As revealed in the Bible, God's plan for our salvation outlines that the Almighty created Adam and Eve and put them in the garden of Eden (Gen 2:18–23) for them to glorify the Creator and have a personal relationship with him (Gen 3:8). Sometime after that, Satan came to Adam and Eve to tempt them to sin against God (Gen 3:1–4). They chose to listen to God's enemy and disobeyed the Creator (Gen 3:6). As a result, sin came into the world, and humanity became separated from God (Gen 3:8). Before the couple left the garden, God provided a way for Adam and Eve to walk in his presence by covering them with the skin of an animal (Gen 3:21). He also made a promise to send the Messiah to rescue them from the power of sin (Gen 3:15). After confirming that promise through the prophets (Acts 3:21), God sent Jesus Christ, his Son, to become one like us and die on the cross for our sins (John 3:16 and Phil 2:8). Jesus rose from the dead (1 Cor 15:3) and returned to heaven (Acts 1:9). Then, he sent the Holy Spirit to dwell in his disciples and bear witness to him (John 15:26). He will come back in glory to judge the world (1 Cor 4:5). Until then, his disciples are called to preach the gospel to the ends of the earth (Acts 1:8) for the eternal glory of God and the joy of the nations (Luke 2:10–14). Those who believe in the gospel will live with God in heaven, and those who do not will spend their eternity in hell (Matt 25:31–46).

Therefore, we have fallen into sin, our relationship with God has been broken, and we need a mediator to reconcile us with God. The Bible teaches that our mediator is Jesus Christ: "For there is one God and one mediator between God and mankind, the man Christ Jesus, who gave himself as a ransom for all people" (1 Tim 2:5).

Theological Controversy 2: The context of the text talks about the Father sending the Holy Spirit in Jesus's name. Is it teaching about three gods? How can I accept the doctrine of the Trinity if the Qur'an rejects it and, as a Muslim, I believe there is only one God (Sura 4:171)?

Apologetic Response: This issue has been discussed multiple times with Fur individuals in Jordan, and it is one of the most frequently cited to illustrate how the Christian faith does not make sense to them. They often claim that the Trinity is not reasonable because this teaching does not follow the rules of reasoning. They claim that human logic will never be able to comprehend the concept that God can be three and, at the same time, be one.

The biblical verse that comes before the passage used for the contextualization of this theme says: "But the Advocate, the Holy Spirit, whom the Father will send in my name, will teach you all things and will remind you of everything I have said to you" (John 14:26). So, the verse presents an excellent example of how the Trinity (Father, Son, and Holy Spirit) works together. The Father sends the Son to the world, the Son goes back to heaven after the resurrection, and the Father sends the Holy Spirit to dwell among the disciples. The doctrine of the Trinity also teaches that relationship is a reality that God has been involved in since before the creation of the world. All of humankind, having been created in his image, is invited to participate in that divine relationship.

Why do Christians believe in the Trinity? Because the Bible itself introduces its concept, as we can find in many passages in the Old and New Testaments, such as 2 Cor 13:14: "May the grace of the Lord Jesus Christ, and the love of God, and the fellowship of the Holy Spirit be with you all."

The Bible teaches that God is Father, Son, and Holy Spirit. Thus, the concept of Trinity is based on the idea of a unity of the three persons that manifest as one God, or as Sproul asserts, "When we confess our faith in the Trinity, we affirm that God is one in essence and three in person."[45]

Like Jews and Muslims, Christians believe that "the LORD our God, the LORD is one" (Deut 6:4). Therefore, to suppose that the doctrine of the Trinity means to believe in three gods (tritheism) is a misunderstanding of the Trinity and a misperception of the Christian faith. Tritheism is not part of the Christian faith, as it has categorically been rejected by the church throughout its history.[46]

---

45. Sproul, *What Is the Trinity?*, 2.
46. Sproul, *What Is the Trinity?*, 1.

Assuming that Mary, the mother of Jesus, is part of the Trinity or that the Trinity implies a sexual relationship between God and Mary are other mistaken interpretations of Christians' beliefs. The doctrine of the Trinity has always been limited to the understanding that God is one God, who is Father, Son, and Holy Spirit.

> We want to make clear that in holding to the doctrine of the Trinity, the Christian church has always denied that there are any other beings alongside the One God. In using the traditional word "person" (hypostasis or "distinct reality") of Father, Son and Holy Spirit, the church has never thought that it is speaking of three personal beings like any persons we know in the world. Nor does it think that God has fathered a child with the same physical process that we see in the world around us. Rather, the church is attempting to express the truth that there are mysterious, unknowable depths to the personal nature of God.[47]

Although the Trinity may be a new concept for individuals who have not been exposed to Christian teachings, why cannot people of faith believe that God can be three in one? Since God is the most powerful, and his essence goes beyond our comprehension, who are we to determine what God can or cannot be? Consider what the Almighty said to Job: "Will the one who contends with the Almighty correct him? Let him who accuses God answer him!" (Job 40:2). Therefore, as people who believe in God, we put our faith in him and humbly submit to the knowledge he shares with us about himself in the Holy Scriptures.

Evaluation

1. How does this contextualization project avoid encouraging syncretism among the Fur people?

The project attempts to avoid any potential syncretism by helping the Fur to have a biblical understanding of God's peace, which produces a Christocentric way of living their faith. Also, differentiating between the world's concept of peace with the peace we find in Jesus will further help prevent syncretism.

As the Fur study about peace in the Scriptures, they will learn that true peace with God is not produced by human effort but by the work of

47. Royal Aal Al-Bayt Institute for Islamic Thought, *Common Word between Us*, 222.

Jesus to reconcile humanity with God, "not counting people's sins against them" (2 Cor 5:19).

2. How does this contextualization project constructively engage the Fur people's worldview?

This project constructively engages the Fur worldview by correcting their misunderstanding about peace and their illusion that there is a place in this world where they can experience heavenly peace. We will warn them not to look for perfect peace in this world, as they will not find it, particularly because, as Jesus prophesied, wars will become a reality even more present in our world as we move to the last days: "You will hear of wars and rumors of wars, but see to it that you are not alarmed. Such things must happen, but the end is still to come. Nation will rise against nation, and kingdom against kingdom. There will be famines and earthquakes in various places" (Matt 24:6–7).

We will also let them know that the peace they want is possible. In Jesus, they can have peace with God and even with those who have been waging war against them and their people. Their Prince of Peace is Jesus, the real peace, God's peace for eternity.

3. How does this contextualization project challenge the Fur people toward (specific) personal change?

Real personal change will happen when they realize that God has a peace plan for them and experience the inner peace that has the potential of healing their hearts from the war violence that has affected their lives and led to their current displacement. This contextualization project will point the Fur to Jesus, who can give them a form of peace that no one can remove from them and will stay with them even among their most challenging life experiences.

Third Theme: Displacement

In the study, participants described the difficulties they faced due to being forcibly displaced from their homeland owing to the conflict in Darfur. Their displacement resulted from the destruction of their villages and the mass killing of their people. Following their displacement, most participants sought safety in a camp for IDPs in Darfur. Because of the surrounding violence, life threats, and inadequate living conditions, they were forced to leave once again, finding shelter beyond their country's borders. The displacement experience has significantly impacted the lives of Fur asylum seekers and refugees, trampling on their sense of dignity, identity, and belonging, among other violations. One of the hardships they bear in their daily journey in Jordan is the uncertainty of whether they will ever return to their homeland and reunite with their family members left behind.

Cultural Exegesis

During their time in Sudan, in addition to the war experience, Fur asylum seekers and refugees had to deal with the reality of forcible displacement. They had to leave not only their village and region but their country too.

Throughout the interviews, participants indicated how challenging it was for them to navigate the experience of displacement. According to one participant, the day he left his village to find refuge in a camp for IDPs was the most heartbreaking day of his life.

Having to leave their homeland and their people meant leaving everything they had. A study participant mentioned that he arrived in Jordan without any luggage because he had lost everything he had in the war.

Displacement has affected participants' ethnic identity and the notion of a temporal connection between the past, present, and future generations. As they began moving to Jordan, they began doubting if they would ever marry a member of their tribe or return to Sudan. In some ways, they feel trapped and lost by their current circumstances: "People of Darfur seem caught between past and future in the prison of the present."[48]

Throughout the interviews, they expressed a feeling of loneliness and a sense that no one understands what they have been through. They even complained of the international community not paying much attention to the crisis that continues to affect the lives of Sudanese from Darfur.

Fur asylum seekers and refugees need to know that they are not alone. Displacement is a phenomenon that has occurred extensively throughout history. The Holy Bible is filled with biblical accounts of people who have undergone what today's refugees have endured. The biblical characters, including baby Jesus, have much to teach the Sudanese.

48. Hastrup, *War in Darfur*, 3.

Biblical Exegesis

As part of the process of biblical exegesis as it relates to the theme of displacement, Matt 2:13–15 will be employed to establish a contextualized approach for evangelism and discipleship among Fur asylum seekers and refugees.

> When they had gone, an angel of the Lord appeared to Joseph in a dream. "Get up," he said, "take the child and his mother and escape to Egypt. Stay there until I tell you, for Herod is going to search for the child to kill him." So he got up, took the child and his mother during the night and left for Egypt, where he stayed until the death of Herod. And so was fulfilled what the Lord had said through the prophet: "Out of Egypt I called my son."

When they had gone. The text refers to the moment that the magi had left Joseph, Mary, and Jesus. The magi were the wise men from the East who had seen the star and traveled to Bethlehem to worship the king of the Jews. Upon arriving at the exact place where Jesus was, they bowed down, worshiped the baby, and opened their treasures, giving him gifts of gold, frankincense, and myrrh. At the end of their time in Bethlehem, they left under divine instruction to take a different route back to their own country so as not to report to King Herod that they had found baby Jesus.

An angel of the Lord appeared to Joseph in a dream. After the magi had left, God moved in a supernatural way to instruct Joseph. It was the second time in his life that God had spoken to Joseph through a dream. The first was when God had told him not to divorce Mary quietly after she had been found to be pregnant by the Holy Spirit (Matt 1:20). By hearing from God in a dream, Joseph joined other people from the Old Testament with whom God had spoken in the same way (Dan 7:1).

Get up. God was calling Joseph to get ready and respond immediately to the heavenly message he was about to receive. It was an urgent matter that could result in the murder of baby Jesus.

Take the child and his mother and escape to Egypt. God was instructing Joseph to take his wife and newborn and leave the country. At that moment, the family was about to become displaced. They did not have time to plan and prepare for the trip, and they had no choice but to depart immediately. They were not migrating as part of a life project or searching for a better life in a foreign country. They were fleeing to protect their lives and did not know how much time they would spend abroad.

The country chosen by God for the family was Egypt, which "had a large Jewish population (a million according to Philo), and it was the closest center of Diaspora Jews for the fleeing family."[49]

Stay there until I tell you. Joseph did not have much information about what was happening or was yet to happen. He had to depend on God's instruction to know exactly what to do.

Herod is going to search for the child to kill him. When King Herod, the head of the government in the country, heard from the magi about the birth of Jesus, who was named the king of the Jews, he became disturbed. Herod was most likely concerned that the new king would launch a revolt against his authority and seize control of the throne. Because the magi did not return to Herod to inform him that they had seen the baby, Herod lost control of the situation, felt deceived, and decided to hunt for the baby boy to kill him:

> Herod is shaken by the Magi's news that a new king has been born. He himself is only half-Jewish and worried by any true claim to his throne. To secure his position, he orders the deaths of all infants in Bethlehem under two years old. It seems that Jesus is a child rather than a baby by the time the Magi visit him.[50]

Why was Jesus so hated while still a baby, and why did Herod take such strong measures to eliminate an infant? The god of this age was using Herod to oppose the manifestation of God's will to humanity: "The coming of the Messiah caused Satan to unleash an arsenal of evil. In this instance, Satan used Herod, a willing vessel. Herod, the king of the Jews, killed all the boys under two years of age in an obsessive attempt to kill Jesus, the newborn King."[51]

So he got up. Joseph, as a just and faithful man, obeyed God as he had done throughout his life (Matt 1:19). He got up after the dream and was immediately ready to leave with his family as God was instructing him.

Took the child and his mother during the night and left for Egypt. During the night, Joseph, Mary, and Jesus were forcibly displaced from the land of Israel by their government and took shelter in Egypt, the same country in which the Israelites had found refuge on different occasions (1 Kgs 11:40; 2 Kgs 25:26).

Like many refugees, they had to leave at night because they did not have time to wait until the next day. Escaping during the night had the advantage of ensuring that no one would notice or prevent them from leaving.

---

49. Osborne and Arnold, *Matthew*, 98.

50. Knowles, *Bible Guide*, 410.

51. Osborne and Comfort, *Matthew*, 33.

Where he stayed until the death of Herod. When Joseph and his family departed from the land of Israel, they had no idea when they would return home. The only thing they knew was that while Herod lived, they would have to stay out of their country. The exact amount of time Joseph and his family remained in Egypt is unknown.

And so was fulfilled what the Lord had said through the prophet: "Out of Egypt I called my son." The forcible displacement Jesus and his parents experienced was part of God's purpose for them. It happened in fulfillment of a prophecy found in the book of Hosea, which states: "When Israel was a child, I loved him, and out of Egypt I called my son" (Hos 11:1).

Principle and Application

Breaking down the phrase "Out of Egypt I called my son," two principles can be applied to evangelism and discipleship among the Fur asylum seekers and refugees in Jordan.

Principle 1—Evangelism Approach: The Gospel of Matthew was written primarily for a Jewish Christian audience and emphasizes that God's purposes to humanity are fulfilled in Jesus Christ. The passage of Matt 2:13–15 narrates three essential events that occurred while Jesus was a young child and involved Joseph and Mary. The events, which relate to asylum seekers and refugees today, are the following: displacement, exile, and voluntary repatriation. They happened in fulfillment of a prophecy that confirmed that Jesus was the Messiah and the eternal Son of God. The passage's context prepares the way for Christians and non-Christians to profoundly understand Jesus's mission as the Savior of the world and completely devote their lives to him as their Lord.

Through the incarnation, Jesus, the Word of God, came into the world and became like us: "Who, being in very nature God, did not consider equality with God something to be used to his own advantage; rather, he made himself nothing by taking the very nature of a servant, being made in human likeness" (Phil 2:6–7).

Jesus became forcibly displaced as a baby and faced many other adversities and temptations. Jesus's life-challenging experiences produced much identification with our weaknesses: "For we do not have a high priest who is unable to empathize with our weaknesses, but we have one who has been tempted in every way, just as we are—yet he did not sin" (Heb 4:15). Jesus was "a man of suffering" (Isa 53:3) who not only knows every struggle we face in life but can address them by his mighty power.

Jesus knows even how it feels to be displaced, to run for his life, and to live in exile. As Smither states:

> Because of their forced displacement due to political tyran-
> ny . . . , Joseph's family fits the modern definition of a refugee.
> Jesus of Nazareth was a refugee. In the Lord's displacement, he
> identified with sojourners, strangers, and the wandering Is-
> raelites in the Old Testament as well as the suffering diaspora
> church in the New Testament. He also identifies with people on
> the move who have sought refuge through the centuries, includ-
> ing those in the present day.[52]

Houston adds, "Jesus can empathize with refugees in their sufferings, enables endurance, and brings hope."[53] Likewise, Pope John Paul II stressed the same point when talking to Palestinian refugees in his speech at Dheisheh refugee camp, located south of Bethlehem in the West Bank, on March 22, 2000. He made it very clear that foreigners and refugees are not less impor-tant in God's eyes, and that God can fulfill his designs in their lives:

> Dear brothers and sisters, dear refugees, do not think that your
> present condition makes you any less important in God's eyes!
> Never forget your dignity as his children! Here at Bethlehem the
> Divine Child was laid in a manger in a stable; shepherds from
> the nearby fields were the first to receive the heavenly message
> of peace and hope for the world. God's design was fulfilled in the
> midst of humility and poverty. Probably the pastors and shep-
> herds of Bethlehem were your predecessors, your ancestors.[54]

When teaching respect and kindness to sojourners in the Old Testa-ment, God highlighted that the Israelites knew the heart of the sojourner because they had been through that experience: "Do not oppress a for-eigner; you yourselves know how it feels to be foreigners, because you were foreigners in the Egypt" (Exod 23:9). Therefore, since Jesus went through displacement, he knows the heart of displaced people. The Messiah knows the pain, he understands the suffering, and he can wipe every tear from the eyes of each Sudanese who has been forcibly displaced.

As people sojourn on this earth and feel tired and overwhelmed, they can find rest in Jesus. He can bring change to their lives and invites them into a healing relationship: "Come to me, all you who are weary and bur-dened, and I will give you rest. Take my yoke upon you and learn from me,

---

52. Smither, *Christian Martyrdom*, 4.

53. Houston, *You Shall Love*, 136.

54. John Paul II, "Speech," 2.

for I am gentle and humble in heart, and you will find rest for your souls. For my yoke is easy and my burden is light" (Matt 11:28–30).

Principle 2—Discipleship Approach: God seeks a personal relationship with his children like he had with Adam and Eve in the garden of Eden before sin entered the world. In those days, God would come to the couple, "walking in the garden in the cool of the day" (Gen 3:8).

Now that Jesus has reconciled humankind with God through "a new and living way opened for us through the curtain, that is, his body" (Heb 10:20), anyone can have free access to God: "For it is by grace you have been saved through faith—and this is not from yourselves, it is the gift of God—not by works, so that no one can boast" (Eph 2:8–9).

Therefore, the creature can approach the Creator on his throne of grace "with a sincere heart and with the full assurance that faith brings," (Heb 10:22) and "with confidence, so that we may receive mercy and find grace to help us in our time of need" (Heb 4:16).

Considering that the Fur people practice a form of Islam influenced by Sufism, a Fur believer can reflect on the biblical teaching that God is omnipresent; therefore, his presence is everywhere in the universe: "'Am I only a God nearby,' declares the LORD, 'and not a God far away? Who can hide in secret places so that I cannot see them?' declares the LORD. 'Do not I fill heaven and earth?' declares the LORD" (Jer 23:23–24). However, God's presence is manifested uniquely in the lives of those who believe. As Jesus revealed to the disciples after his ascension, the Father sent the third person of the Trinity, the Holy Spirit, to make a permanent residence in them: "Do you not know that your bodies are temples of the Holy Spirit, who is in you, whom you have received from God? You are not your own" (1 Cor 6:19).

The presence of the Holy Spirit in the believer is a treasure, it is God living in him: "But we have this treasure in jars of clay to show that this all-surpassing power is from God and not from us" (2 Cor 4:7). Besides, the manifestation of the Holy Spirit gives life to our bodies and takes us to God in our acts of worship and daily devotion. When we don't know how to pray, the Holy Spirit intercedes for us: "In the same way, the Spirit helps us in our weakness. We do not know what we ought to pray for, but the Spirit himself intercedes for us through wordless groans" (Rom 8:26).

Once an individual believes in Jesus and becomes born again (2 Cor 5:17), the Holy Spirit gives the believer the life of God, eternal life, which is really his very nature: "But when the kindness and love of God our Savior appeared, he saved us, not because of righteous things we had done, but because of his mercy. He saved us through the washing of rebirth and renewal by the Holy Spirit, whom he poured out on us generously through

Jesus Christ our Savior, so that, having been justified by his grace, we might become heirs having the hope of eternal life" (Titus 3:4–7).

Those who believe and become born again have the Holy Spirit dwelling in them and are members of the universal church of Christ, in which there is no distinction or favoritism: "For we were all baptized by one Spirit so as to form one body—whether Jews or Gentiles, slave or free—and we were all given the one Spirit to drink" (1 Cor 12:13). Furthermore, the Holy Spirit seals the believer unto the day of redemption: "And you also were included in Christ when you heard the message of truth, the gospel of your salvation. When you believed, you were marked in him with a seal, the promised Holy Spirit, who is a deposit guaranteeing our inheritance until the redemption of those who are God's possession— to the praise of his glory" (Eph 1:13–14).

Jesus, the Son of God who was called from Egypt, is also the Immanuel, which means God with us (Isa 7:14). Jesus became one like us through his incarnation, and now in his glory, he wants us to be one like him. This is possible through a personal relationship of the believer with God led by the Spirit, which produces transformed life: "And we all, who with unveiled faces contemplate the Lord's glory, are being transformed into his image with ever-increasing glory, which comes from the Lord, who is the Spirit" (2 Cor 3:18).

Bearing in mind the possibility of a church planting movement among the Fur, new believers need to be encouraged to develop a biblical relationship with the Holy Spirit who will guide them into all truth (John 16:13–15).

Regarding believers from outside of the Fur community working with Fur individuals, a fruitful practice proposed to address the theme of displacement is biblical witness, which involves sharing Scripture with the Fur people about God's perspective on diaspora to equip them with a biblical worldview.

Implementation and Communication

Considering the possibility that members of the Fur people in Jordan will believe in the gospel, the following are proposals for attitudes that disciplers should encourage the new believers to adopt throughout their discipleship process.

Continue to maintain a personal relationship with Jesus and pray for healing and growth in different areas of your life. Ask the Holy Spirit to help you forgive all the people who have produced suffering in your life, including those who carried out armed violence against you and your people in Sudan.

Expand your knowledge of the Holy Spirit. Study the distinct role of the Holy Spirit in the Old Testament compared to the New Testament. Note that in the Old Testament, the Spirit would come upon people on occasion (Judg 6:34), while in the New Testament, the Holy Spirit dwells in the believer (1 Cor 3:16).

Encourage believers to consider the qualities of the fruit of the Spirit in their lives manifested in different scenarios. Discuss with them the qualities of the fruit that they need to express the most in this season of their lives.

Reject any confusion between past or present Sufi practices and the new spiritual growth practices you are learning to nourish your everyday journey with Christ. How can you explore your personal and corporate relationship with the transcendent and immanent God yourself without maintaining practices that do not follow the Holy Scriptures' teachings?

Go beyond having a personal relationship with God and be intentional about having fellowship with other believers in the body of Christ. Make sure you meet with other believers for worship, prayer, and fasting. Invite new believers who resist fellowshipping to serve one another, "not giving up meeting together, as some are in the habit of doing, but encouraging one another— and all the more as you see the Day approaching" (Heb 10:25).

Apologetics Issue

Theological Controversy 1: How can I believe that Jesus is the Son of God if the Qur'an says that God "begets no son" (Sura 17:111)?

Apologetic Response: Some of the conversations about Jesus and attempts to explain the Christian faith to Fur individuals were influenced by this controversy in one way or another. The following statement was made in a conversation by one individual from the community: "I find it difficult to believe that Jesus is the Son of God. If I believe that he is, I automatically become a Christian."

When attempting to help Fur individuals to understand the Scriptures, explain to them that the meaning of the title "Son of God" given to Jesus in the Bible is generally misunderstood in Islam. Most Muslims believe that the expression Son of God, when used by Christians, suggests that God had a son because of a sexual relationship (Sura 19:88–92).

In dialogue with Fur asylum seeker and refugee friends, contend, using biblical texts, that according to the teachings of the Holy Scriptures, the title Son of God does not carry any implication of a sexual relationship between the God the Father and Mary, the mother of Jesus. In fact, Christians believe in the virgin birth of Jesus, which means that Mary miraculously conceived Jesus by the power of the Holy Spirit and without sexual intercourse of any kind (Matt 1:18).

Also say that in the biblical sense, the language used for *son* has a spiritual meaning. Emphasize that the suggestion that God had sex with Mary sounds like blasphemy to the ears of all Christians around the world. Next, try to explain that God is described as a Father in the Scriptures because of the spiritual relationship that he has with Jesus and with those who receive him as Father by faith in the work of Christ: "So in Christ Jesus you are all children of God through faith" (Gal 3:26).

The sonship of Jesus is not a concept limited to the New Testament: instead, it is affirmed in the Old Testament, as in the prophecy that Jesus would be called out from Egypt: "Out of Egypt I called my son" (Hos 11:1).

Believing that Jesus is the Son of God is essential for everyone who wants to overcome this world: "Who is it that overcomes the world? Only the one who believes that Jesus is the Son of God" (1 John 5:5).

Theological Controversy 2: How can I believe that Jesus was God if he became a baby and even had to run for his life?

Apologetic Response: "Can you tell me who Jesus is to you? Is Jesus the Son of God?" A Fur man asked these two questions throughout the research. Even though he did not express strong opposition to the divinity of Christ, he presented other questions to challenge this subject. However, many other individuals have openly questioned the fact that Christians believe in Jesus not only as a prophet but as God. It is critical to address this issue.

Following his incarnation, Jesus united two natures: the divine nature and the human nature, which theologians refer to as the doctrine of the hypostatic union (also known as the theory of the union of the two natures). An illustration of this reality is found in the New Testament, where the Messiah was referred to as both the Son of Man (Matt 8:20) and the Son of God (Matt 14:33). Therefore, Jesus was fully man and fully God, as the witness of the Holy Scriptures:

> In your relationships with one another, have the same mindset as Christ Jesus: Who, being in very nature God, did not consider equality with God something to be used to his own advantage; rather, he made himself nothing by taking the very nature of a servant, being made in human likeness. And being found in appearance as a man, he humbled himself by becoming obedient to death—even death on a cross! (Phil 2:5–8).

Throughout history, the existence of Jesus's two natures combined has produced much controversy and division. However, both Jesus's humanity and his divinity are a biblical reality. Grudem comments on Jesus's humanity:

> He was born just as all human babies are born (Luke 2:7). He grew through childhood to adulthood just as other children grow: "And the child grew and became strong, filled with wisdom; and the favor of God was upon him" (Luke 2:40). Moreover, Luke tells us that "Jesus grew in wisdom and in stature, and in favor with God and man" (Luke 2:52).[55]

Jesus had a human body, as the apostles, who were eyewitnesses, testified: "While they were there, the time came for the baby to be born, and she gave birth to her firstborn, a son. She wrapped him in cloths and placed him in a manger, because there was no guest room available for them" (Luke 2:6–7). He had physical needs, such as hunger: "The next day as they were leaving Bethany, Jesus was hungry" (Mark 11:12). Jesus got tired and slept: "Jesus was in the stern, sleeping on a cushion" (Mark 4:38). Also, he was tempted: "Then Jesus was led by the Spirit into the wilderness to be tempted by the devil" (Matt 4:1).

However, Jesus also had a divine nature. Considering Jesus's divinity, Grudem comments once again:

> The New Testament, in hundreds of explicit verses that call Jesus "God" and "Lord" and use a number of other titles of deity to refer to him, and in many passages that attribute actions or words to him that could only be true of God himself, affirms again and again the full, absolute deity of Jesus Christ. "In him *all the fulness of God* was pleased to dwell" (Col. 1:19), and "in him the whole fulness of deity dwells bodily" (Col. 2:9). In an earlier section we argued that Jesus is truly and fully man. Now we conclude that he is truly and fully God as well. His name is rightly called "Emmanuel," that is, "God with us" (Matt. 1:23).[56]

Jesus had power over nature, which brought great admiration from his disciples: "They were terrified and asked each other, 'Who is this? Even the wind and the waves obey him!'" (Mark 4:41). He had authority over the evil spirits: "The demons begged Jesus, 'Send us among the pigs; allow us to go into them'" (Mark 5:12). Jesus gave life to the dead: "When he had said this, Jesus called in a loud voice, 'Lazarus, come out!' The dead man came out, his hands and feet wrapped with strips of linen, and a cloth around his face. Jesus

---

55. Grudem, *Systematic Theology*, 532.
56. Grudem, *Systematic Theology*, 552.

said to them, 'Take off the grave clothes and let him go'" (John 11:43–44). He forgave sins: "When Jesus saw their faith, he said to the paralyzed man, 'Son, your sins are forgiven'" (Mark 2:5). Jesus knew the thoughts of people: "Knowing their thoughts, Jesus said, 'Why do you entertain evil thoughts in your hearts?'" (Matt 9:4). Jesus is directly referred to as the Creator of the universe: "Through him all things were made; without him nothing was made that has been made" (John 1:3). Also, Jesus claimed to be one with the Father: "I and the Father are one" (John 10:30).

The baby Jesus who went to Egypt with his parents looking for shelter was both man and God. He already had the two natures, and they were not in conflict but absolutely combined. The two natures of Jesus are a reality and a divine revelation. Therefore, as people of faith who want to please our God, we must accept the witness of the Holy Scriptures.

Evaluation

1. How does this contextualization project avoid encouraging syncretism among the Fur people?

The project will avoid syncretism by helping Sudanese build their relationship with God through the Holy Spirit who lives in them. Also, they are encouraged to list all the old religious practices that they keep. New believers are then asked to analyze whether the practices are against God's word and to determine if they could lead them into a condition of bondage to the world of darkness.

2. How does this contextualization project constructively engage the Fur people's worldview?

The project's approach presents the possibility of engaging in a personal relationship with a loving God who meets their need of relating to both a transcendent and immanent God. Also, participants are encouraged to know a God who is close to them, understands what they have gone through in life, and is willing to meet them where they are.

3. How does this contextualization project challenge the Fur people toward (specific) personal change?

It provides a sense of dignity to Fur asylum seekers and refugees by revealing that Jesus himself experienced similar circumstances in life, such as forcible displacement from his homeland and threats from his own government. Therefore, Jesus can communicate in a very particular way with them. Additionally, it emphasizes that what they have experienced in life doesn't make them inferior to other people or less important in God's eyes.

Fourth Theme: Exile

Exile in Jordan has not been a pleasant experience for the Fur people. Along with the interview responses, they described various difficulties they have endured to survive in this setting. Among the most pressing concerns is the ban of legal employment in an environment marked by high living costs, restricted access to public services, and a shortage of resources that other refugees receive but asylum seekers do not. Additionally, they deal with challenges such as the prejudice that isolates Sudanese even from places of worship, the bullying their children face in schools, and the long wait for resettlement without knowing whether it will ever happen. All the participants in this study hope for the opportunity for a different kind of life in their future resettlement site. The ongoing violence in Darfur indicates that their exile experience will continue, and voluntary repatriation will not be an option in the foreseeable future.

Cultural Exegesis

Participants have shared much information and personal stories about their current place of exile. Throughout the interviews, they have made it particularly clear that even though they are grateful to the country for welcoming them, their life in Jordan is filled with adversities. Among the challenges that the Fur people face are racial discrimination, the limited assistance that only some of them receive from the UNHCR, and the ban on legal employment. This scenario makes their exile a quite difficult experience.

Many of the participants showed a strong desire to relocate from Jordan to a third country. In fact, resettlement is the only hope Sudanese in Jordan have for a better future, because they can neither voluntarily return to Sudan nor experience local integration. However, due to the small number of refugees who are ever accepted in a resettlement program, when

Fur asylum seekers and Sudanese talk about their future, they express that resettlement is like a dream. Some participants have been waiting for this dream to come through for several years now and struggle to renew their hope and patience.

Fur individuals have a high expectation of moving to a place where they will have a new citizenship and which they will call home, which is an expected desire for people who have been displaced and living in exile for several years.

While we are in this world, regardless of whether we live in the country where we were born or hold citizenship, we are "foreigners and exiles" (1 Pet 2:11), and at some point, we will depart from it, because our destination is heaven. Our merciful God has prepared a house with many rooms for us in heaven. All we need to do is believe and obey his words: "My Father's house has many rooms; if that were not so, would I have told you that I am going there to prepare a place for you?" (John 14:2).

Biblical Exegesis

As part of the process of biblical exegesis as it relates to the theme of exile, Heb 11:8–10 and 13–16 will be employed to establish a contextualized approach for evangelism and discipleship among Fur asylum seekers and refugees.

> By faith Abraham, when called to go to a place he would later receive as his inheritance, obeyed and went, even though he did not know where he was going. By faith he made his home in the promised land like a stranger in a foreign country; he lived in tents, as did Isaac and Jacob, who were heirs with him of the same promise. For he was looking forward to the city with foundations, whose architect and builder is God.

> All these people were still living by faith when they died. They did not receive the things promised; they only saw them and welcomed them from a distance, admitting that they were foreigners and strangers on earth. People who say such things show that they are looking for a country of their own. If they had been thinking of the country they had left, they would have had opportunity to return. Instead, they were longing for a better country—a heavenly one. Therefore God is not ashamed to be called their God, for he has prepared a city for them.

By faith Abraham, when called to go to a place he would later receive as his inheritance. In the book of Genesis, God called Abraham to make a geographical journey that would take him from his homeland: "Go from your country, your people, and your father's household to the land I will show you" (Gen 12:1). It was one of the most significant movements of people recorded in the Scriptures directly instigated by God's instruction. Throughout the book of Hebrews, the author reiterates the teachings of the Old Testament. In Genesis, the Lord sent Abraham out of Mesopotamia and granted him and his descendants the land of Canaan.

Obeyed and went, even though he did not know where he was going. When Abraham left his country, he had no idea where he would be heading next in his life's journey. He was most likely challenged by the curiosity, if not the fear, of moving to a place that he knew nothing about, not even how far away it was located. Regardless of any feeling, Abraham walked by faith into his exile experience and followed God's leading in his life.

By faith he made his home in the promised land like a stranger in a foreign country. When Abraham arrived at the promised land, he established himself in it but did not dwell there as if it were his destination. He chose to live as a foreigner in his new country as if he had not yet found a country of his own.

He lived in tents, as did Isaac and Jacob, who were heirs with him of the same promise. Abraham and his descendants did not place a high value on earthly possessions but lived as people who were transitioning. Even Isaac and Jacob, who were born in the land, lived there as strangers. While they inherited a land given to them by God, they considered themselves to be a people in exile.

For he was looking forward to the city with foundations, whose architect and builder is God. Abraham realized that we are strangers in this world, and he was looking for a country in heaven to call home. He had in mind a city that God is preparing for those who put their trust in him by believing in his words.

All these people were still living by faith when they died. Through the course of their lives, they remained steady in their beliefs. Their faith was tested, like when God asked Abraham to sacrifice his son: "Take your son, your only son, whom you love—Isaac—and go to the region of Moriah. Sacrifice him there as a burnt offering on a mountain I will show you" (Gen 22:2). However, the faith of such people was unshakeable through all life's circumstances, and they died believing in God and his promises.

They did not receive the things promised; they only saw them and welcomed them from a distance. When God called Abraham, the Almighty gave his servant promises, which are registered in Gen 12. The most significant promise made to Abraham was that "all peoples on earth will be blessed through you" (Gen 12:3). According to the apostle Paul, this promise is fulfilled in Jesus Christ, since he is the Messiah, the seed of Abraham who would bless all peoples: "The promises were spoken to Abraham and to his seed. Scripture does not say 'and to seeds,' meaning many people, but 'and to your seed,' meaning one person, who is Christ" (Gal 3:16). Abraham did not see the whole fulfillment of God's promises in his life, just the beginning, and greeted it from afar.

Admitting that they were foreigners and strangers on earth. People like Abraham, Isaac, and Jacob understood and admitted the fact that we do not belong to this world. We live as foreigners and strangers on earth. We may be here for a short or long time, but as "foreigners and exiles" (1 Pet 2:11) in this world we will depart from it at some point and will not be able to take anything with us when we leave.

People who say such things show that they are looking for a country of their own. Abraham and his descendants who lived in the land promised and given by God not only believed they were foreigners and strangers on earth but expressed this belief verbally. Therefore, they provided evidence that they had their eyes fixed on the horizon of eternity with their God. They were looking for something even more significant than the land that had been given to them. Their focus was on the country of their own waiting for them in heaven. They had understood the same concept that the apostle Paul communicated in one of his letters: "Our citizenship is in heaven" (Phil 3:20).

If they had been thinking of the country they had left, they would have had opportunity to return. Abraham, Isaac, and Jacob showed no attachment to what was past. They were not looking back to the country they had left in obedience to God, and that is why they never returned to it. They were walking by faith and looking forward to something more significant.

Instead, they were longing for a better country—a heavenly one. Their eyes were fixed on heaven, because they knew that what God had prepared for them in eternity was far superior to any possession they could acquire on earth.

Therefore God is not ashamed to be called their God, for he has prepared a city for them. God was pleased with them for their life example and had a room prepared for them in eternity, just as he has for all those who are his children, as Jesus told the disciples: "My Father's house has many rooms" (John 14:2).

Principle and Application

Breaking down the phrase "God is not ashamed to be called their God, for he has prepared a city for them," two principles can be applied to evangelism and discipleship among the Fur asylum seekers and refugees in Jordan.

Principle 1—Evangelism Approach: The Letter to the Hebrews was written to a Christian audience. The purpose of the letter was to encourage believers who were facing hardship and suffering. Although it is primarily directed at believers, it nevertheless has significant implications for non-Christians, as it emphasizes the divinity, the supremacy, and the sufficiency of Jesus Christ. In addition, it highlights Jesus's role as a mediator between God and people, who brings forgiveness to those who believe in him and obey his teachings. The passage in Heb 11:8–10 and 13–16 speaks about a country in heaven and an eternal life prepared for those who believe in God. It invites people to place their faith in God and prepare themselves to enter the city that he has prepared for them.

We live in a condition of spiritual exile. Since sin entered the world in the garden of Eden (Gen 3:1–7), contaminating Adam and Eve and consequently all their descendants, humanity fell into a horrible spiritual position: "For all have sinned and fall short of the glory of God" (Rom 3:23). Religious affiliation cannot achieve a way out of this condition. We have no power to transform ourselves and get us out from the state of "enmity against God" (Jas 4:4). This spiritual reality can be illustrated by the life of the apostle Paul. Before Paul had an encounter with Jesus on the way to Damascus (Acts 9:4), he was considered a religiously irreproachable man. His religious credentials were enviable. Educated in Jerusalem under Gamaliel, a teacher of the law who was honored by all the people, Paul was steeped in the best traditions of Jewish orthodoxy, as he affirms: "Circumcised on the eighth day, of the people of Israel, of the tribe of Benjamin, a Hebrew of Hebrews; in regard to the law, a Pharisee" (Phil 3:5).

But while in the eyes of men Paul was an impeccably religious person when receiving divine light on his spiritual condition, Paul himself concluded that he was the greatest of sinners: "Here is a trustworthy saying that deserves full acceptance: Christ Jesus came into the world to save sinners—of whom I am the worst" (1 Tim 1:15). The experience narrated by the apostle leaves no doubt that religion is incapable of abrogating our sinful condition. This helps us understand why the Janjaweed can profess a religion but still kill their fellow Muslim brothers and sisters in Darfur. Religion alone doesn't heal.

Only the Messiah can remove us from this condition of spiritual exile and take us back home to enjoy a personal relationship with God. Those who believe will have eternal life: "Very truly I tell you, whoever hears my word and believes him who sent me has eternal life and will not be judged but has crossed over from death to life" (John 5:24).

Principle 2—Discipleship Approach: Christ has done for humanity a work that no one else could ever do. As disciples, we must trust him and base our relationship with God on what Jesus has done instead of on what we can do to be saved.

Religions center on human effort to get closer to the Creator, based on the awareness that our relationship was once broken and we must do something to restore it. Consciously or unconsciously, men began to create religions, seeking to rebuild or reconnect their relationship with God.

The first expression of religiosity in human history was carried out by Adam and Eve. As soon as they sinned, they began to have a very different worldview. They realized their nakedness, understood that they had sinned, and tried to cover their shame with a garment woven from fig leaves (Gen 3:7). The couple's attitude represented an effort to solve the problem caused by their disobedience: the dishonor arising from sin and separation from God. But the Lord rejected the initiative, the effort, and the proposed solution. Instead, God clothed the couple in clothing made from animal skins—an allusion to the spotless Lamb who would come as the Messiah and be sacrificed to cover our spiritual nakedness: "The LORD God made garments of skin for Adam and his wife and clothed them" (Gen 3:21).

The attitude of the first couple was rejected not by divine whim, but because, through the spiritual death caused by sin, man became incapable of approaching God on his own initiative or on merit. Therefore, the solution to repair the damage caused by sin is beyond the reach of human beings. Thus, it was necessary for the Eternal to reject the human enterprise and institute the path to be trodden by those who desire to have communion with him.

Outlining the gospel message for the first time in the garden, God performed the first sacrifice in the Bible by preparing fur garments and clothing for the couple. With this action, God made it very clear that there was nothing Adam and Eve could do to resolve their spiritual condition and instituted a principle later reaffirmed in Scripture, to which we will return in chapter 7: "Without the shedding of blood there is no forgiveness" (Heb 9:22).

Later in the history of mankind, God again took the initiative on behalf of human beings. Fulfilling the promise made in Eden, he came down from heaven and graciously came to us in the person of his Son, Jesus, the Lamb of God, to punish sin and do justice in the universe: "The next day John saw Jesus coming toward him and said, 'Look, the Lamb of God, who takes away the sin of the world!'" (John 1:29). Keller makes an essential distinction between the gospel of Jesus Christ and religion: "The gospel is, therefore, radically different from religion. Religion operates on the principle: 'I obey, therefore I am accepted.' The gospel operates on the principle: 'I am accepted through Christ, therefore I obey.'"[57]

Bearing in mind the possibility of a church planting movement among the Fur, new believers need to be encouraged to focus on basing their relationship with God on the work of Jesus. God is more interested in giving them a new life than a new religious affiliation: "But because of his great love for us, God, who is rich in mercy, made us alive with Christ even when we were dead in transgressions—it is by grace you have been saved. And God raised us up with Christ and seated us with him in the heavenly realms in Christ Jesus" (Eph 2:4–6).

Regarding believers from outside of the Fur community working with Fur individuals, a fruitful practice proposed to address the theme of exile is to build a network of followers of Jesus who will care for the Fur, give them a sense of belonging, and welcome them into groups of prayer and Bible study.

Implementation and Communication

Considering the possibility that members of the Fur people in Jordan will believe in the gospel, the following are proposals for attitudes that disciplers should encourage the new believers to adopt throughout their discipleship process.

Continue to reflect on the concept of exile in the Bible. Consider how common the exile experience is in the Holy Scripture and meditate on the fact that many biblical characters understood the earth as a place of pilgrimage through which all must pass. People like Jacob would even refer to their age as their years of pilgrimage: "Pharaoh asked him, 'How old are you?' And Jacob said to Pharaoh, 'The years of my pilgrimage are a hundred and thirty. My years have been few and difficult, and they do not equal the years of the pilgrimage of my fathers'" (Gen 47:8–9).

Expand your knowledge of the historical scattering of God's people, often encouraged by religious persecution. Note in the Scriptures how they responded. Also, observe the treatment God prescribed for his people regarding loving and caring for the foreigners living among them.

Encourage other Fur asylum seekers and refugees to maintain hope amid the uncertainty in which they live. Write down verses from the

57. Keller, "Gospel," 2.

Scriptures that could be used to encourage them. Consider safe ways you can share the truth found in the verses with them.

Reject any thought or suggestion that refugees are inferior to people living in other social circumstances. Remember that we are all refugees in this world, regardless of whether we live in the country of our birth. Keep in mind the whole earth belongs to God, and regarding the nations, "he marked out their appointed times in history and the boundaries of their lands" (Acts 17:26). So, God leads us from place to place according to his eternal purposes (Acts 17:27).

Go beyond and consider what social structures can be created to help refugees feel more supported in Jordan. Share your ideas with the Fur community, hear the opinions of individuals of different ages, education levels, and genders. Invite people from outside the community to cooperate with their knowledge, abilities, and resources.

Apologetics Issue

Theological Controversy 1: How can I believe that Jesus was the seed of Abraham to bless the nations (Gal 3:16) if Jesus said, "Before Abraham was born, I am!" (John 8:58)?

Apologetic Response: Since the divinity of Jesus has been questioned by several Fur individuals in this context, as previously stated, this issue related to Jesus's divinity is included as a potential theological controversy.

As God, Jesus is eternal. Jesus has been there throughout all eternity. The expression *I am* was the same one used when God called Moses to take the Israelites from Egypt, he asked God's name, and the Almighty answered: "I AM WHO I AM" (Exod 3:14). The Jews became furious with Jesus, because when he made this statement, he was affirming his divinity.

Since Jesus is divine, the phrase he used was correct, both theologically and chronologically: "Before Abraham was born, I am!" However, Jesus is the second person of the Trinity, the Son, who through the incarnation assumed human form and was born from his mother, Mary. Jesus's genealogy takes us back to Abraham: "This is the genealogy of Jesus the Messiah, the son of David, the son of Abraham" (Matt 1:1). So, as a man, Jesus descended from Abraham to fulfill the prophecy that through Abraham, God would bless the nations: "He redeemed us in order that the blessing given to Abraham might come to the Gentiles through Christ Jesus, so that by faith we might receive the promise of the Spirit" (Gal 3:14).

Therefore, there is no contradiction in this statement, because the two realities coexist. As God, Jesus is before Abraham. As man, born from Mary, Jesus is the seed of Abraham to bless the nations.

Theological Controversy 2: How can I submit myself to the authority of the Bible if the Qur'an also claims to be the word of God?

Apologetic Response: A Fur individual argued in a conversation: "Islam is the best religion, and the Qur'an is the word of God." In other interactions people affirmed the authority of the Qur'an over the Bible. In fact, there were individuals who stated that they do not need the Bible because they have the Qur'an. The Fur people need to know that the Bible is the word of God. Throughout history, God inspired about fifty faithful servants whom the Holy Spirit instructed to transmit God's message to the world. In the Old Testament, God used prophets like Moses. In the New Testament, God used apostles like Paul to give us one of the most preserved ancient books in the world, with over two-thousand-year-old scroll manuscripts in existence.

The Bible is the bestselling book of all time, with more than five billion copies distributed. It has shown its power in the lives of uncountable people who have been healed, delivered from evil spirits, raised from the dead, and transformed by its power.

Although the Holy Spirit inspired and used humans to write the Bible, its message come from the Almighty God: "We also have the prophetic message as something completely reliable, and you will do well to pay attention to it, as to a light shining in a dark place, until the day dawns and the morning star rises in your hearts. Above all, you must understand that no prophecy of Scripture came about by the prophet's own interpretation of things. For prophecy never had its origin in the human will, but prophets, though human, spoke from God as they were carried along by the Holy Spirit" (2 Pet 1:19–21).

Whereas there are many translations or versions of the Bible, their variations are due to the translation process alone. These types of differences don't reflect changes in the manuscripts. Any book translated by more than one person will face the same situation.

The Bible is God's word with a clear salvation message to humanity, which provides a way for the sinners to be reconciled with God through Jesus Christ and by the forgiveness of their sins.

Considering that some people doubt whether they can trust the Bible, suggest that they apply to the Bible the same idea found in Ps 34:8: "Taste and see that the Lord is good." Each person is invited to taste for themselves and see if the Bible is the word of God. In other words, give yourself a chance to read the Bible with a sincere heart and ask God to reveal to you if the Bible is worthy to be trusted.

Evaluation

1. How does this contextualization project avoid encouraging syncretism among the Fur people?

The project reaffirms Jesus's divinity and dispels the misconception that he was simply a prophet, like all the others. Also, it explains that Jesus was both God and man. As God, Jesus existed before Abraham, and as God incarnate, he was after Abraham.

2. How does this contextualization project constructively engage the Fur people's worldview?

The project engages the Fur people's worldview by helping the Sudanese believers understand that we are all pilgrims and foreigners in this world (1 Pet 2:11). When seen in the context of eternity, we are on this planet for a remarkably short period. We are here primarily to fulfill God's purposes in and through our lives. However, by faith in Christ, we become citizens of heaven and gain access to the eternal promised land.

The approach also provides points of connection between the Fur people and prophets like Abraham, Isaac, and Jacob, who saw themselves as pilgrims in this world. The essential component of their identities was not in having land but in having God and trusting his promise of a better country in heaven. This understanding influenced them through several generations.

3. How does this contextualization project challenge the Fur people toward (specific) personal change?

The fruitful practices of this project encourage the Fur not to put their hope in the things of this world, calling their attention instead to the fact that expecting too much from this life can bring frustration and disappointment: "Do not store up for yourselves treasures on earth, where moths and vermin destroy, and where thieves break in and steal. But store up for yourselves treasures in heaven, where moths and vermin do not destroy, and where thieves do not break in and steal" (Matt 6:19–20).

The Fur are also reminded that resettlement is not the only possibility for their future and are asked to trust the plans God has for them: "'For I know the plans I have for you,' declares the Lord, 'plans to prosper you and not to harm you, plans to give you hope and a future'" (Jer 29:11).

Fifth Theme: Suffering

Another theme that emerged during the study's interviews was suffering. Participants expressed that suffering has been a constant in their lives, especially after the war started in Darfur in 2003. The Fur people have endured a great deal of pain and suffering, in their villages in Darfur, in Sudanese camps for IDPs, and in the neighborhoods of Amman. Six participants experienced peace in Darfur before the outbreak of the war, but four had been born during the civil war and have known peace only since relocating to Jordan. In the interviews, the participants revealed that suffering is present in different areas of their lives. As can be seen from the participants' responses, their painful experiences have resulted in loss, grief, mistrust, fear, anxiety, trauma, and mental health disorders, such as anxiety, depression, and post-traumatic stress disorder (PTSD). They keep going with their lives and hoping that resettlement in a third country will alleviate some of their grief. While they make every effort to overcome suffering, they greatly need restoration and healing.

Cultural Exegesis

Fur asylum seekers and refugees have experienced an incredible amount of suffering. The suffering they have been dealing with is not only physical. They carry emotional wounds because of all they have experienced, both back in Sudan and here in Jordan. They sometimes feel paralyzed. Keller highlights, "Suffering seems to destroy so many things that give life meaning that it may feel impossible to even go on."[58]

Spelman defines suffering as "a universal human experience described as a negative basic feeling or emotion that involves a subjective character of unpleasantness, aversion, harm or threat of harm to body or mind."[59]

In general, participants have a negative perspective on suffering. They have suffered so much, and they want to get rid of all the suffering they face in their lives. However, they are aware that this is not possible, because suffering is part of the human experience.

They need to access the biblical teaching about suffering and contemplate how God works through sorrow and pain. By understanding God's perspective regarding suffering, they will be better prepared to deal with their painful experiences and to realize that the sufferings of Jesus brought salvation to humanity.

58. Keller, *Walking with God*, 13.
59. Spelman, *Fruits of Sorrow*, 171.

Biblical Exegesis

As part of the process of biblical exegesis as it relates to the theme of suffering, 2 Cor 1:3–7 (NKJV) will be employed to establish a contextualized approach for evangelism and discipleship among Fur asylum seekers and refugees.

> Blessed be the God and Father of our Lord Jesus Christ, the Father of mercies and God of all comfort, who comforts us in all our tribulation, that we may be able to comfort those who are in any trouble, with the comfort with which we ourselves are comforted by God. For as the sufferings of Christ abound in us, so our consolation also abounds through Christ. Now if we are afflicted, it is for your consolation and salvation, which is effective for enduring the same sufferings which we also suffer. Or if we are comforted, it is for your consolation and salvation. And our hope for you is steadfast, because we know that as you are partakers of the sufferings, so also you will partake of the consolation.

Blessed be the God and Father of our Lord Jesus Christ, the Father of mercies and God of all comfort. The apostle Paul refers to God in this passage as "the God of all comfort." This title given to God joins other titles such as "the God and Father of our Lord Jesus Christ" and "the Father of mercies." God reveals himself in a variety of ways throughout the Scripture. Therefore, the Bible teaches that God is love, God is kindness, and God is a comforter. We witness God's kindness through what he has done and still does. How do we get to know the God of all comfort? Only when we suffer. If we don't suffer, we do not experience God's comfort.

Who comforts us in all our tribulation. The text teaches that our God is not distant and unconcerned about our suffering. The Almighty has his eyes on his children and sends them comfort in all their tribulation. Like a doctor who has healing medication to administer to his patients when they have a wound, God has appropriate comfort to give to people amid their suffering for all their tribulation. As a result, no sorrow is too great or too minor for God to address and provide comfort for those who are experiencing it. God is the source of all our comfort in our times of adversity, as Vroegop highlights: "For the Christian, the exodus event—the place where we find ultimate deliverance—is the cross of Christ. This is where all our questions—our heartaches and pain—should be taken. The cross shows us that God has already proven himself to be for us and not against us."[60]

---

60. Vroegop, *Dark Clouds, Deep Mercy*, 37.

That we may be able to comfort those who are in any trouble. We are comforted both to overcome our tribulation and to provide comfort to others based on the comfort we have received. As a comforter, one way God works is to use people to bring comfort to others who are in need. Later, in this same letter, the apostle Paul confirms this teaching: "But God, who comforts the downcast, comforted us by the coming of Titus" (2 Cor 7:6).

With the comfort with which we ourselves are comforted by God. It is God who has entrusted us with the responsibility of passing on his comfort to others around us. The greater our suffering, the greater the comfort we receive from God. The greater our level of comfort, the greater our ability to offer to others what we have received from God.

For as the sufferings of Christ abound in us, so our consolation also abounds through Christ. The sufferings of Christ should not surprise people who know the Holy Scriptures or pay attention to the words of Jesus, like his disciples did. Still, some people find it difficult to assimilate the idea that Jesus had to face much suffering to fulfill his mission. Peter behaved in this way. He even reprimanded Jesus for talking about his death and resurrection: "Never, Lord!" he said. "This shall never happen to you!" (Matt 16:22). In response, Peter received a stern rebuke from Jesus for opposing God's will: "Get behind me, Satan! You are a stumbling block to me; you do not have in mind the concerns of God, but merely human concerns" (Matt 16:23).

The suffering of the Messiah was accurately predicted and recounted by the prophets of the Old Testament. The prophets were so detailed in their descriptions of Christ's suffering that one of them, Isaiah, even foretold the event of Jesus's crucifixion: "He was despised and rejected by mankind, a man of suffering, and familiar with pain. Like one from whom people hide their faces he was despised, and we held him in low esteem. Surely, he took up our pain and bore our suffering, yet we considered him punished by God, stricken by him, and afflicted. But he was pierced for our transgressions, he was crushed for our iniquities; the punishment that brought us peace was on him, and by his wounds we are healed" (Isa 53:3–5).

Suffering was such a central aspect in Jesus's life that he received the title "a man of suffering" from the prophet Isaiah seven hundred years before his incarnation. The sufferings of Christ had a divine purpose and led him to fulfill his mission in the world. In the book of Isaiah, the sufferings of Christ are presented as a way God brings comfort to humanity: "to proclaim the year of the LORD's favor and the day of vengeance of our God, to comfort all who mourn" (Isa 61:2).

As disciples of Jesus Christ, we are also called to suffer for Jesus, as the Scripture says: "For it has been granted to you on behalf of Christ not only to believe in him, but also to suffer for him" (Phil 1:29).

One reason we suffer is to preach the gospel because "the gospel will always be countercultural anywhere in the world as it collides with human fallenness and with the religions and worldviews that the Bible insists to be delusions stemming from the suppression of God's revelation."[61] However, the more suffering we bear for Christ's sake, the greater the amount of encouragement that will be showered upon us through our Lord.

Now if we are afflicted, it is for your consolation and salvation. Suffering serves a valuable purpose. The suffering we experience in life is intended to bring us comfort and salvation. In this regard, Jesus serves as a model. As his suffering promoted our consolation and salvation to the world, our suffering will fulfill the same purposes. "He accepted suffering. He willingly laid down His life. He poured out His very soul unto death. Shall not we, His servants, tread the same pathway?"[62]

Which is effective for enduring the same sufferings which we also suffer. Paul and the other apostles suffered for the sake of the gospel. They were often persecuted and endured suffering for announcing Christ to the world, as Paul narrates his testimony in 2 Cor 11:24–28:

> Five times I received from the Jews the forty lashes minus one. Three times I was beaten with rods, once I was pelted with stones, three times I was shipwrecked, I spent a night and a day in the open sea, I have been constantly on the move. I have been in danger from rivers, in danger from bandits, in danger from my fellow Jews, in danger from Gentiles; in danger in the city, in danger in the country, in danger at sea; and in danger from false believers. I have labored and toiled and have often gone without sleep; I have known hunger and thirst and have often gone without food; I have been cold and naked. Besides everything else, I face daily the pressure of my concern for all the churches.

The apostles demonstrated a strong identification with Jesus and were willing to suffer because of their efforts to spread the Christian faith in a world that was hostile to it. It should come as no surprise that they are the ones in the Scriptures inviting all the other disciples to do the same.

Or if we are comforted, it is for your consolation and salvation. In many contexts, suffering is frequently regarded as a negative experience and as a form of divine punishment. Nevertheless, Jesus told his disciples, living in

61. Dowsett, "Deliver Us from Evil," 63.
62. Elliot, *Path through Suffering*, 39.

this fallen world, it is impossible not to face suffering: "In this world you will have trouble" (John 16:33). Therefore, we should not despise suffering or take a negative stance. Suffering has a determined purpose; it is intended to promote maturity, consolation, and salvation.

And our hope for you is steadfast, because we know that as you are partakers of the sufferings, so also you will partake of the consolation. Those who were partaking in the sufferings of the apostles would also partake in their consolation. Those who would join them in their sorrow would also share their joy. This partnership happens because we are the body of Christ (1 Cor 12:27). As members of the same body, we are all connected and can fellowship with our brothers and sisters no matter where they are, physically or temporally, since we share fellowship with other sufferers across both space and time.

Suffering is a temporary reality. No matter how long we have suffered, our pain will pass when we are finally redeemed, and it cannot be compared to what God is preparing for us: "I consider that our present sufferings are not worth comparing with the glory that will be revealed in us" (Rom 8:18).

As Christians, we have a long history and a legacy of people who have suffered to promote God's kingdom. We are called to do the same, joining them today by reproducing their example of love, faith, and obedience to God.

Principle and Application

Breaking down the phrase "the Father of mercies and God of all comfort, who comforts us in all our tribulation," two principles can be applied to evangelism and discipleship among the Fur asylum seekers and refugees in Jordan.

Principle 1—Evangelism Approach: In the selected passage, 2 Cor 1:3–7, the apostle Paul is writing a second letter to the believers in the city of Corinth. As Paul addresses the church that he had planted there, he speaks of the God of all comfort. He encourages the believers by reminding them that anyone who believes in Jesus will experience earthly suffering and heavenly comfort. The passage has an essential application to people outside of the Christian community by highlighting that God has much comfort to give to people facing tribulation if their faith is placed in Jesus.

Since we live in a fallen and broken world, we find suffering everywhere, including in our own lives. Occasionally, such suffering results in significant consequences: "We are all vulnerable, and the world fractures us in many ways throughout our lives. Consequently, we are unable to avoid traumas, some of which leave long-lasting scars."[63]

Fur asylum seekers and refugees in Jordan have endured substantial suffering because of the Darfur crisis. However, their suffering is not limited to the events in their past. Their current situation causes continual pain and trauma:

> The trauma of refugee status is particularly corrosive. It does the usual harm of devastating our own self-image and sense of permanence in the world, but it does more. It is a dislocation from our familiar domestic geography and culture; and that must wrench from our grasp all the external markers by which we know ourselves and our worth.[64]

Fur individuals desperately need refreshment for their souls (Ps 23:3). Amid this reality, the Holy Scriptures present our Creator as the God of all comfort. In our times of suffering, if we turn to God in faith, he will be there to comfort us in all our tribulations and trials. The Scriptures assure us that there is no tribulation that God's comfort will not address.

The only path we can take to experience God's comfort is Jesus Christ, who says: "I am the way and the truth and the life. No one comes to the Father except through me" (John 14:6). In God alone, we can find the amount of comfort we need to fill our hearts and even share with others who may be experiencing similar difficulties.

Principle 2—Discipleship Approach: Suffering is an inevitable reality, even for those who believe in God. Therefore, we shall not be deceived by the illusion that because we follow Jesus, and he has suffered for us on the cross, we will not need to suffer anymore. Instead, we must be aware that when we suffer, divine peace will be there amid the adversities, as Keller asserts: "Walking with God through suffering means that, in general, you will not experience some kind of instant deliverance from your questions, your sorrow, your fears. There can be, as we shall see, times in which you receive a surprising, inexplicable 'peace that passes understanding.'"[65]

When we are facing trials in our lives, as believers, we will naturally pray to ask God to stop the ongoing situation that is making us suffer. However, we must always consider that God can use that exact situation to transform our lives. So, we need to submit ourselves to God and proceed to trust him amid the adversity:

---

63. Friesen, *Living from the Heart*, 24.
64. Hinshelwood, "Foreword," xiii.
65. Keller, *Walking with God*, 237.

Storms will come. Our peace and faith come with the knowledge that Jesus has power over all storms, whatever their source or strength. He can quiet them if he chooses. Often the early Christians hoped for Jesus to quiet the storm of persecution, but he did not. So in the middle of the storm, they relied, instead, on their faith in the power of their Savior and the eternal rest promised to them.[66]

When we believe in God and become a new creation, we tend to trade one kind of suffering for another. As we put on the new self and grow in maturity in our spiritual life, we are expected to stop our wrongdoings (Eph 4:20–24). This prevents us from causing unnecessary problems and producing suffering from our sinful choices. However, we begin suffering for doing what is right in God's sight in a world that is in rebellion with God. As we grow as believers, all our suffering should be because of our faith, not because of our sinful desires: "If you suffer, it should not be as a murderer or thief or any other kind of criminal, or even as a meddler. However, if you suffer as a Christian, do not be ashamed, but praise God that you bear that name" (1 Pet 4:15–16).

Jesus was very clear with his disciples that the Christian life is a road of suffering: "Enter through the narrow gate. For wide is the gate and broad is the road that leads to destruction, and many enter through it. But small is the gate and narrow the road that leads to life, and only a few find it" (Matt 7:13–14). It's clear that the disciples fully understood the Messiah's teachings because later when facing adversities and persecution for their faith in Jesus, they did not complain, but rejoiced: "The apostles left the Sanhedrin, rejoicing because they had been counted worthy of suffering disgrace for the Name" (Acts 5:41).

There are several adversities that Jesus's disciples can experience when following their Lord. Sittser describes some of them: "Discipleship implies suffering, leads to persecution, tests mettle, demands steadfastness, requires endurance and even leads to death. It demands that we confess Jesus as Lord."[67]

Preaching the gospel has always produced persecution for God's people. The very word *witness* carries in it a sense of the danger of proclaiming God's word in the world we live in: "By definition, a martyr is a witness. The New Testament speaks about the act of witnessing (*martyreō*) and the

---

66. Osborne and Comfort, *Matthew*, 164.

67. Sittser, *Water from Deep Well*, 28.

person who witnesses (*martys*)."[68] Nevertheless, we suffer for many reasons in life. Why not suffer for the cause of the gospel?

Martyrdom is a legacy of the Christian faith, and every believer must be willing to embrace it if God gives him the honor of laying down his life for Jesus: "Suffer for Jesus and even to die for Him: Jesus of Nazareth, ten of the twelve disciples, and the apostle Paul all died as martyrs. Their testimonies shaped the early Christian community, setting the tone for an expectation and embrace of suffering."[69] Sittser explains the concept of martyrdom and presents an essential difference between Christian martyrdom and Islamic *jihad* as proclaimed in the religious views of Muslim fundamentalists:

> Not that we should glorify or seek martyrdom as a good in itself, as if the Christian faith validates or even encourages the use of violence. Much of the martyrdom we read about today, especially in the form of suicide bombing, is the complete opposite of the martyrdom that Christians suffered in the first few centuries. These modern "martyrs"—if we dare even use the word to describe such horrific acts—bear witness to a God of vengeance, hate and murder, not a God of love. The early Christian martyrs were victims of such hate, not perpetrators. They absorbed violence; they did not inflict it. They were called to martyrdom; they did not force it on innocent people, which is what suicide bombers do today.[70]

Even though people may have a negative view of suffering, God uses suffering to perfect the lives of his children, like the goldsmith uses fire to refine gold by removing its impurities. For this reason, when the disciples would suffer for Jesus, they would rejoice. They had a positive view on suffering based on what they had learned from Jesus: "And when they had called in the apostles, they beat them and charged them not to speak in the name of Jesus, and let them go. Then they left the presence of the council, rejoicing that they were counted worthy to suffer dishonor for the name" (Acts 5:40–41 ESV).

Sometimes, God allows suffering into our lives to test our faith and make us complete: "Count it all joy, my brothers, when you meet trials of various kinds, for you know that the testing of your faith produces steadfastness. And let steadfastness have its full effect, that you may be perfect and complete, lacking in nothing" (Jas 1:2–4 ESV). Besides, as we endure suffering, we need to remember that our God can enrich us in the most

---

68. Smither, *Christian Martyrdom*, 31.

69. Smither, *Christian Martyrdom*, 10.

70. Sittser, *Water from Deep Well*, 28.

unlikely circumstances, giving us treasures from darkness and riches from secret places (Isa 45:3).

Facing suffering for Jesus should not be a surprise or a cause for sadness to God's people but, instead, a reason for rejoicing, as there will be a divine reward: "Beloved, do not think it strange concerning the fiery trial which is to try you, as though some strange thing happened to you; but rejoice to the extent that you partake of Christ's sufferings, that when His glory is revealed, you may also be glad with exceeding joy" (1 Pet 4:12–13 NKJV).

God even uses persecution and martyrdom to build his church and promote the proclamation of the gospel to the nations. In the book of Acts, the church in Jerusalem began preaching the gospel widely after they experienced great persecution of their faith, as in Acts 8:1–4:

> On that day a great persecution broke out against the church in Jerusalem, and all except the apostles were scattered throughout Judea and Samaria. Godly men buried Stephen and mourned deeply for him. But Saul began to destroy the church. Going from house to house, he dragged off both men and women and put them in prison. Those who had been scattered preached the word wherever they went.

In the body of Christ, events of suffering and joy become a shared experience, "so that there should be no division in the body, but that its parts should have equal concern for each other. If one part suffers, every part suffers with it; if one part is honored, every part rejoices with it" (1 Cor 12:25–26).

Although there is a positive aspect concerning suffering and the persecution of believers, we shall not provoke, promote, or seek suffering. Any of these behaviors would be antagonistic to the Christian faith:

> No one should seek this suffering; to be sought is not its nature. Nor is there cause and effect in it; it is beyond what is "deserved." When in its grasp, the suffering has the appearance of hell, but beauty arises from the ashes. The suffering involved in the death of the ego, the self, is not in itself joyous, but the flowers of this death are a sweet fragrance to God.[71]

One of the purposes of suffering in the Christian life is to bring the believer into a closer relationship with the Lord. Elliot brings more understanding to this perception: "There is a much deeper fellowship into which

---

71. Arthur, *Theology of Suffering*, 1.

the Christian who suffers may enter. It is the fellowship of Christ's suffering. Christ's cup of suffering overflows and we suffer with Him."[72]

Furthermore, suffering is intended to bring the believer into a closer relationship with others. When we suffer, we naturally connect with people experiencing similar suffering. As social creatures by nature, human beings tend to band together in the face of suffering. One of the purposes of experiencing God's comfort when we suffer is to be able to comfort others with the "comfort we ourselves receive from God" (2 Cor 1:4).

I am convinced that the body of believers is divinely projected to be a caring community in which emotional and spiritual healing can happen. Love, care, and joy experienced among brothers and sisters as they relate to their Creator can have a significant therapeutic effect, as Dr. Bell emphasizes the significance of people who have suffered experiencing healing together: "The best way to promote healing from trauma is to get as many traumatized parties who share a common event together and begin processing the feelings, thoughts, and memories together."[73]

As I encourage the formation of healing community groups, I want to highlight that they are not intended to serve as a substitute for professional medical advice, diagnosis, or treatment; instead, they highlight the critical role of faith communities in supporting healing among their members, which is highly effective as they process their traumas, Dr. Bell adds:

> When people share their memories of the event, they all have different perceptions of how things happened and how fast. Also, many people forget traumatic events or sequences. By establishing a shared perspective immediately after an event, the event becomes safer and a support group has come to life. Guess what this does?
>
> It creates an enormous opportunity for all in the group to re-evaluate their relationships with each other and with God. What this also does is makes the brain re-evaluate the memory collectively and pulls this information from the Limbic system back into the Memory glands, where it belongs. This basically drops a window between the person and the event. They remember the event, but no longer feel it from a fight or flight perspective.[74]

Considering that there are over one hundred million forcibly displaced people in the world, it is hard to think that every displaced person, not to

---

72. Elliot, *Path through Suffering*, 82.

73. Bell, "Healing from Trauma," para. 7.

74. Bell, "Healing from Trauma," para. 9–10.

mention other groups who have been exposed to other potentially traumatic experiences, will have access to professional trauma care. This scenario becomes even more challenging when displaced people move to a context where they feel isolated. According to Alayarian, "Social and cultural isolation is probably the major factor resulting in mental disorder in refugees."[75] Therefore, Christians have a critical contribution to give in creating environments in which displaced people can build healthy relationships, process their traumatic experiences, and find healing and renewal. Additionally, as co-workers in God's service (1 Cor 3:9), Jesus's disciples must extend to others the comfort they have received from him, trusting that our God "wants to transform every form of human suffering into something glorious. He can redeem it. He can bring life out of death."[76]

Providentially, there are several tools available to equip Christians who are not professional therapists and would like help building healing communities and promoting mental health. One of the most used tools in the Middle East is called the THI (Trauma Healing Institute) method. The method engages the mind, body, and spirit by combining mental health best practices and engagement with God through the Bible. It is based on the book *Healing the Wounds of Trauma: How the Church Can Help*, and it has been offered as a training by the Bible Societies of many countries, particularly in countries dealing with the effects of the world migration crisis.[77] Another tool is called the Life Model, which is based on the book, *The Life Model: Living from the Heart Jesus Gave You*. The program is recommended by Dr. Dallas Willard: "The Life Model is the best model I have seen for bringing Christ to the center of counseling and restoring the disintegrating community fabric within Christian churches."[78] Additionally, the Christian community can benefit from a movement called the Truth Collective, which is headed by a group of Christian women in the United States. The organization produces resources to assist Muslim women all over the world in finding healing through art therapy activities.[79] "We invite Muslims into trauma healing only after we have had the courage to entrust our own heart wounds to Jesus Christ. This humbles us as ministers, allowing us to experience a friendship with Muslim women that is honest and equal," says Jami Staples, the founder and CEO of the Truth Collective.[80]

75. Alayarian, *Resilience, Suffering and Creativity*, xix.

76. Alayarian, *Resilience, Suffering and Creativity*, xix.

77. See https://www.traumahealingbasics.org.

78. Friesen, *Living from the Heart*, xii.

79. See https://www.thetruthcollective.org/resources.

80. Staples, email to author, Feb. 24, 2022.

Bearing in mind the possibility of a church planting movement among the Fur, new believers need to be encouraged to express their sufferings, listen respectfully to each other, and practice the spiritual disciplines as a way of relating to God and bringing before his throne anything that could be troubling their hearts: "Cast all your anxiety on him because he cares for you" (1 Pet 5:7).

Regarding believers from outside of the Fur community working with Fur individuals, a fruitful practice proposed to address the theme of suffering is to serve Fur individuals by meeting their tangible needs as an expression of the gospel. Also, help them build confidence to share their needs, express their feelings, and seek solutions to their physical, emotional, and spiritual challenges.

Implementation and Communication

Considering the possibility that members of the Fur people in Jordan will believe in the gospel, the following are proposals for attitudes that disciplers should encourage the new believers to adopt throughout their discipleship process.

Continue to reflect on the benefits of suffering. Consider how much more mature you are today because of the suffering you have experienced. What are the "hidden treasures, riches stored in secret places" (Isa 45:3), that the Lord has given you amid the experiences you had dealing with suffering?

Expand your impact by creating spaces in which relationships are stimulated, built, and affirmed. Encourage everyone to share, listen, and support each other. Keep in mind that people tend to hide their experiences, vulnerabilities, and traumas to protect their emotions, reputation, and sense of honor. Be respectful, patient, and supportive.

Encourage people who are suffering to look for professional help and to take their sufferings to Jesus. Discuss with them the biblical practice of lament as a way of bringing their sorrows to God in an "honest cry of a hurting heart wrestling with the paradox of pain and the promise of God's goodness."[81] According to Vroegop's definition of lament, "in the Bible lament is more than sorrow or talking about sadness. It is more than walking through the stages of grief. Lament is a prayer in pain that leads to trust."[82]

Reject any teaching that believers in Christ do not suffer or that if they suffer, they are living a sinful life. Do not blame yourself or God for all the

81. Vroegop, *Dark Clouds, Deep Mercy*, 26.

82. Vroegop, *Dark Clouds, Deep Mercy*, 28.

suffering you have experienced in life. Pursue God's healing amid your sufferings and share the comfort you receive with others.

Go beyond a limited approach to suffering by recognizing the three dimensions of our lives: physical, emotional, and spiritual. Consider creating biblical counseling groups on trauma and connect those in need of professional help with recommendations and referrals.

Apologetics Issue

Theological Controversy 1: Why did a merciful God let a good prophet like Jesus suffer so much?

Apologetic Response: This is a common objection among Muslims even though it was not directly raised by participants in the research.[83] As 2 Cor 1:3–7 will be introduced to the Fur people, there is a great probability that this objection will be brought up. Due to the relevance of the subject of suffering in the process of helping them to trust Jesus, this controversy needs to be addressed with a proper response.

It is significant for the Fur people to understand that in Christ we have a God who both understands human suffering and has experienced it to the fullest. Suffering was very present throughout Jesus's life on earth. He began embracing suffering at his birth when there was no place for him to be born (Luke 2:7). He was then forcibly displaced from his country, and later in his life, he did not have a home: "Foxes have dens and birds have nests, but the Son of Man has no place to lay his head" (Matt 8:20). Besides deprivation, the Messiah faced suffering in many other areas, as Isaiah foretold: "He was despised and rejected by mankind, a man of suffering, and familiar with pain. Like one from whom people hide their faces he was despised, and we held him in low esteem" (Isa 53:3).

Muslim scholars use Sura 33:40 to argue that God cares for his prophets and would not let them suffer: "Those who deliver the messages of Allah and fear Him, and do not fear anyone but Allah; and Allah is sufficient to take account." However, the Holy Scriptures show that many prophets suffered. In fact, some of them were killed because of the message they were preaching. Calling people to repent from their sins makes them uncomfortable and can create great problems in society, particularly when prophets speak against those who hold much power in their hands. For instance, John the Baptist was beheaded by Herod Antipas for denouncing sin in his household (Matt 14:3–12). This explains why a prophet is not loved among his people, as Jesus said: "A prophet is not without honor

83. Lodahl, Claiming Abraham, 158.

except in his own town, among his relatives and in his own home" (Mark 6:4). There are many examples in the Old Testament of prophets being killed for preaching God's word. Prophethood was a dangerous task, as we can witness in the words of Elijah: "I have been very zealous for the LORD God Almighty. The Israelites have rejected your covenant, torn down your altars, and put your prophets to death with the sword. I am the only one left, and now they are trying to kill me too" (1 Kgs 19:14).

To have a correct perspective on suffering, we must remove our eyes from the suffering itself and its associated pain, realizing that God had a purpose for each suffering that Jesus faced, particularly at his crucifixion. God's purpose is rooted in his wisdom, which exceeds our limited human understanding: "'For my thoughts are not your thoughts, neither are your ways my ways,' declares the LORD. 'As the heavens are higher than the earth, so are my ways higher than your ways and my thoughts than your thoughts'" (Isa 55:8–9).

Theological Controversy 2: How can I believe that Jesus was crucified if the Qur'an says, "They killed him not, nor crucified him" (Sura 4:157)?

Apologetic Response: "In truth, Jesus was not crucified as some people claim. Let me tell you something, you Christians believe Jesus was crucified, but this did not take place. The religion of Islam teaches that God spared Jesus from the crucifixion experience, but many people are unaware of this, and still think that Jesus was crucified," said a study participant in a conversation. Therefore, it is essential to teach the Fur people that as individuals willing to please God, we must listen to what the Almighty spoke through the prophets many centuries before the Messiah's incarnation. The suffering servant "took up our pain and bore our suffering," as the prophet Isaiah writes in Isa 53:4. Besides, we have to pay attention to Jesus's own words when he spoke objectively about his crucifixion: "From that time on Jesus began to explain to his disciples that he must go to Jerusalem and suffer many things at the hands of the elders, the chief priests and the teachers of the law, and that he must be killed and on the third day be raised to life" (Matt 16:21). In addition, the apostles who were eyewitnesses to the events of the crucifixion testified of Jesus's death: "For Christ also suffered once for sins, the righteous for the unrighteous, to bring you to God. He was put to death in the body but made alive in the Spirit" (1 Pet 3:18).

Jesus's crucifixion was a pivotal event that mobilized the entire city of Jerusalem, and numerous people were following each step that preceded the crucifixion and the crucifixion itself: "When all the people who had gathered to witness this sight saw what took place, they beat their breasts and went away" (Luke 23:48). Also, Jesus was crucified in a distinct place where the multitudes could not miss him: "Carrying his own cross, he went out to the place of the Skull (which in Aramaic is called Golgotha). There they crucified him, and with him two others—one on each side and Jesus in the middle" (John 19:17–18).

The Jewish leaders did not deny Jesus's death. How could they do so if the whole city had seen it? After Jesus rose again, they lied about the resurrection by inventing a story about his body being stolen, but they never denied the event of the crucifixion: "You are to say, 'His disciples came during the night and stole him away while we were asleep'" (Matt 28:13).

Josephus, a Jewish historian from the first century (around 93–94), registered Jesus's crucifixion by saying that Pontius Pilate "condemned him to the cross,"[84] corroborating the witness and writings of the apostles.

Therefore, there is much evidence of Jesus's crucifixion, as Maurer argues: "We have clear evidence of his crucifixion: it was foretold by prophets in the OT, Jesus predicted his death, and eye-witness and historians testify to this event."[85]

The crucifixion had a divine purpose to benefit the world, bringing salvation to those who believe: "It was the mission of Jesus, to die at the cross as the final perfect sacrifice so that death could be conquered and all who believe in him have forgiveness of sins and eternal life (Jn 3:16, 20:31)."[86]

Yes, the crucifixion was an expression of human cruelty but also a manifestation of God's love. It is crucial to look at the crucifixion through God's eyes: "If the cross is the place where the worst thing that could happen happened, it is also the place where the best thing that could happen happened. Ultimate hatred and ultimate love met on those two crosspieces of wood. Suffering and love were brought into harmony."[87]

Considering all the sufferings Jesus endured during his life on earth, a question that arises is this: Why would God eliminate suffering from him only at his death?

Evaluation

1. How does this contextualization project avoid encouraging syncretism among the Fur people?

The project attempts to avoid any potential conflation of Christian martyrdom and Islamic jihad. It will clarify that Christians who die for their

84. Josephus, *New Complete Works*, 590.

85. Maurer, "Answering," 1.

86. Maurer, "Answering," 1.

87. Elliot, *Path through Suffering*, 26.

faith do not provoke or promote their deaths. Christian martyrs are neither suicide bombers nor harbingers of terror; instead, they are killed
while demonstrating peace, love, and forgiveness. Besides the example of
Jesus at the cross (Luke 23:34–43), the stoning of Stephen also illustrates
the biblical core of martyrdom: "While they were stoning him, Stephen
prayed, 'Lord Jesus, receive my spirit.' Then he fell on his knees and cried
out, 'Lord, do not hold this sin against them.' When he had said this, he
fell asleep" (Acts 7:59–60).

2. How does this contextualization project constructively engage the Fur people's worldview?

The project seeks to communicate that suffering is not a curse but a challenging component of life that touches everybody in their earthly journey.
Depending on the circumstances, it may have physical, emotional, and
spiritual consequences. However, it can also produce good results in us,
such as maturity, empathy, and endurance. Suffering will continue to be a
part of our human experience for the time we spend in this world. As we
face trials, our sufferings need to be addressed and always taken to God,
who can provide the comfort we need: "Even though I walk through the
valley of the shadow of death, I will fear no evil, for you are with me; your
rod and your staff, they comfort me" (Ps 23:4 ESV).

3. How does this contextualization project challenge the Fur people toward (specific) personal change?

The message of the project is that we can overcome suffering in Christ and
find comfort and peace amid our trials. Also, we can learn how to make
use of suffering for our personal growth and the advancement of God's
kingdom. Furthermore, the prophets have left us an example of how to be
patient as we deal with suffering: "Brothers and sisters, as an example of
patience in the face of suffering, take the prophets who spoke in the name
of the Lord" (Jas 5:10).

Summary

The chapter presented a contextualization project addressing the five
themes that emerged in the analysis of the ethnographic findings: discrimination, war, displacement, exile, and suffering. Each section devoted

to the themes had subsections, including Cultural Exegesis, Biblical Exegesis, Principle and Application, Implementation and Communication, Apologetics Issue, and Evaluation.

The next chapter, the conclusion of this study, will revisit the research questions, discuss the implications and contributions of the study, provide personal reflections, highlight prospects for future research, introduce questions raised in the study, and make final remarks. The content of this section will highlight lessons that Christians from inside and outside the Arab world can learn from the evangelism and discipleship project used in Jordan among the Fur asylum seekers and refugees.

7

Conclusion

Faith has to do with things that are not seen and hope
with things that are not at hand.

—Thomas Aquinas

Introduction

THIS STUDY PROPOSES A contextualization model for ministry among the Fur, a Sudanese people group living as asylum seekers and refugees in Jordan. Since the war broke out in Darfur in 2003, the whole region has been destabilized and the people have been displaced to many countries, including Jordan. Considering that their lives have been impacted in many ways and even transformed in their new living context, this study asks the question: *What are the best approaches for evangelism and discipleship to be employed in the process of planting a church among Fur asylum seekers and refugees in Jordan?*

The emphasis is that using themes regularly discussed among the people allows the gospel message to connect with the hearts of the Fur people. We see how Jesus used this kind of personal connection to present the gospel message to people throughout his ministry. One of the examples we find in Matt 13:3–5, when Jesus delivered the parable of the four soils to people who were well versed in agricultural matters: "Then he told them many things in parables, saying: 'A farmer went out to sow his seed. As he was scattering the seed, some fell along the path, and the birds came and ate it up. Some fell on rocky places, where it did not have much soil. It sprang up quickly, because the soil was shallow."

This principle can be applied to reaching the Fur people by considering the pertinent themes among the Fur asylum seekers and refugees living in Jordan to be approached in a conversation and used in a gospel presentation.

Five themes emerged during the interviews with Fur refugees: discrimination, war, displacement, exile, and suffering. Based on these five themes, I built a contextualization project that focuses on evangelism and discipleship, envisioning a church planting movement among the people.

Hopefully, the insights shared in this chapter will help Christians from both inside and outside the Arab world benefit from the evangelism and discipleship project developed for the Fur asylum seekers and refugees living in Jordan.

Response to the Study Question

The analysis of the Fur people's ways of life, which was based on the survey conducted in this specific context, was essential to respond to the research question and the supporting questions proposed in chapter 2 of this study.

The central question in this study is:

What are the best approaches for evangelism and discipleship to be employed in the process of planting a church among Fur asylum seekers and refugees in Jordan?

The best approach is to identify the themes that the Fur people consider the most significant and engage them through a contextualization project that actively communicates the good news of Jesus.

The supporting questions are:

1) What is the spiritual worldview of the Fur people?

The Fur people are Sunni Muslims who adhere mainly to the Maliki school of jurisprudence, which they consider the most authoritative. They adhere to a version of Islam that has been heavily affected by Sufism, and as a result, they believe that they can have a personal relationship with God. They think that God is both transcendent and immanent.

2) How do the Fur people in Jordan currently regard Islam?

Both the war in Darfur, led by fellow Muslims, and the discrimination faced in Jordan, particularly perpetrated by Arab Muslims, have discouraged many Fur individuals from continuing to practice the religion of Islam as they did before the war began. Many Fur individuals in Jordan do not pray in mosques and are now highly receptive to talking about Christianity and other faith expressions.

3) What challenges that the Fur people face as asylum seekers and refugees in Jordan should be addressed during the pre-evangelism process?

Challenges that should be faced pre-evangelism include the following: the everyday struggle to survive, concerns about family members in Darfur, fear of going to jail and being deported for engaging in illegal employment, anxiety for resettlement, and uncertainty for the future.

4) In a gospel presentation, what themes will make the most sense to Fur asylum seekers and refugees in Jordan?

The themes that will make the most sense to Fur asylum seekers and refugees in Jordan are the five emerging themes from the analysis of the findings: discrimination, war, displacement, exile, and suffering.

5) Which themes need to be discussed first in the discipleship process with Fur individuals?

The themes that need to be discussed first in the discipleship process with Fur individuals are the five emerging themes from the analysis of the findings: discrimination, war, displacement, exile, and suffering.

6) What fruitful practices ought to be adopted for ongoing ministry among Fur asylum seekers and refugees in Jordan?

This study has designed a list of five fruitful practices based on each of the five emerging themes to help Jesus's disciples from outside of the Fur community to work with Fur individuals and bear fruit among them for the glory of God (John 15:8).

Fruitful Practice 1: Nurture positive relationships with Fur individuals based on biblical equality, respect, and love, allowing them to experience a relationship that recognizes God's image in all human beings.

Fruitful Practice 2: Pray with Fur individuals for peace in Sudan and throughout the world, creating a culture of prayer and encouraging them to enter a relationship with the Prince of Peace.

Fruitful Practice 3: Share Scripture with the Fur people about God's perspective on the diaspora to equip them with a biblical worldview.

Fruitful Practice 4: Build a network of followers of Jesus who will care for the Fur, give them a sense of belonging, and welcome them into groups of prayer and Bible study.

Fruitful Practice 5: Serve Fur individuals by meeting their tangible needs as an expression of the gospel. Also, help them build confidence to communicate their needs, express their feelings, and seek solutions to their own physical, emotional, and spiritual challenges.

Implications and Contributions of the Study

The context of the study reinforces three global missions realities that define our world. The realities are 1) Islam is the fastest growing religion globally; 2) the current migration crisis is the largest in recorded history; and 3) there are still unreached people groups who are waiting to hear the gospel of Jesus Christ. These global missions realities are shaped by significant challenges that impact our world, such as poverty, racial discrimination, and suffering. All these realities must be taken into consideration as the global church strives to join God in his mission in our world and as it goes about its mission of spreading the gospel to the ends of the earth.

Personal Reflections

Listening to the people was an enriching experience. Although I previously had lived in Sudan for nearly three years and have been relating to the Sudanese people for approximately seventeen years, I learned so much in this research experience. However, it was not easy listening to some of their stories. The suffering they have experienced is heartbreaking and overwhelming.

The war in Darfur is cruel. No human being deserves what the Fur people, together with the other people from the region, are enduring. The violence against civilians in Sudan and many other places of the world must stop.

War is a strong force behind the humanitarian crisis we have in the world today. Therefore, everybody needs to raise their voices against violence and engage in peacemaking. Even though biblical prophecy suggests that armed conflicts will tend to increase globally, Christians worldwide and the international community must work together to oppose all kinds of conflicts. We must do our best to prevent more people from enduring physical, emotional, and spiritual suffering.

Although not ignoring the potential risks, I would like to reaffirm the importance of ordinary people becoming actively involved in healing communities. Through partnerships with professional counselors, appropriate basic training, and sharing with others what participants have learned, more people can become involved. A traditional professional solution is desirable but, unfortunately, not accessible to all displaced people in countries like Jordan, where an overwhelming population of asylum seekers and refugees need immediate help to overcome their sufferings as they continue to fight for life.

> The clinical solutions currently are expensive and cumbersome; they require extreme levels of education and do not spread on their own. Even those people who are able to benefit from modern treatments are not able to then help others without undergoing the same extensive training that therapists need. From a global perspective, factors such as wars, AIDS, societal disintegration, child abuse, violent crime, human trafficking, addictions, and terrorism have left about a quarter of the world's population showing significant signs of trauma.[1]

Another reflection is that refugees are not a homogenous group of people. They have a lot of things in common, but many differences as well. We must look at them individually, even when contemplating a specific people group. Although I hope this study will be applied to other contexts, caution and careful consideration are important to make sure that applying this research in a different context is useful and applicable.

In a world filled with suffering, we must be prepared to deal with the suffering of the people we interact with regularly. Many Christians lack a theology of suffering. As Christians, we tend to think that we will no longer suffer because we are blessed "in the heavenly realms with every spiritual blessing in Christ" (Eph 1:3). Some Christians may wrongly infer that those who suffer are experiencing the result of disobedience to God. Often, Christian workers are trained in theology, missiology, anthropology, and linguistics. Still, they do not learn enough about dealing with suffering in their own lives and then in the lives of those who are suffering around them.

When dealing with people who have experienced great suffering, we must be equipped to respond as Christians and to handle suffering so that we can avoid developing burnout and indirect trauma as consequences.[2]

---

1. Friesen, *Living from the Heart*, x.

2. Sometimes also referred to as secondary trauma, compassion fatigue, or vicarious trauma.

Sin has heavily affected our world, bringing to the human experience sickness (physical suffering), trauma (emotional suffering), and darkness (spiritual suffering). Therefore, suffering affects our bodies, our emotions, and our souls.

Christians need to learn how to care for those who need comfort. Specific resources related to dealing with suffering were mentioned in chapter 6, in the section on suffering. We need to be God's voice to a world immersed in suffering by taking people from darkness to light, from a place of despair to God's presence. Then we will be able to say about them: "The people living in darkness have seen a great light; on those living in the land of the shadow of death a light has dawned" (Matt 4:16).

Prospects for Future Study

As of early 2022, I am unaware of any Fur believers in the country. However, since this project proposes a strategy for engaging the Fur asylum seekers and refugees in Jordan with the gospel, there is a possibility that there will be a group of Fur believers in this context in the coming years. Therefore, one area for future research would be to conduct an anthropological study with the new believers, employing an approach called *critical contextualization*. Paul Hiebert developed this approach to promote the process of contextual theology among indigenous churches.[3] Hiebert's approach follows a four-step process to enable biblical teachings to produce the transformation of cultural beliefs and practices of the new gospel believers. It requires the cross-cultural worker and new believers to work jointly to analyze their beliefs and practices according to the Holy Scriptures.

The four steps are as follows: 1) The cross-cultural worker and the local believers discuss a cultural belief or practice to get a better understanding of it; 2) The cross-cultural worker and the local believers analyze together various Scriptures that speak to all parts of the belief or practice; 3) The local believers critically evaluate the specific belief or practice in light of the Holy Scriptures and decide what they will keep, reject, modify, or create regarding new indigenous forms; and 4) The local believers decide how to implement the new practice in the context of the community of believers.

It is impossible to determine when a group of believers will be formed among the Fur community in Jordan. However, by listening to the voices of Fur individuals, examining the themes they embrace in their conversations, and presenting the gospel, taking into consideration their current circumstances, this research paves the way for a new study on critical

---

3. Hiebert, *Anthropological Reflections*, 88–91.

contextualization. Applying Paul Hiebert's approach or method to a church planting movement among the Fur people will be vital as a subsequent study project. Since the Fur people in Jordan are getting in touch with the gospel for the first time, a study on critical contextualization would allow the word of God to reshape their worldview and prevent religious syncretism from suffocating their faith in the Messiah.

Questions Raised in the Study

In approaching the end of this study, some of the questions I have raised are:

1. Is there a need to revisit the findings to identify other relevant themes?

2. How soon will the themes relevant to the Fur people today change?

3. Since this study has been done with a group of adults (ages ranging from twenty-two to fifty-five), is it necessary to conduct a similar study with other age groups, like teenagers and youth? Are the same themes relevant to them, or are other themes even more relevant to their age groups?

4. If this contextualization project becomes effective and a group of Jesus's disciples is formed, what can be done to prevent new disciples from placing too much emphasis on this project rather than highlighting the importance of Scripture?

5. What other approaches will future believers be able to use in this context? What strategies can they develop to reach out to their own people and other people groups in this context?

Final Remarks

The reality of life for the Fur asylum seekers and refugees needs to be known. Their voices must continue to be heard. Solutions to their problems must be found. The suffering they experience day by day cries out to heaven and requires an adequate response from Christians worldwide and the international community.

Fur individuals are special people—above all because they were created in God's image, as Schaeffer asserts: "All men bear the image of God. They have value, not because they are redeemed, but because they are God's creation in God's image."[4] Therefore, they must be seen and treated as people who hold significance, value, and dignity.

I want to humbly propose some suggestions for actions that need to be taken by different groups in favor of the Fur asylum seekers and refugees and the entire refugee community in Jordan.

I understand that the UNHCR personnel face tremendous pressures every day as they deal with an unmeasurable task. However, the refugees are crying out and saying that some of the solutions proposed to them are not addressing their humanitarian crisis. It is unreasonable for refugees and their families to live in conditions of suffering like those they faced in their country of origin. It is not permissible to subject human beings to live permanently in conditions designed for emergency or temporary situations. One cannot try to solve the challenge of the migratory crisis by producing similar or even bigger problems. Short-term solutions developed for emergencies, in practice, do not have an effect, and are not solutions, for individuals who need to live with them for an extended period. May the UNHCR find new strategies, proposals, and approaches to properly address the current migration crisis that affects the lives of over one hundred million people worldwide.

Governments need to make every diplomatic effort possible to bring about peaceful conditions in the world by mediating between countries at war, discouraging the emergence of new conflicts, and denouncing those who benefit from financing armed conflicts. They also need to consider the resettlement of refugees a humanitarian issue and be more generous in welcoming those seeking refuge.

NGOs need to make every effort to provide quality services to refugees. They must equip refugees to develop activities that promote their self-support. They need to act broadly, addressing the deepest needs of refugees rather than just emergency needs. They need to constantly seek new solutions to the migratory crisis and discuss them with the international community.

More ordinary citizens like me need to pressure their governments, asking them to stop supporting armed conflicts, which represent the main reason fueling the global migration crisis. Also, they must pressure them to be more generous in resettling refugees. They must participate in the refugee resettlement process by welcoming, facilitating, and assisting each one in their process of rebuilding life in the new country of residence.

I conclude this work by praying for my dear Fur asylum seekers and refugee friends living in Jordan:

---

4. Schaeffer, *Mark of the Christian*, 15.

Dear Father in Heaven, by your eternal grace, open the spiritual eyes and the door of faith to the Sudanese people, particularly those from the Fur tribe. Let them come to the fountain and drink the living water, never to be thirsty again. Give them the grace of experiencing a new life in Jesus. Touch their bodies, heal their souls, and enlighten their spirits. I also ask you, Lord Jesus, to redeem them from their current situation of segregation, humiliation, and oppression. Have compassion on them, as they are harassed and helpless, like sheep without a shepherd. Holy Spirit, guide their feet, bless them with a real opportunity to rebuild their lives, and restore their relationships with family and friends in Sudan. May the peace of the Almighty be manifested in Sudan and his light shine brightly among the people in Darfur. In Jesus's name, Amen.

Appendix A

Map of Sudan

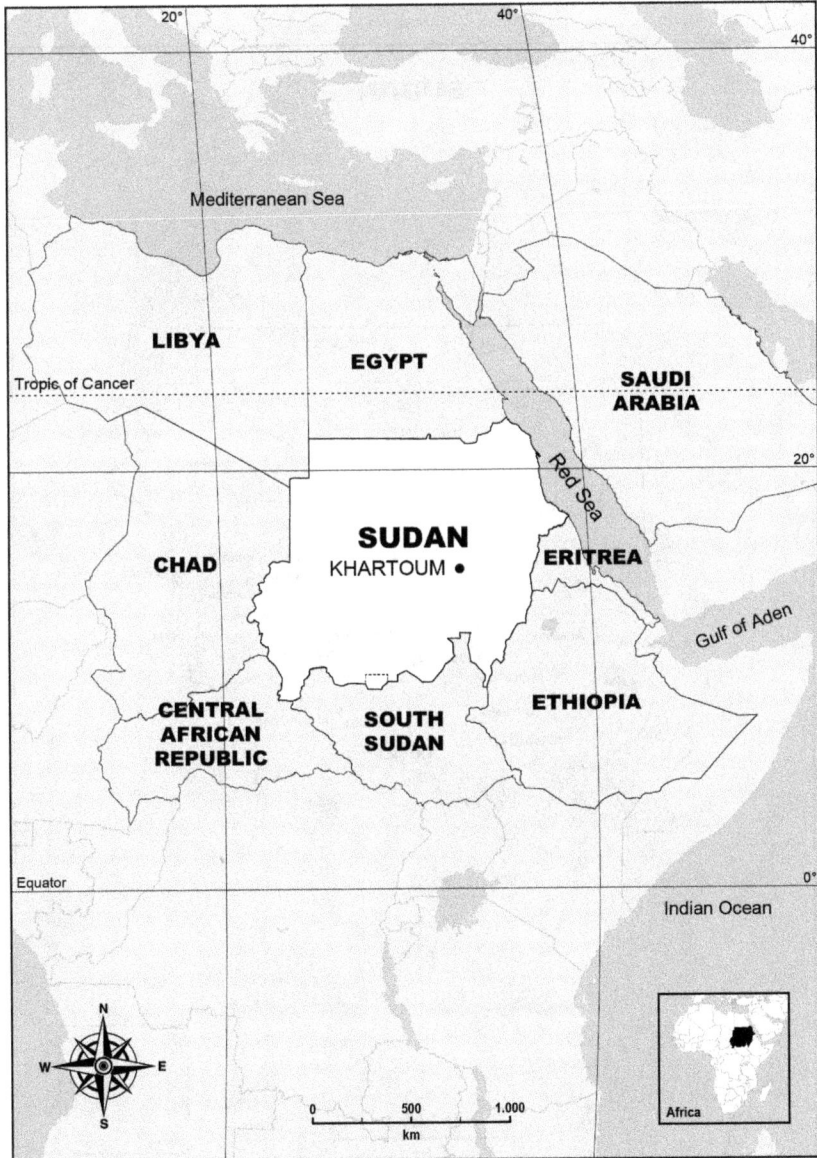

Appendix B

Political Map of Sudan

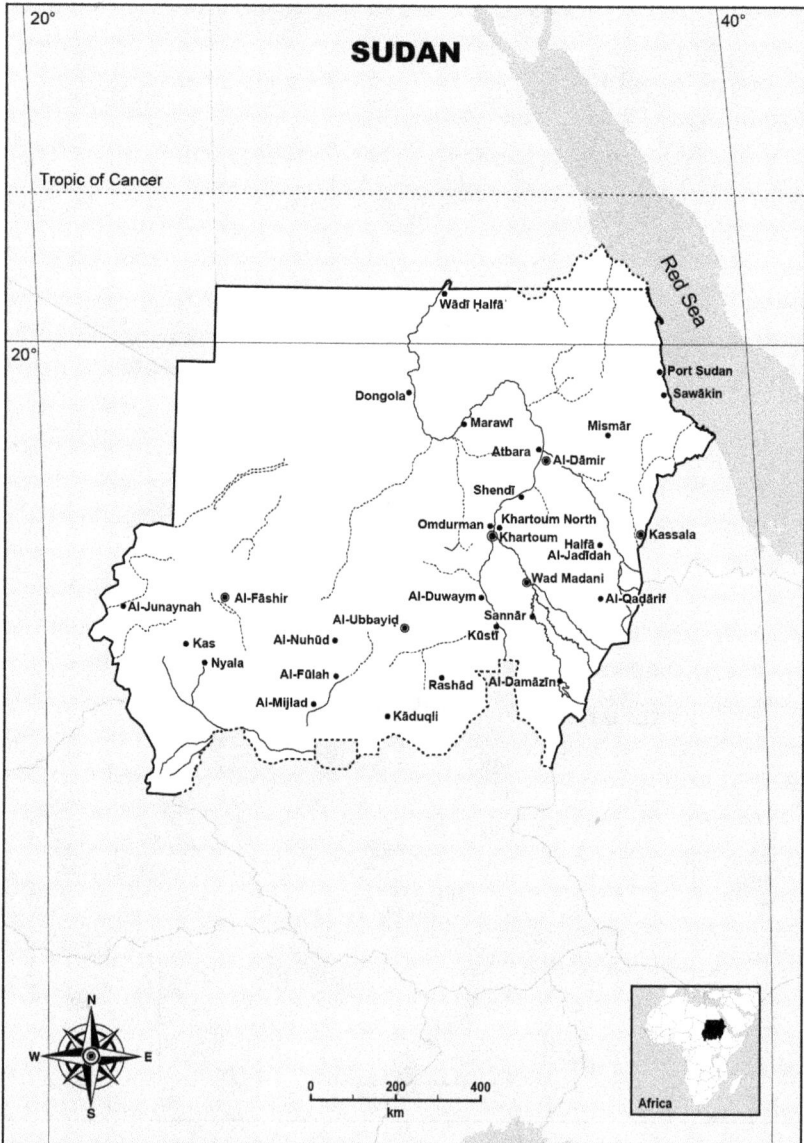

Appendix C

Map of States of Sudan

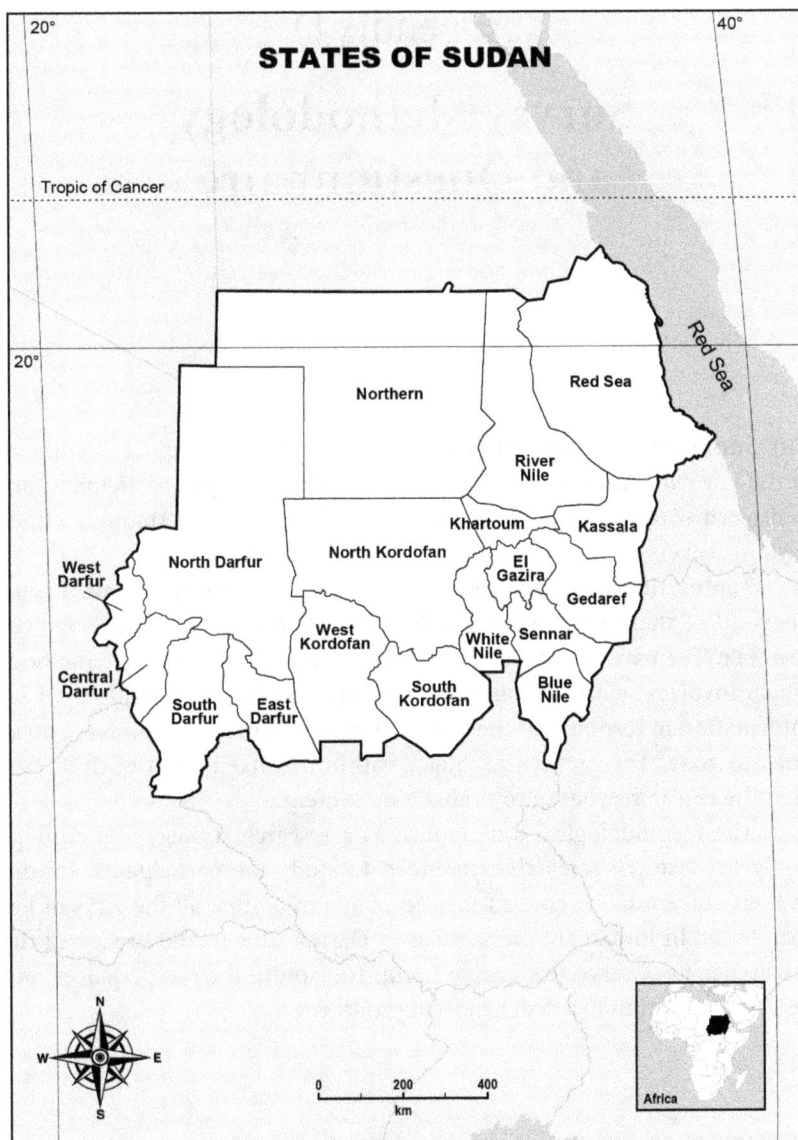

Appendix D

Survey Methodology
and Questionnaire

The Survey

THE SUDANESE PARTICIPANTS OF this cross-sectional study are members of the Fur tribe, the target group being examined. All the participants are registered with the UNHCR Jordan and hold the official status of either asylum seekers or refugees.

The participants were selected by a Fur community member who knew all of them personally and introduced the participants to the researcher. The participants were determined using the purposive method, which involves selecting community members who can provide the best information in response to the survey. The time horizon of the survey was 2020 to 2022. The survey took place within this fixed point of time, and next the researcher began to evaluate its content.

The methodological tool applied as a research strategy was ethnography because the researcher intended to study the participants' culture in their current living context instead of assuming that all the ways of life manifested in Jordan are the same as in Darfur. This method required the researcher to observe the people group to capture their experiences and perceptions within their current living context.

Characteristics of the Interviews

The interviews took place over two weeks, in October 2020, and all were conducted in person. Interviews were conducted at the participants' houses, and during all of them, meals were served. The duration of each interview was approximately one hour and fifty minutes. A total of fifteen hours was spent conducting all the interviews.

A total of ten adults were interviewed: eight men and two women. The two female participants were wives of male participants. The wives had their husbands sitting next to them during the entire time of the interview. The participants' ages ranged from twenty-two to fifty-five.

A facilitator assisted the researcher: a Fur, male, adult, fluent in Arabic, English, and Fur, who took responsibility for setting up the meetings and translating whenever necessary. Other than the translator, the researcher also relied on the work of a cultural consultant: a Fur male, fluent in Arabic, English, and Fur, who provided information, ideas, and perspectives based on his cultural expertise.

All the participants speak Fur and Arabic fluently. Some of them speak limited English. Therefore, the languages used during the interviews were Arabic, English, and Fur. Participants had the opportunity to choose their preferred language to respond to the survey questionnaire. Five of the ten participants preferred to respond in Arabic, three chose to respond in English, and two opted to respond in Fur. The facilitator translated the Arabic and Fur language responses into English, and all responses were transcribed in English.

The Questionnaire

1. Do you understand and agree to participate in this survey?

2. What is your name?

3. What is your marital status?

4. How long have you lived as a refugee here?

5. Where exactly are you from in Sudan?

6. Have you lived as a refugee in any other country beyond Jordan?

7. How was life in Sudan when you decided to leave the country?

8. How big is your family?

9. Do you have more relatives in Sudan?

10. How do people marry in your culture?

11. What do you think of a Muslim having more than one wife?

12. Whom will your children marry here?

13. How do you explain this pandemic situation? What is the origin of coronavirus?

14. Are you a Muslim?

15. Do you practice your faith?

16. How do you describe God?

17. Do you go to the mosque?

18. How do you think this world came into existence?

19. How do you know if something is right or wrong?

20. How do you know the truth?

21. How do you make decisions in your life?

22. What do you consider to be the most important thing in your life?

23. How is life in Jordan?

24. Do you want to go back to Sudan?

25. What do you think of the Jordanians?

26. How do people treat you here?

27. Can you practice your faith here the same way you could in Sudan?

28. What do you like most about life in Jordan?

Appendix E

Literature Review

SUDAN IS A MUSLIM-MAJORITY country. More than half of the Sudanese population identify as Arabs and speak Sudanese Arabic, the country's official language.

- In the book *Understanding Arabs*, Margaret Nydell provides information to help understand Arabs in general. Nydell describes Arab beliefs, values, and concepts related to friendship, family, social structure, and many other areas. The book offers an up-to-date representation of the Arab world and provides an introduction for those who want to know about Arab cultures and their influence in countries like Sudan.

- Harold A. MacMichael's *A History of the Arabs in the Sudan*, in its first volume, takes the reader many years back into history, presenting accounts of the tribes who lived in Sudanese land before the Arabs came to the country. MacMichael shares stories that express unique information gleaned directly from local people, including genealogical records known in Sudan as *nisbas*.

- Robert O. Collins unpacks two centuries of Sudan's history in his book *A History of Modern Sudan*, demonstrating the link between past challenges and present issues in the country, including the breeding ground of Islamist terrorism and the recent war in Darfur. The chapter "Disaster in Darfur" is particularly significant for this study because it examines the current situation of Darfuri refugees, with a focus on the Fur people.

- Kim Searcy talks about the expansion of Islam in Sudanese territory in the first chapter of his book *The Formation of the Sudanese Mahdist State: Ceremony and Symbols of Authority: 1882–1898*. The book gives a historical perspective on significant events in Sudan that paved the way for the country's Islamization. It also touches on important topics that help us understand the Sudanese worldview, such as the Islamic mysticism manifested in Sufi brotherhoods.

- The book *The River War: An Account of the Reconquest of the Sudan* is a text produced by a Nobel Prize-winning writer and historian. It provides an account of Britain's reconquest of Sudan. This book on the history of Sudan was written by the legendary statesman Winston Churchill. In his early years, before he became the prime minister of England or even started his political career, Churchill served as a soldier in Sudan. In 1899, he wrote the book based on his treasured field experience. It recounts the conflict of British soldiers led by Lord Kitchener against the Islamic Jihadists seeking to take control of the country during the Mahdiya Period.

- *The Darfur Sultanate: A History* is a text written by a scholar highly knowledgeable about the context of which he is writing. R. S. O'Fahey addresses historical events and aspects of life in Darfur from a unique perspective, having worked for the United Nations Mission to Sudan (UNMIS) and the African Union during the peace talks in Abuja, which were initiated intending to resolve Darfur's current crisis. The author presents an in-depth overview of the Darfur Sultanate, which includes information on various topics, such as culture, history, and geography, among other things.

- P. M. Holt and M. W. Daly's book *A History of the Sudan: From the Coming of Islam to the Present Day* provides a comprehensive understanding of the history of Sudan, covering more recent events, including the civil war that started in Darfur. Besides that, the authors detail the strange relationship between Sudanese authorities and Osama bin Laden, who lived in Sudan's capital, Khartoum, before moving to Afghanistan and creating the international terrorist organization called Al-Qaeda.

- In *Sudan, South Sudan, and Darfur: What Everyone Needs to Know*, Andrew S. Natsios, a former special envoy to Sudan and director of US-AID, discusses events covering twenty-five years of Sudan's recent history. He focuses on the two major conflicts in recent decades in Sudan.

- In his book *Sudan: Darfur, Islamism and the World*, Richard Cockett, the Africa editor of the *Economist*, gives perspective on the ongoing conflict in Darfur. Since the war began in 2003, more than 300,000 people have been killed, and over 2.7 million have been forcibly displaced. Also, living conditions in the region have significantly deteriorated. Throughout the book, Cockett brings together various viewpoints on the war and the different voices of people involved in the clashes.

- Following the failure to stop the genocide in Rwanda in 1994, the international community informally agreed to raise their voices against any other genocide. In a book published in 2011, *Fighting for Darfur: Public Action and the Struggle to Stop Genocide*, Rebecca Hamilton and Mia Farrow write about a compassion campaign to draw international attention to the genocide unfolding in Darfur since 2003. The global protest movement mobilized millions of people worldwide who took to the streets to march, calling for an end to the genocide. Besides ordinary people, celebrities like Steven Spielberg, George Clooney, and Angelina Jolie joined the movement. The book highlights the power of advocacy on behalf of those facing much suffering.

- The book *Explaining Darfur: Four Lectures on the Ongoing Genocide* provides background information for the ongoing conflict in western Sudan.[1] The contributors to this volume show that people involved in the war in Darfur are highly vulnerable and in need of support. They need help to achieve a peaceful solution. Darfurians need the international community to cooperate with them. They need international leaders to pressure the Khartoum administration for a peace agreement. The book provides a detailed description of Darfur, analyzes the Darfur conflict, and makes policy recommendations to governments and international organizations partnering with Sudanese people to resolve Sudan's current problems.

- *Darfur in the Shadows: The Sudanese Government's Ongoing Attacks on Civilians and Human Rights*[2] focuses on the conflicts in Darfur that started in 2003. It exposes how the Sudanese government has led attacks on populated areas and used airstrikes to massacre the civilians in different villages in Darfur. It helps the reader understand some of the sufferings endured by Sudanese people, the human rights violations in western Sudan, and the reasons the international community considers the atrocities committed in Darfur to constitute genocide.

1. Van Ardenne et al., *Explaining Darfur*.
2. Henry, *Darfur in the Shadows*.

- Halima Bashir's book *Tears of the Desert: A Memoir of Survival in Darfur* recounts her life story as a member of the Zaghawa tribe from Darfur, where she was born and grew up. As the village's first formal doctor, Bashir was able to use her knowledge and skills as a health professional to help war victims. Amid the armed conflict, Halima was sexually abused, her village was attacked by the Janjaweed militia, and she was forced to flee Sudan to save her life. The book gives readers the perspective of someone who has lived through the civil war in Darfur. Also, the book demonstrates how the stories and testimonies of those who have lived through the horrors of the conflict are critical in providing a much-needed perspective of what is happening in Darfur. Their voices are crucial in helping the world understand the sufferings experienced by war victims worldwide and reminding humanity of its moral obligation to join their voices in solidarity.

- In the book *Darfur Genocide: The Essential Reference Guide*, Alexis Herr presents an overview of the civil war in Darfur. The author puts together nearly one hundred articles written by experts who discuss several topics and multiple aspects of the conflict. The book considers crucial moments in Sudanese history, such as the Sudanese Lost Boys and Girls. The authors examine religious, cultural, political, and social factors contributing to the outbreak of violence in Darfur in 2003.

- Professor Mahmood Mamdani, a Columbia University scholar, examines the situation in Darfur in his book *Saviors and Survivors: Darfur, Politics, and the War on Terror*. Based on an approach that considers historical, geopolitical, and international relations issues, Mamdani looks at Sudan and analyzes what is happening in Darfur. The author contests the world's response to that crisis and disagrees with the assessment that describes the conflict in Darfur as a genocide. According to the author, the current conflict stems from disputes between nomadic and peasant tribes over fertile land in the south and efforts by British colonial officials to artificially tribalize Darfur by dividing its population into "native" and "settler" tribes. He believes that the involvement of opposition parties in the region's challenges in 2003 resulted in the formation of the two rebel movements, causing the violence that destabilized the region. The book takes a unique perspective on the Darfur civil war, and it helps the reader gain a broader understanding of the situation.

- In a journal article called "Who Are the Darfurians? Arab and African Identities, Violence and External Engagement," Alex de Waal examines the processes of identity formation in Darfur. He talks about past and present processes of identity formation, which both help explain how people see themselves in the region. He discusses the importance of the singularities of Darfur and the recent polarization of Arab and African identities in Darfur, which the civil war helped to strengthen.

- The Janjaweed are a Sudanese militia group that takes part in the violence in Darfur. They are responsible for fighting rebel groups in the region on behalf of the Sudanese government. In the book, *Darfur: A New History of a Long War*, Julie Flint and Alex de Waal discuss the humanitarian tragedy in Darfur, focusing on essential aspects of the violence produced since 2003.

- The book *Refugee Diaspora: Missions amid the Greatest Humanitarian Crisis of the World* presents a biblical basis for refugee ministry and provides an overview of the refugee situation worldwide.[3] The twenty-three authors reflect on the broader picture of migration and cross-cultural missions, challenging the reader to consider the reality of immigrants living in different parts of the world. The book discusses migration in the Middle East and has a chapter focused on Jordan called "Jordan, Home for Refugees: Two Challenges." The chapter's author, J. Wu, presents the historical context of refugee work in the country, the current initiatives carried out by Christians, and some challenges they face to develop their work.

Fortunately, a considerable number of books about Sudan help to explain the events that impact the country today and represent a valuable contribution to this research. However, there is scarce literature about the Fur people specifically, although they are among the most prominent people groups from Darfur. Also, most of the available publications do not specifically discuss evangelism and discipleship among the people groups from Darfur living in Sudan or overseas. Because of the scarcity of resources, this research is doubly needed to address such a challenge and fill the literature gap.

---

3. George and Adeney, *Refugee Diaspora*.

Recommended Reading

Abusharaf, Rogaia Mustafa. *Transforming Displaced Women in Sudan Politics and the Body in a Squatter Settlement*. Chicago: University of Chicago Press, 2009.

Ali, Mohamed Hassan Fadlalla. *Short History of Sudan*. New York: iUniverse, 2007.

Anderson, G. Norman. *Sudan in Crisis the Failure of Democracy*. Gainesville: University Press of Florida, 1999.

Baas, Saskia. *From Civilians to Soldiers and from Soldiers to Civilians: Mobilization and Demobilization in Sudan*. Amsterdam: Amsterdam University Press, 2012.

Barker, Geoff. *Sudan*. New York: Marshall Cavendish Benchmark, 2009.

Barker, Jeff Allen. *Sioux Center Sudan: A Farm Girl's Missionary Journey*. Peabody, MA: Hendrickson, 2018.

Bassil, Noah R. *The Post-Colonial State and Civil War in Sudan: The Origins of Conflict in Darfur*. London: Tauris, 2013.

Blaker, Lisa French. *Heart of Darfur*. London: Hodder, 2008.

Cheadle, Don, and John Prendergast. *Not on Our Watch: The Mission to End Genocide in Darfur and Beyond*. New York: Hyperion, 2007.

Collins, Robert O. *Civil Wars and Revolution in the Sudan: Essays on the Sudan, Southern Sudan and Darfur, 1962–2004*. Hollywood: Tsehai, 2005.

———. *A History of Modern Sudan*. Cambridge: Cambridge University Press, 2012.

Daly, M. W. *Darfur's Sorrow: The Forgotten History of a Humanitarian Disaster*. Cambridge: Cambridge University Press, 2010.

de Waal, Alex. *Famine That Kills: Darfur, Sudan*. New York: Oxford University Press, 2005.

———. *War in Darfur and the Search for Peace*. Cambridge: Harvard University Press, 2007.

———. "Who Are the Darfurians? Arab and African Identities, Violence and External Engagement." *African Affairs* 104 (Apr. 2005) 181–205.

Eltigani, Eltigani El Tahir. *War and Drought in Sudan: Essays on Population Displacement*. Gainesville: University Press of Florida. 1995.

Hagan, John, and Wenona Rymond-Richmond. *Darfur and the Crime of Genocide.* Cambridge: Cambridge University Press, 2008.

Hari, Daoud. *The Translator: A Tribesman's Memoir of Darfur.* New York: Random House, 2008.

Hassan, Salah M., and Carina E. Ray. *Darfur and the Crisis of Governance in Sudan: A Critical Reader.* Ithaca, NY: Cornell University Press, 2009.

Jok, Jok Madut. *Sudan: Race, Religion, and Violence.* Oxford: Oneworld, 2015.

Marlowe, Jen, et al. *Darfur Diaries: Stories of Survival.* New York: Nation, 2006.

Miller, Debra A. *Darfur.* Detroit: Greenhaven, 2009.

Prunier, Gérard. *Darfur: A 21st Century Genocide.* Ithaca, NY: Cornell University Press, 2011.

Reitz, Hazel. *The Winds of Darfur.* Charleston, SC: BookSurge, 2009.

Steele, Philip. *Sudan, Darfur and the Nomadic Conflicts.* New York: Rosen Central, 2013.

Trimingham, Spencer J. *Islam in the Sudan.* London: Oxford University Press, 1965.

Tubiana, Marie-José. *Forced to Flee: Stories of Asylum Seekers from Darfur, Sudan.* Paris: Harmattan, 2017.

Vaughan, Chris. *Darfur Colonial Violence, Sultanic Legacies and Local Politics, 1916–1956.* Suffolk, UK: Currey, 2015.

Willemse, Karin. *One Foot in Heaven: Narratives on Gender and Islam in Darfur, West Sudan.* Women and Gender: The Middle East and the Islamic World 5. Leiden: Brill, 2007.

Zaki, Victor. *My Life Journey from Darfur, Sudan to Boston, USA.* Bloomington, IN: Xlibris, 2020.

Bibliography

Abdullah II. "The Hashemites." King Abdullah II, n.d. https://kingabdullah.jo/en/page/the-hashemites/hashemites.

———. *Our Last Best Chance: The Pursuit of Peace in a Time of Peril.* New York: Viking, 2011.

Abū Salīm, Muḥammd Ibrāhīm. *Manshūrāt al-Mahdī.* Beirut: Dār al-Jīl, 1983.

ACAPS. "Chad Darfur Refugees." ACAPS, last modified Feb. 24, 2021. https://www.acaps.org/country/chad/crisis/darfur-refugees.

Alayarian, Aida. *Resilience, Suffering and Creativity: The Work of the Refugee Therapy Center.* New York: Routledge, 2018.

Aljadid, Renad. "Amman Ranked Most Expensive Arab City, 28th Worldwide." *The Jordan Times*, May 29, 2018. http://jordantimes.com/news/local/amman-ranked-most-expensive-arab-city-28th-worldwide.

Andrews, Edward D. *New Testament Documents: Can They Be Trusted?* Cambridge, OH: Christian, 2020.

Arthur, J. Bryson. *A Theology of Suffering.* Carlisle, UK: Langham Creative Projects, 2020.

Attard, Carmel Paul. *Is the Bible Infallible?* Bloomington, IN: iUniverse, 2019.

Barnabas Aid. "Christian Converts from Islam Arrested and Tortured in Darfur, Sudan." Barnabas Aid, Nov. 6, 2018. https://barnabasfund.org/en/news/christian-converts-from-islam-arrested-and-tortured-in-darfur-sudan.

Barth, Karl. "The Christian Life: Church Dogmatics IV." In *Lecture Fragments*, edited by G. W. Bromiley and T. F. Torrance, 1956–57. Edinburgh: T&T Clark, 1981.

Barth, Markus. *Ephesians: Introduction, Translation, and Commentary on Chapters 1–3.* London: Yale University Press, 2008.

Bashir, Halima. *Tears of the Desert: A Memoir of Survival in Darfur.* New York: One World/Ballantine, 2008.

BBC. "Guide: Christians in the Middle East." *BBC*, Oct. 11, 2011. http://www.bbc.com/news/world-middle-east-15239529.

————. "Jordan Deports Hundreds of Sudanese Asylum Seekers." *BBC*, Dec. 18, 2015. https://www.bbc.com/news/world-africa-35130797.

Bell, Gary. "Healing from Trauma for Christians." Seattle Christian Counseling, Jan. 17, 2019. https://seattlechristiancounseling.com/articles/healing-trauma-christians.

Berlatsky, Noah, and Frank Chalk. *Darfur*. Farmington Hills, MI: Greenhaven, 2015.

Bert, Francesco. *Jordan*. UNHCR, Feb. 2021. https://reporting.unhcr.org/sites/default/files/Jordan%20country%20factsheet%20-%20February%202021.pdf.

Bevans, Stephen B. *Essays in Contextual Theology*. Theology and Mission in World Christianity 17. Boston: Brill, 2018.

————. *Models of Contextual Theology*. Revised and expanded ed. Faith and Cultures. Maryknoll, NY: Orbis, 2002.

Bickerton, Ian J., et al. "Jordan." *Encyclopaedia Britannica*, July 20, 1998; last modified Aug. 13, 2021. https://www.britannica.com/place/Jordan.

Braswell, George W., Jr. *Islam: Its Prophet, Peoples, Politics and Power*. Nashville: Broadman and Holman, 1996.

Britannica, The Editors of Encyclopaedia. "Anglo-Egyptian Condominium." *Encyclopaedia Britannica*, July 20, 1998; last modified Apr. 17, 2018. https://www.britannica.com/place/Anglo-Egyptian-Condominium.

————. "Conflict in Darfur." *Encyclopaedia Britannica*, last modified Dec. 19, 2018. https://www.britannica.com/place/Sudan/Conflict-in-Darfur.

————. "Darfur." *Encyclopaedia Britannica*, July 20, 1998; last modified June 15, 2015. https://www.britannica.com/place/Darfur.

Campbell, Jonathan. "Releasing the Gospel from Western Bondage." *International Journal of Frontier Missions* 16 (1999) 167–71.

Campo, Juan E. *Encyclopedia of Islam*. New York: Facts on File, 2009.

Cashin, David G. *The Seven Essential Questions of Life*. Edited by Brian T. McGregor. Scotts Valley, CA: Createspace, 2016.

Chapman, Colin. *Cross and Crescent: Responding to the Challenge of Islam*. Nottingham, UK: InterVarsity, 1995.

Chatelard, Géraldine. "Jordan: A Refugee Haven." Migration Policy Institute, Aug. 31, 2010. https://www.migrationpolicy.org/article/jordan-refugee-haven.

Churchill, Winston. *The River War: An Account of the Reconquest of the Sudan*. Mineola, NY: Skyhorse, 2013.

Cockett, Richard. *Sudan: Darfur, Islamism and the World*. New Haven, CT: Yale University Press, 2010.

Collins, Robert O. *A History of Modern Sudan*. Cambridge: Cambridge University Press, 2012.

Creswell, John W., and J. David Creswell. *Design: Qualitative, Quantitative, and Mixed Methods Approaches*. Los Angeles: SAGE, 2003.

Creswell, John W., and Cheryl N. Poth. *Qualitative Inquiry and Research Design: Choosing among Five Approaches*. Thousand Oaks, CA: SAGE, 2018.

Davis, Rochelle, et al. "Sudanese and Somali Refugees in Jordan: Hierarchies of Aid in Protracted Displacement Crises." Middle East Research and Information Project, Summer 2016. http://www.merip.org/mer/mer279/sudanese-somali-refugees-jordan.

Dodd, Carly. "The 10 Longest Rivers in the World." World Atlas, Nov. 22, 2022. https://www.worldatlas.com/articles/which-are-the-longest-rivers-in-the-world.html.

Dowsett, Rose. "Deliver Us from Evil." In *Sorrow and Blood: Christian Mission in Contexts of Suffering, Persecution, and Martyrdom*, edited by William David Taylor et al., 59–64. Pasadena, CA: William Carey, 2012.

———. "Dry Bones in the West." In *Global Missiology for the 21st Century: The Iguassu Dialogue*, edited by William David Taylor, 447–62. Grand Rapids: Baker, 2001.

Economist Intelligence Unit, et al. "Sudan." *Encyclopaedia Britannica*, Jan. 25, 1999; last modified Jan. 26, 2022. https://www.britannica.com/place/Sudan.

Elliot, Elisabeth. *A Path through Suffering*. Grand Rapids: Baker, 2014.

Elliston, Edgar J. *Introduction to Missiological Research Design*. Pasadena, CA: William Carey, 2011.

Erickson, Richard J. *Commentary on Ephesians*. Baker Illustrated Bible Commentary. Grand Rapids: Baker, 2012.

Ernst, Carl W. *The Shambhala Guide to Sufism*. Boston: Shambhala, 1997.

Esposito, John L., and Dalia Mogahed. *Who Speaks for Islam? What a Billion Muslims Really Think*. New York: Gallup, 2007.

Evans, Kirsten. "Genocide: The Weight of a Word." *National Review*, Mar. 19, 2016. http://www.nationalreview.com/article/432993/isiss-genocide-christians-recognized-john-kerry-congress.

Fallah, Belal, et al. *Moving beyond Humanitarian Assistance: Supporting Jordan as a Refugee-Hosting Country*; World Refugee & Migration Council Research Report. WRM Council, Sept. 2021. https://wrmcouncil.org/wp-content/uploads/2021/09/Jordan-Syrian-Refugees-WRMC.pdf.

Fedorak, Shirley A. *Anthropology Matters*. Ontario: University of Toronto Press, 2013.

Flint, Julie, and Alex de Waal. *Darfur: A New History of a Long War*. London: Zed, 2008.

Foster, Richard J. *Celebration of Discipline: The Path to Spiritual Growth*. San Francisco: HarperOne, 2018.

Frank, Audrey. *Covered Glory: The Face of Honor and Shame in the Muslim World*. Eugene, OR: Harvest, 2019.

Friesen, James G. *Living from the Heart Jesus Gave You: The Essentials of Christian Living*. Pasadena, CA: Shepherd's, 2010.

Gangel, Kenneth O. *Toward a Harmony of Faith and Learning: Essays on Bible College Curriculum*. Eugene, OR: Wipf & Stock, 2002.

George, Sam, and Miriam Adeney. *Refugee Diaspora: Missions amid the Greatest Humanitarian Crisis of the World*. Littleton, CO: William Carey, 2018.

Government of Sudan. "Understanding Darfur Conflict." Reliefweb, Jan. 19, 2005. https://reliefweb.int/report/sudan/understanding-darfur-conflict.

Grudem, Wayne. *Systematic Theology: An Introduction to Biblical Doctrine*. Leicester, UK: InterVarsity, 1994.

Grzyb, Amanda F. *The World and Darfur: International Response to Crimes against Humanity in Western Sudan*. Montreal: McGill-Queen's University Press, 2010.

Guelich, Robert A. *Sermon on the Mount: A Foundation for Understanding*. Waco: Word, 1991.

Hamilton, Rebecca, and Mia Farrow. *Fighting for Darfur: Public Action and the Struggle to Stop Genocide*. New York: St. Martin, 2011.

Hammad, Hussam. *Jordânia: Passo a Passo*. Translated by Jairo de Oliveira. Amman: N.p., 2018.

Harlan, Mark A. *A Model for Theologizing in Arab Muslim Contexts*. PhD diss. Pasadena, CA: Fuller Theological Seminary, 2005.

———. "De-Westernizing Doctrine and Developing Appropriate Theology in Mission." *International Journal of Frontier Mission* 22 (2005) 159–64.

Hastrup, Anders. *The War in Darfur: Reclaiming Sudanese History.* Hoboken, NJ: Taylor and Francis, 2013.

Henry, Jehanne. *Darfur in the Shadows: The Sudanese Government's Ongoing Attacks on Civilians and Human Rights.* New York: Human Rights Watch, 2011.

Herr, Alexis. *Darfur Genocide: The Essential Reference Guide.* Santa Barbara, CA: ABC-CLIO, 2020.

Hesselgrave, David J. *Communicating Christ Cross-Culturally: An Introduction to Missionary Communication.* Grand Rapids: Zondervan, 1991.

Hesselgrave, David J., and Edward Rommen. *Contextualization: Meanings, Methods, and Models.* Pasadena, CA: William Carey, 2000.

Hiebert, Paul G. *Anthropological Insights for Missionaries.* Grand Rapids: Baker, 1985.

———. *Anthropological Reflections on Missiological Issues.* Grand Rapids: Baker, 1994.

———. *Transforming Worldviews: An Anthropological Understanding of How People Change.* Grand Rapids: Baker, 2008.

Hinshelwood, R. D. "Foreword." In *Resilience, Suffering and Creativity*, edited by Aida Alayarian, xiii–xv. New York: Routledge, 2018.

Holt, P. M., and M. W. Daly. *A History of the Sudan: From the Coming of Islam to the Present Day.* New York: Taylor & Francis, 2014.

Houston, Fleur S. *You Shall Love the Stranger as Yourself: The Bible, Refugees, and Asylum.* New York: Routledge, 2015.

Howard, W. Stephen. *Modern Muslims: A Sudan Memoir.* Athens: Ohio University Press, 2016.

Hull, Bill. *The Complete Book of Discipleship: On Being and Making Followers of Christ.* Colorado Springs, CO: NavPress, 2006.

ICC. "Al Bashir Case." International Criminal Court, n.d. https://www.icc-cpi.int/darfur/albashir.

International Commission of Inquiry on Darfur. *Report to the Secretary-General.* Google, Jan. 25, 2005. https://www.google.com/url?sa=t&rct=j&q=&esrc=s&sour ce=web&cd=&cad=rja&uact=8&ved=2ahUKEwjdv4L-q671AhWNpZUCHXj1A dQQFnoECAsQAw&url=https%3A%2F%2Fwww2.ohchr.org%2Fenglish%2Fdoc s%2Fdarfurreport.doc&usg=AOvVaw3q4bQwqkKyb1l4JMWodLCR.

Jamieson, Robert, et al. *Commentary Critical and Explanatory on the Whole Bible.* Grand Rapids: Christian Classics Ethereal, 2005.

John Paul II. "Speech of the Holy Father John Paul II: Visit to the Refugee Camp of Dheisheh." Vatican, Mar. 22, 2000. https://w2.vatican.va/content/john-paul-ii/en/speeches/2000/jan-mar/documents/hf_jp-ii_spe_20000322_deheisheh-refugees.pdf.

Johnston, Rochelle, et al. *Realizing the Rights of Asylum Seekers and Refugees in Jordan from Countries Other Than Syria with a Focus on Yemenis and Sudanese.* Reliefweb, Apr. 2019. https://reliefweb.int/sites/reliefweb.int/files/resources/71975.pdf.

Josephus, Flavius. *The New Complete Works of Josephus.* Grand Rapids: Kregel, 1999.

Kato, Byang H. "The Gospel, Cultural Context, and Religious Syncretism." In *Let the Earth Hear His Voice*, edited by J. D. Douglas, 1216–23. Minneapolis: World Wide, 1975.

Keller, Timothy. *Generous Justice: How God's Grace Makes Us Just.* New York: Riverhead, 2012.

———. "The Gospel—Key to Change." CRU, Jan. 2013. https://www.cru.org/content/dam/cru/legacy/2013/01/Gospel_KeytoChange_TimKeller.pdf.

———. Walking with God through Pain and Suffering. New York: Riverhead, 2013.

Knowles, Andrew. The Bible Guide. Minneapolis: Augsburg, 2001.

Kraft, Charles H. Appropriate Christianity. Pasadena, CA: William Carey, 2005.

Lenegan, Sonia, and C. J. McKinney. "What Is the Difference between Refugee Status and Humanitarian Protection?" Free Movement, June 2019; updated at unspecifed date. https://www.freemovement.org.uk/what-is-the-difference-between-refugee-status-and-humanitarian-protection.

Lidorio, Ronaldo. "Gospel and Culture." God, Church and Mission, Jan. 1, 2020. https://godchurchmission.com/v2/index.php/3-gospel-and-culture.

Lodahl, Michael E. Claiming Abraham: Reading the Bible and the Qur'an Side by Side. Grand Rapids: Brazos, 2010.

Love, Rick. Muslims, Magic, and the Kingdom of God. Pasadena, CA: William Carey, 2000.

MacMichael, Harold A. A History of the Arabs in the Sudan. 2 vols. Charleston, SC: Bibliolife, 2009.

Macrotrends. "Jordan Refugee Statistics 1960–2022." Macrotrends, n.d. https://www.macrotrends.net/countries/JOR/jordan/refugee-statistics.

Mamdani, Mahmood. Saviors and Survivors: Darfur, Politics, and the War on Terror. New York: Crown, 2010.

Maurer, Andreas. "Answering 10 Popular Muslim Objections." Global Connections, n.d. https://www.globalconnections.org.uk/sites/newgc.localhost/files/papers/Answering%2010%20Popular%20Muslim%20Objections%20-%20iNet.pdf.

———. Ask Your Muslim Friend: An Introduction to Islam and a Christian's Guide for Interaction with Muslims. Cape Town: AcadSA, 2008.

Mennonite Central Committee. On the Basis of Nationality: Access to Assistance for Iraqi and Other Asylum-Seekers and Refugees in Jordan. Akron, PA: Mennonite Central Committee, 2017. https://reliefweb.int/sites/reliefweb.int/files/resources/On%20the%20Basis%20of%20Nationality.pdf.

Miaschi, John. "What Languages Are Spoken in Jordan?" World Atlas, Aug. 1, 2017. https://www.worldatlas.com/articles/what-languages-are-spoken-in-jordan.html.

Mohamed, Yasien. Fitrah: The Islamic Concept of Human Nature. London: Ta-Ha, 1996.

Moreau, A. Scott. Contextualization in World Missions: Mapping and Assessing Evangelical Models. Grand Rapids: Kregel, 2012.

Natsios, Andrew S. Sudan, South Sudan, and Darfur: What Everyone Needs to Know. New York: Oxford University Press, 2020.

Nehls, Gerhard. Dear Abdallah. Nairobi: Life Challenge Africa, 1992.

Nelson, Harold D. Sudan: A Country Study. Washington, DC: US Government, 1982.

Netton, Ian Richard. Encyclopedia of Islamic Civilization and Religion. London: RoutledgeCurzon, 2004.

Nicholls, Bruce J. "Theological Education and Evangelization." In Let the Earth Hear His Voice, edited by J. D. Douglas, 634–45. Minneapolis: World Wide, 1975.

Nydell, Margaret K. Understanding Arabs: A Guide for Modern Times. Boston: Intercultural, 2006.

Oberlin, Kevin. "What Is Contextualization?" Center for Global Opportunities, Mar. 3, 2017. https://www.bjucgo.com/blog/what-is-contextualization.

O'Fahey, Rex S. Darfur and the British. London: Hurst, 2017.

————. *The Darfur Sultanate: A History*. New York: Columbia University Press, 2008.

Osborne, Grant, and Clinton E. Arnold. *Matthew*. Exegetical Commentary on the New Testament. Grand Rapids: Zondervan, 2010.

Osborne, Grant, and Philip W. Comfort. *Matthew*. Life Application Bible Commentary. Wheaton, IL: Tyndale, 1996.

Payne, J. D., and John Mark Terry. *Developing a Strategy for Missions: A Biblical, Historical, and Cultural Introduction*. Grand Rapids: Baker, 2013.

Peters, George W. "Issues Confronting Evangelical Missions." In *Evangelical Missions Tomorrow*, edited by Wade T. Coggins and E. L. Frizen Jr., 169–94. Pasadena, CA: William Carey, 1977.

Petterson, Donald. *Inside Sudan: Political Islam, Conflict, and Catastrophe*. Boulder, CO: Westview, 1999.

Pocock, Michael, et al. *The Changing Face of World Mission: Engaging Contemporary Issues and Trends*. Encountering Mission Series. Edited by A. Scott Moreau. Grand Rapids: Baker, 2005.

Porter, Stanley E. "Peace." In *New Dictionary of Biblical Theology*, edited by T. Desmond Alexander and Brian S. Rosner, 682–83. Nottingham, UK: InterVarsity, 2020.

Prince, Andrew James. "Contextualisation of the Gospel: Towards an Evangelical Approach in the Light of Scripture and the Church Fathers." PhD diss., Australian Catholic University Faculty of Theology and Philosophy, 2015.

Qureshi, Javed Ahmed. "Muslim Law." Jiwaji University, Apr. 4, 2020. http://www.jiwaji.edu/pdf/ecourse/law/MALIKI%20SCHOOL.pdf.

Qureshi, Nabeel. *No God but One: Allah or Jesus? A Former Muslim Investigates the Evidence for Islam and Christianity*. Grand Rapids: Zondervan, 2016.

Rheenen, Gailyn Van. *Contextualization and Syncretism: Navigating Cultural Currents*. Pasadena, CA: William Carey Library, 2006.

Royal Aal Al-Bayt Institute for Islamic Thought, The. *A Common Word between Us and You*. Amman: Royal Aal Al-Bayt Institute for Islamic Thought, 2009.

Ryle, John, et al. *The Sudan Handbook*. Nairobi: Rift Valley Institute, 2011.

Schaeffer, Francis A. *The Mark of the Christian*. Westmont, IL: InterVarsity, 2013.

Schiller, Nina Glick, et al. "From Immigrant to Transmigrant." *Anthropological Quarterly* 68 (1995) 48–63.

Searcy, Kim. *The Formation of the Sudanese Mahdist State: Ceremony and Symbols of Authority: 1882–1898*. Islam in Africa 11. Boston: Brill, 2011.

Security Council. "Security Council Demands Sudan Disarm Militias in Darfur, Adopting Resolution 1556 (2004) by Vote of 13–0–2." United Nations, July 30, 2004. https://www.un.org/press/en/2004/sc8160.doc.htm.

Segura-Guzmán, Osías. "The Practice of Theology, in Local Theology for the Global Church." In *Local Theology for the Global Church: Principles for an Evangelical Approach to Contextualization*, edited by Matthew Cook et al., 77–78. Pasadena, CA: William Carey, 2010.

Short Comments on Every Chapter of the Holy Bible. London: Religious Tract Society, 1838.

Sibson, Robert. *Jordan: UNHCR Operational Update*. UNHCR, Apr. 2017. https://reporting.unhcr.org/sites/default/files/UNHCR%20Jordan%20Operational%20Update%20-%20April%202017.pdf.

Sidahmed, Abdel Salam, and Alsir Sidahmed. *Sudan: The Contemporary Middle East*. London: Routledge, 2011.

Sittser, Gerald L. *Water from a Deep Well: Christian Spirituality from Early Martyrs to Modern Missionaries*. Downers Grove, IL: InterVarsity, 2015.

Smither, Edward L. *Christian Martyrdom: A Brief History with Reflections for Today*. Eugene, OR: Wipf & Stock, 2020.

Spelman, Elizabeth V. *Fruits of Sorrow: Framing Our Attention to Suffering*. Boston: Beacon, 1997.

Sproul, R. C. *What Is the Trinity?* San Diego: EChristian, 2014.

Stacey, Aisha. "The Concept of Ummah in Islam." The Religion of Islam, Apr. 2, 2018; last modified Jan. 11, 2021. https://www.islamreligion.com/articles/11312/concept-of-ummah-in-islam.

Stott, John. *Basic Christianity*. London: InterVarsity, 2021.

Stott, John, et al. "Lausanne Covenant." Lausanne, 1974. https://lausanne.org/content/covenant/lausanne-covenant#cov.

Tano, Rodrigo D. *Theology in the Philippine Setting: A Case Study in the Contextualization of Theology*. Quezon City: New Day, 1981.

Thompson Coon, Rose, et al. *Knowledge for Children in the Middle East and North Africa (Mena)*. UNICEF, 2017. https://www.unicef.org/mena/media/2841/file/MENA-KnowledgeReport-2018.pdf.

Totten, Samuel, and Eric Markusen. *Genocide in Darfur: Investigating the Atrocities in the Sudan*. New York: Routledge, 2006.

UN. "Sudan: Intercommunal Clashes Displace Tens of Thousands in Volatile Darfur Region." United Nations, Jan. 7, 2020. https://news.un.org/en/story/2020/01/1054911.

———. "UNHCR Delivers Much-Needed Aid to Sudanese Refugees in Chad." United Nations, Mar. 20, 2020. https://news.un.org/en/story/2020/03/1059842.

———. "Violence, Insecurity and Climate Change Drive 84 Million People from Their Homes." United Nations, Nov. 11, 2021. https://news.un.org/en/story/2021/11/1105592.

UNHCR. "Asylum-Seekers: Seeking International Protection." UNHCR, Dec. 11, 2016. https://www.unhcr.org/ceu/86-enwho-we-helpasylum-seekers-html.html.

———. "Jordan: Statistics for Registered Persons of Concern (as of 15 December 2021)." Operational Data Portal, Dec. 16, 2021; uploaded Dec. 20, 2021. https://data2.unhcr.org/en/documents/details/90152.

———. *Resettlement Handbook*. UNHCR, n.d. www.unhcr.org/46f7c0ee2.pdf.

———. *UNHCR Global Trends 2012*. UNHCR, June 19, 2013. https://www.unhcr.org/ph/wp-content/uploads/sites/28/2017/03/GlobalTrends2012.pdf.

———. *UNHCR Global Trends 2014*. UNHCR, June 18, 2015. https://www.unhcr.org/statistics/country/556725e69/unhcr-global-trends-2014.htmlb.

———. *UNHCR Global Trends 2016*. UNHCR, June 19, 2017. https://www.unhcr.org/statistics/unhcrstats/5943e8a34/global-trends-forced-displacement-2016.html.

———. *UNHCR Global Trends 2020*. UNHCR, June 18, 2021. https://www.unhcr.org/flagship-reports/globaltrends.

———. *UNHCR Global Trends 2021*. UNHCR, June 16, 2022. https://www.unhcr.org/62a9d1494/global-trends-report-2021.

———. *UNHCR Service Guide*. UNHCR, Aug. 2018. https://www.unhcr.org/jo/wp-content/uploads/sites/60/2018/08/WEB-FINAL_Service-Guide-August2018_ENG-HighRes.pdf.

————. *Universal Periodic Review: Jordan.* Ref World, Mar. 2013. https://www.refworld. org/pdfid/513d90172.pdf.

Van Ardenne, Agnes, et al. *Explaining Darfur: Four Lectures on the Ongoing Genocide.* Amsterdam: Amsterdam University Press, 2011.

Van der Smissen, Sheila. *Drinking from the Nile: Twelve Years in Sudan, a Memoir.* Independently Published, 2019.

Van Pelt, P. *Bantu Customs in Mainland Tanzania.* Tabora, Tanz.: TMP, 1984.

Voll, John Obert. *Historical Dictionary of the Sudan.* London: Scarecrow, 1978.

Vroegop, Mark. *Dark Clouds, Deep Mercy: Discovering the Grace of Lament.* Wheaton, IL: Crossway, 2019.

Waal, Alex de. "Who Are the Darfurians? Arab and African Identities, Violence and External Engagement." *African Affairs* 104 (Apr. 2005) 181–205.

Wahba, Wafik. "Witnessing to the Gospel through Forgiveness: A Living Example from the Persecuted Christians in Egypt." *Lausanne Global Analysis* 7 (Jan. 2018). https://www.lausanne.org/content/lga/2018-01/witnessing-gospel-forgiveness.

Walker, Jenny, and Paul Clammer. *Lonely Planet Jordan.* Amman: Lonely Planet Global Limited, 2018.

Willard, Dallas. *The Spirit of the Disciplines: Understanding How God Changes Lives.* New York: HarperOne, 2009.

Wolterstorff, Nicholas. *Until Justice and Peace Embrace: The Kuyper Lectures for 1981 Delivered at the Free University of Amsterdam.* Grand Rapids: Eerdmans, 1983.

Zwemer, Samuel. *The Influence of Animism on Islam.* London: Central Board of Missions, 1920.

Scripture Index

www.ingramcontent.com/pod-product-compliance
Lightning Source LLC
Chambersburg PA
CBHW060335100426

42812CB00003B/999